The material in this book is not intended as a substitute for
trained medical or psychological advice. Readers are advised
to consult their personal healthcare professionals prior to
attempting the activities and exercises presented in this book.
The publisher and the author assume no liability for any injuries
caused to the reader that may result from the reader's use of
the content contained herein and recommend common
sense when contemplating the practices described.

About the Author

Yasmin Henkesh is a dedicated performer, teacher, trainer, and workshop instructor with over forty years of cabaret and folkloric Middle Eastern Dance experience. As a performer, she has captivated audiences around the world, particularly in Egypt where she lived for a number of years. She has shared stages with Arab superstars Sabah, Ahmed Adaweya, Walid Toufic, Mohammed Al Azabi, Hassan Abou El-Saoud, Mona Said, Sahar Hamdi, Fifi Abdo, and Shoo Shoo Amin. As a teacher, she offers lively, fun, and invigorating classes that help students connect with their natural rhythm and passion. Her workshops are widely acclaimed for their depth of research, grasp of the region's dance history, and easy-to-follow movement explanations. Her adopted family is from a long line of Cairo's Muhammad Ali Street musicians and can be heard on albums released by her Sands of Time Music label. *Trance Dancing with the Jinn* is her first book.

To Write to the Author

If you wish to contact the author or would like more information about this book, please write to the author in care of Llewellyn Worldwide, Ltd. and we will forward your request. The author and publisher appreciate hearing from you and learning of your enjoyment of this book and how it has helped you. Llewellyn Worldwide, Ltd. cannot guarantee that every letter written to the author can be answered, but all will be forwarded. Please write to:

Yasmin Henkesh
℅ Llewellyn Worldwide
2143 Wooddale Drive
Woodbury, MN 55125-2989

Please enclose a self-addressed stamped envelope for reply,
or $1.00 to cover costs. If outside the USA, enclose
an international postal reply coupon.

YASMIN HENKESH

Foreword by Orion Foxwood

The Ancient Art of Contacting
Spirits Through Ecstatic Dance

TRANCE
DANCING
with the
JINN

Llewellyn Publications
Woodbury, Minnesota

FIRST EDITION
First Printing, 2016

Book design by Bob Gaul
Cover design by Lisa Novak
Cover photo by Jason Sayada/Serpentine Communications
Additional image by iStockphoto.com/3841794/©akarelias
For interior art credits see page 377.
Llewellyn Publications is a registered trademark of Llewellyn Worldwide Ltd.

Library of Congress Cataloging-in-Publication Data (Pending)
ISBN: 978-0-7387-3794-2

Llewellyn Publications
A Division of Llewellyn Worldwide Ltd.
2143 Wooddale Drive
Woodbury, MN 55125-2989
www.llewellyn.com

Printed in the United States of America

Contents

Part Three: Kinetic Trance Techniques
••

Foreword
by Orion Foxwood

How beautiful they are,
The lordly ones
Who dwell in the hills,
In the hollow hills.

They have faces like flowers
And their breath is wind
That stirs amid grasses
Filled with white clover.

Their limbs are more white
Than shafts of moonshine
They are more fleet
Than the March wind.

They laugh and are glad
And are terrible:
When their lances shake
Every green reed quivers.

From *The Immortal Hour* by Fiona Macleod

This poem speaks of "the Lordly Ones," a class of spirits that are the subject of many Celtic ballads, stories, folktales, and folk practices. They are also known as the "Faery," "the Shining Ones," and the "People of Peace." But these figures are not the diminutive or whimsical figures of modern media and children's tales. No, they are powerful spirits that are as mystical as the wind and as ominous as storm clouds, living in a realm of existence that interpenetrates the world of form and the domain of humanity. The depiction of the Faery presented in this poem is reflective of the traditional view before their image was demonized and trivialized, and speaks of their power, beauty, and awesome presence. These elements and their profound effect on humanity are attributes they share with what may be their Middle Eastern cousins … the jinn.

The Faery and the jinn share other characteristics as well, such as living in the hollow places of the earth (caves, caverns, etc.), having secret or arcane knowledge, and possessing the ability to effect altered states of consciousness in humans, causing us both fear and reverence. However, where there are several authors who teach the importance of human/faery alliances, there are few who uphold and defend the integrity of the jinn and the value and importance of the human/jinn alliance. For this and many other reasons, Yasmin has been called to be such a voice.

There are many types of "invisibles" (including divinities, jinn, faery, angels, exalted human ancestors, nature spirits, and other spirit-beings) currently commanding our attention and urgently advising our species to re-engage with them so we may collectively heal. They are extending invitations to us to enter into co-creative partnerships with them, just as they did with our ancient and indigenous human ancestors. They hold vital information and guidance about cultivating and/or restoring a healthy living relationship with our individual selves, and with the global family (human and other, seen and unseen) that is sharing life on Earth with us.

The tone of escalating urgency that is energizing this call is shaped, in part, by increasing levels of toxic chemical and energetic pollutants and by humanity's disruption to life-supportive ecological systems, which is endangering or destroying life forms (including humans). In short, we have neglected to consistently consider our effects on a planet that is shared with, *but not owned by,* humanity. As every indigenous wisdom tradition of the world has advised for centuries, we share this world not only with the life forms that can be observed by the five senses and categorized by current science, but also with beings that are not so easily observed. Many of them, such as jinn and faery, have knowledge about the more subtle qualities of life and about their powers to heal and help.

Yasmin is being guided by the jinn for a similar, or same, call to action. Through decades of painstaking research, she has documented and integrated a wealth of information, which she presents here in a way that not only illustrates traditional folklore, but gives the reader a means to access the jinn's strata of existence through modifying consciousness with trance and one of its most beloved companions, dance. This will be of great value, for all those who are called into partnership with any type of invisibles, in supporting a healthy interaction with the spirits, particularly the ones that have never been human. Yasmin provides current and understandable information on types of trance, the nature of trance, and the signs and symptoms of altered states of consciousness (useful for building familiarity and confidence when using broader ranges of perception), giving the reader signposts for the thresholds of inner perception that occur as one shifts into ranges of consciousness where spirits can be contacted. These types of discussions are extremely helpful when developing the subtle senses, and in mastering methods for shifting into altered consciousness and then bringing back and translating the information shared there.

When reading the book, you can feel the love and respect Yasmin has for the jinn, the source cultures that have preserved their lore, and the sacred use of trance dance as the vehicle for contact. Her book opens a literary door through which the reader can step into a "living tradition" as it is being practiced today within its culture. Through this and other examples of real-life experiences, the living existence of the jinn becomes almost palpable. Yasmin spent many years in Egypt researching and immersing herself in the culture, and she personally witnessed traditional techniques for entering and exiting specific types of trance to engage, sever, or mitigate a human/jinn interaction. This is a particularly pivotal aspect of her work, for if a teaching is not *alive* in the life of a teacher, which only happens through immersion, application, and integration, it lacks soul. Without this soul, teachers or authors can only transmit words and information, but none of the nuances and subtleties that truly ignite the teachings into an active awareness. With it, however, they can transmit wisdom that transports the student beyond mere mental constructs and into the living presence of the tradition and the jinn. To this, Yasmin adds her detailed academic research on the subject and her personal experience, creating the priceless gem you hold in your hands.

Of all the guiding spirits that have come forward to engage with humanity, the jinn have been the most vilified. There have been few to no books on the sacred side of the jinn and how to cultivate interactions with them. Yasmin provides us one such book, and she expands its usefulness in the modern world by presenting clear, science-based, and practical ways to access the realm of awareness within us. For this is the "dancing floor of the divine."

Now, folks often ask me if I think there are harmful spirits, or, better stated, "those not in harmony with us." Well, of course there are! But then, there are harmful humans, and we do not cast out all of humanity because of it. So why should we cast out the jinn, when they have much to offer us if we would only take the responsibility to develop our subtle senses? We should develop this discernment, the ability to feel which spirits are harmonious to our inner spirit and which ones are not, the same way we develop the capacity to discern who is the best human company for us and who is not. The development of subtle senses in human/spirit interaction has other benefits as well. It refines our understanding of other subtleties in life, such as those powerful invisible forces we encounter every day in human interaction: love, authenticity, connection, and compassion. Thus engagement with the invisible brings so much life…to life!

It is my hope that more humans who have been contacted by some form of the sacred invisibles will, in the interests of our shared world, come into a type of "convocation of the contacts" to build alliances of healing, magic, and wisdom, and give voice to some of the most helpful guiding spirits that have walked a parallel mystic journey with humanity since the beginning of our life on Earth. I cannot speak for the jinn, but my spirit-wife Brigh, the guiding force for the teachings of my Faery Tradition, has made it clear that the Faery can repair the threads of interconnection in the living web, threads that have been disrupted by humanity's damage to many of the world's ecosystems. But she further informs us that "We will not come unbidden."

In my opinion, Yasmin, myself, and the readers of this book are all listening and responding to a co-creative call to action. The sacred spirit-world works its magic in synchronous and mystical ways, to find voices for its message and the means to open the road for the work at hand. My first meeting with Yasmin is a great example of their wondrous ways. Let me tell you a true tale about a Faery Seer and a Jinn Wise Woman who were drawn together by the Holy to bring forth this treasure which you now hold in your hands…

It was a cold, overcast winter day in Maryland and I was doing spiritual readings at the home of my dear friend and esteemed Middle Eastern dancer and dance anthropologist Artemis Mourat. Artemis informed me that her friend Yasmin was scheduled for a reading that day. I had heard all about Yasmin and her highly disciplined teaching style, and already respected her. The scheduled time for her appointment was at hand, and in walked this radiant woman with long, elegant hair and a refined stature; I knew we would be friends, very dear friends, colleagues in the field of human and "other" companionship. There was a powerful energy in the air that informed me that this reading was a voice for a different kind of spirit…and powerful it was! My spirit-wife and the powerful forces that work through my tradition made it overwhelmingly clear: Yasmin was called to be a voice for the jinn. They want to help humanity attain the vision that God has for planet Earth…Eden.

So, how do we get from where we are as a species (disconnected from our relationships as a member of life on Earth) to a state that is healthier for the planet, ourselves, and the rest of nature? In my opinion, we must return to a living awareness of the profound way that the Creator's love and vision for all life flows through what is seen and unseen, and the thresholds in between. The sacred invisibles are here to help midwife human consciousness back to the intimate side of life.

I leave you now to walk your awareness through the tome that lies before you. As Machaelle Small Wright, a wise and inspired author and trailblazer in human and nature co-creative science, says, "Only those who can see the invisible can achieve the impossible."

It took her under a minute to fall into a trance—literally. One second her arms were flailing, the next she was sprawled on the floor unconscious. The musicians paused while her sister propped her up, her head dangling like a tetherball on a rope. The Rattler pressed his hands to her temples and twisted her neck this way and that. Then he yanked on her arms. Someone sprinkled rose water on her face. She took time to return; she was a long way away. Fifteen minutes later, though, she was back on her feet, dancing. Her possessor liked the music and refused to let her sit out the song. Who knew when they would find another zar?

Introduction

Spirit possession is real to many Egyptians, as it is to other cultures around the world. Zar practitioners in Egypt and elsewhere believe that invisible entities called *zar* (a subspecies of *jinn*) crave the sensations of solid bodies—of blood coursing through veins and electrical impulses throbbing along nerves—and infiltrate Earth's creatures to satisfy their desires. Their names may change from culture to culture, but their *modus operandi* remains the same. They make hosts sick to attract attention, but once their presence is acknowledged during dance-induced trances, they cease their noxious activity and form symbiotic relationships with their humans. In Brazil, for example, the spirits are called *orishas* instead of zar or jinn, but they still descend into trained initiates during trance dance rituals. In Haiti, *loa* visit Vodun practitioners in the same way, facilitated by frenetic drumming. In West Africa, *bori* manifest during all-night dance ceremonies, similar to Balinese and Vietnamese possession spirits. Native American shamans speak to animal guides during percussion-heavy vision quests, as do their Siberian counterparts. And in raves around the globe, many young adults see spirits as they trance dance the night away to blaring, percussion-heavy music. Yes, the Earth is full of people who believe that invisible entities inhabit living creatures or manifest when loud rhythmic music is played.

This belief evolved with our species during the Paleolithic era, along with higher-order consciousness, art, and music. And what is music without dance? After all, Paleolithic *Homo sapiens* were anatomically modern humans. Their brains generated the same electrical impulses along the same "wiring" as ours. They slept and dreamt just as we do. So on occasion, they must also have seen visions. And if present-day humans

1

see spirits after prolonged dancing, it is only logical that early dancers must have seen them, too. Those first visionaries became shamans, or seers, for their tribes—Chosen Ones that visited invisible worlds, communicated with their inhabitants, and returned with invaluable knowledge. And when these interlopers taught others their skills, their disciples corroborated the experiences—since their brains reacted similarly.

Eventually, visions turned into myths that were passed down by word of mouth from generation to generation until they ended up in humanity's first texts. *The Epic of Gilgamesh* (2500 BCE) and the *Pyramid Texts*[1] (2400 BCE) are based on images, magical powers, and otherworldly inhabitants from eons of shamanic journeys. Once belief in a single creative force emerged, God was deemed responsible for life's animating spark— from the solid bodies of Earth's creatures to the angels, demons, gods, goddesses, and spirits fleetingly glimpsed during moments of altered consciousness. Others disagreed. They maintained there was no single creator, only multitudes of spirits, or later, with the Renaissance, no spirits at all, only scientific logic. Hence, in the twenty-first century, belief in one (invisible) entity is far from unanimous. Nevertheless, those who do believe—in something—vastly outnumber those who don't.

Today, research into the anatomy of the brain is illuminating why humans see Invisibles during altered states of consciousness. Evidence suggests that when the human brain focuses on a limited set of thoughts (concentrates), as during problem-solving, improvisation, or listening to rhythmic music, or when it is bombarded with overwhelming, monotonous, or emotion-inducing stimuli, it isolates what it considers pertinent and begins to ignore the rest. This is why perception changes during trance. As focus narrows, the brain stops processing extraneous stimuli and blocks signals from regions it deems nonessential, particularly areas of the prefrontal cortex, the seat of critical reasoning and learned inhibition. This reduction is key. It allows a barrage of unfiltered information to pass into and out of the subconscious and unusual synaptic connections (i.e., new ideas) to occur. This altered mental processing is the essence of "trance."

Do all human brains do this? Can the process be controlled? Does reality actually vary depending on our state of mind or the chemicals flooding our neural synapses? Are

---

1   The *Pyramid Texts* are a collection of resurrection spells, found on one Fifth Dynasty and many Sixth Dynasty pyramid walls.

the visions real? Are spirits actually trying to communicate with us when the reasoning, inhibitory parts of our brains are shut down? Or is everything merely hallucination?

Hopefully, by the end of this book, you can answer a few of these questions from personal experience. Not everyone will reach the same conclusions, of course, but consensus isn't important. It's the journey that matters. Scientists are continually discovering new information. What is unknown today may be crystal clear tomorrow.

Personally, I have found that Middle Eastern trance induction techniques, supplemented with insights from modern brain research, permit almost everyone to experience kinetic, or moving (i.e., dancing) trance—with practice. The trick is to discover how the movements affect you personally. Everyone reacts differently, although most people encounter similar landmarks. The region's trance rituals—Sufi whirling, Sufi zikr, and zar trance dancing—are particularly effective. The first two, performed by men (although in Turkey women now whirl), are associated with Islam and the divine spirit of Allah, or God. The third, zar, is done by women to communicate with the jinn, examples of which are sprinkled throughout the book. Yet the depth of altered consciousness often achieved at zars, i.e., "possession," is not easy to attain or necessary to benefit from the state's healing and meditative properties. Plus, it is difficult to control, which is why in Part Three, the "How To" section, I only present milder "lucid trance" techniques.

Parts One and Two of the book explore trance history, actual trance sensations, the science behind "altered states," and the spirits, methods, and religious traditions associated with the three Middle Eastern trance rituals mentioned above. The use of trance, particularly for healing, is rooted in humanity's ancestral, perhaps original, religious belief systems. Sadly, many traditions may soon be lost forever. The zar cult, for example, is dying out, as both modernity and fundamentalist Islam cut away at its tenants. Perhaps after another generation, it will disappear completely, along with its unique prehistoric spirituality, music, and rhythms.

Nevertheless, one element, the jinn, is still very much alive to Islam's almost two billion Muslims because the Quran, like the Bible, takes the existence of Invisibles for granted. And while spirits in general are a popular subject in the Middle East, the jinn in particular hold an elevated status because of their prominence in Islam's sacred book.

The Muslim version of Satan, Iblis, is "of the jinn,"[2] while different jinn, "on a righteous path,"[3] gave Muhammad hope in his darkest hour. As you can see, they occupy both ends of the good/bad spectrum, and all the gray areas in between … just like humans.

But what do you think? Do you believe in Invisibles or do you consider them an outdated tradition from an ignorant past? What if you had a safe, drug-free way to see for yourself? Would you be curious enough to try it—even though the method takes practice and you probably won't succeed on your first attempt? Not that the techniques are difficult. Those of you with a spiritual nature who like exercise should find them quite enjoyable. Those of you who don't like to dance … well, maybe not! But what follows isn't really "dancing" in the modern sense of the word anyway. "Kinetic meditation" is a better description. More to the point, what have you got to lose? A few pounds? The movements could even make you feel better—but you won't know until you try.

---

2   Quran 18:50: "And when We said to the angels, 'Bow to Adam,' they bowed, except for Iblis. He was of the jinn and disobeyed the command. Will you take him and his progeny as guardians in My stead while they are enemies to you?"

3   See the Quran, Surah 72, *al-Jinn* ("The Jinn").

PART ONE

Trance

Dancing with Genies—A Zar Hadra

Cairo, Egypt

The taxi dropped us off next to the Islamic Museum on Muhammad Ali Street, in the heart of the furniture district. Dollies stacked with faux Louis XIV chairs blocked the road. Donkeys pulling carts of upholstery stuffing hogged the sidewalk. We followed the wagons into the warren of carpentry workshops behind the museum, picking our way past ramshackle medieval hovels filled with tools, guilt armchairs, and baroque loveseats wrapped in plastic. Eventually, we stopped outside a decrepit four-story building. Excited chatter echoed into the street from the stairwell. It grew louder as we climbed to a landing piled with lumpy couches and a bed frame.

Old women in black cover-ups stepped aside to let us enter a tight two-bedroom apartment. Children ran up and down the hallway as their mothers chatted near the door. The living room, bathed in afternoon sunlight, had been cleared of furniture except for twenty blue metallic folding chairs lining the walls. The balcony door, propped open by a *tabla* drum, looked out over the main alley and the setting sun. A string of multicolored light bulbs decorated the ceiling.

A makeshift altar, the *kursi al-arousa* (or "throne"), was set up in a corner diagonally across from the balcony. It was nothing more than a stool covered with a sheet and a white lace tablecloth. But hidden underneath it sat a metal tub filled with popcorn, peanuts, fried chickpeas and hard candy wrapped in foil—treats for Rouqash, a young zar spirit. Another bowl of candy sat on top, covered with a pita loaf sprinkled with sugar. And towering above it all loomed a three-foot cream-colored candle shoved into a sand-filled paint can smeared with either red latex or blood. Two more cans on the floor flanked the kursi on either side, a purple candle in one and a dark green candle in the other. A Golden Era photograph of the family's deceased patriarch hung on the wall behind them.

Five women aged forty to sixty-five sat cross-legged on the room's tattered oriental carpet, smoking cigarettes. Large frame drums about two feet in diameter lay beside them, along with a dented aluminum wash basin holding a tarnished incense burner and a bowl of red incense (*bakhour*). The women wore loose, multicolored cotton shifts, or galabeyas. Their hair was covered by black gauze tied behind their ears and long black scarves draped over their heads or around their necks. They were the Harim Masri (or Firqa Saidi), female zar musicians from the Saidi region of Upper Egypt and the first of three groups scheduled to perform.

Unfortunately, I was informed, all the performances would be short. The rise of Islamic fundamentalism in Egypt meant that zars were now considered taboo pagan rituals. If the neighbors complained there would be hell to pay, even for a simple two-hour *hadra* ...

1

·········

What Is Trance?

And so began my odyssey into the realm of the Invisibles. But before I finish the story or show you how to visit the invisible world, I would like to review some basics first. Just as there are many human races, numerous tribes of Invisibles populate the Earth, each with distinctive energy signatures. Angels and human ancestor spirits (the souls of the dead) are the most well known, but regional entities (such as the jinn and faerie) also exist. I would also like to discuss a few fundamentals about trance and the visible world we live in—like the nature of matter and what makes our brains tick. Physics and biology are probably not the best subjects to begin a dance manual with, but meeting the spirit world requires preparation—and knowledge is power. I promise I will try to make this as brief and painless as possible.

We know our universe exists because our ancestors evolved sensory organs that detect its matter and a few of the electromagnetic radiations (radio waves, light, X-rays, etc.) it emits. But, believe it or not, this matter, the substance we are made of, is the exception to the universe's rule. According to NASA's website, "everything on Earth, everything ever observed with all of our instruments, all normal matter … adds up to less than 5 percent of the Universe." The rest "is a complete mystery. But it is an important mystery. It turns out that roughly 68 percent of the universe is dark energy. Dark matter makes up about 27 percent."[4] This energy and matter are called "dark" because they do not reflect light (photons) or interact with electromagnetic forces. We only know they

---

4 NASA, "Dark Energy, Dark Matter," *NASA Science: Astrophysics.*

are there by their effects on gravity, a force governed by Albert Einstein's general theory of relativity. In fact, dark energy is what is pushing our universe apart, while dark matter forms the giant lattice in space that keeps galaxies in place and prevents them from spinning apart.[5] As for our 5 percent … it resides in different states; solid, liquid, gas, and plasma (earth, water, air, and fire). While the first three states are easily observable (think ice, water, and steam), the fourth, plasma, is less obvious. Again, from NASA:

> [Plasma is] a mixture of electrons (negatively charged) and ions (atoms that have lost electrons, resulting in a positive electric charge). [It] is not a gas, liquid, or solid—it is the fourth state of matter. Plasma often behaves like a gas, except that it conducts electricity and is affected by magnetic fields. On an astronomical scale, plasma is common. The Sun is composed of plasma, fire is plasma, fluorescent and neon lights contain plasma. "99.9 percent of the Universe is made up of plasma," says Dr. Dennis Gallagher, a plasma physicist at NASA's Marshall Space Flight Center. "Very little material in space is made of rock like the Earth.[6]

Plasma is and always has been crucial to our existence. "Smokeless fire," to quote an expression in the Quran ("*marij an-nar*," the tip of a flame), provided our hominid ancestors with food, light, heat, and protection—and on a planetary scale, it protects the air we breathe. Plasma descends to Earth from the outer atmosphere through the magnetic vortexes at the North and South poles and through tears in our magnetic field. And although plasma appears during the process of combustion (fire), it is not necessarily "hot." Plasma fingers reaching toward each other from ground and sky during thunderstorms pass entirely unnoticed—until they connect and a bolt of electricity shoots through them (lightning)!

OK, that's enough physics for now. I don't want to overwhelm you, but I did want to point out how little we (including scientists) really know about the world around us. I hope you will keep this in mind later as we discuss potentially controversial subjects— such as the cerebral mechanisms of trance or the possibility of non-solid life forms.

---

5   "Dark Matter," *The Economist*, 13; "Fractional Distillation," 72.

6   NASA, "Plasma, Plasma, Everywhere."

So What Is Trance?

Nothing like asking the hard questions first! The Harvard philosopher, psychologist, and physiologist William James once wrote that "our normal waking consciousness, rational consciousness as we call it, is but one special type of consciousness, whilst all about it, parted from it by the filmiest of screens, there lie potential forms of consciousness entirely different."[7] Before I teach you how to part the "rational consciousness" screen, however, we should talk about what lies beyond it first.

The truth is that even leading consciousness researchers can't say for sure what trance is or how it's caused—although they have some good ideas. And new facts are continually coming to light. Another truth is that you don't have to understand neurobiology to experience different forms of consciousness, but some basic knowledge helps put the mind at ease. And since mental surrender is essential to trance induction, familiarity with the basics will make the process easier.

Before we begin, though, take a minute to think about what the word "trance" means to you. If it elicits fear, this could prevent you from stepping over the altered consciousness threshold. For those with prior trance experience, try to relive your first encounter. For novices who inadvertently conjure up images of zombies or hypnotized magicians' assistants... understand that trance is not a recent trick "discovered" by Mesmer or Freud to analyze the troubled or sick. It is a natural phenomenon that *Homo sapiens* have cultivated since the dawn of our species. And because it is ubiquitous (all humans can alter their mental landscapes, although some are better at it than others), the underlying biology must have contributed to our survival early in our evolution, according to Darwin's natural selection theory. But how? Modern humans hardly use this ability. Or do they?

It depends on how you define the word "trance."

Okay, so we should look for answers in the dictionary then, right? Unfortunately, the most common definition of "trance" is "an altered state of consciousness," a vague catchall phrase that can mean many things to many people, including mental illness. And although this definition does describe states produced while daydreaming, listening to music, watching television, meditating, concentrating, praying, while under hypnosis or

---

7   *The Varieties of Religious Experience.*

deep relaxation, it also describes sleep, unconscious states such as comas, and personality disorders such as bipolar or schizophrenia. These are all "altered states."

Which brings up another question—altered from what? "Rational consciousness"? Altering something implies a normal baseline condition, "a psychological sense of self and the identification of that self with our bodies."[8] While altered states can be profound, light, or even pass unnoticed, like missing an exit while driving because you're listening to music, they can also be controlled or take on a life of their own. They can occur spontaneously or be induced. In fact, many different levels and types of consciousness are thrown into the same "altered" basket simply because they do not conform to society's definition of normal or "rational."

For our purposes then, we need to define both states, normal and altered … and a simple non-committal phrase like "a half conscious state" won't do. The etymology of "trance," however—the Latin *transir*, "to go across, pass over," as in from life to death—supplies an important clue: the description of a pivotal underlying sensation, entering a passageway such as a hall or alley, i.e., a vortex. Collins English Dictionary (10th edition) offers slightly more: "Any mental state in which a person is unaware or apparently unaware of the environment, characterized by loss of voluntary movement, rigidity, and lack of sensitivity to external stimuli"—like pain. But trance dancing or other forms of kinetic trance do not prevent movement, so this description doesn't work either … Collins also mentions "a state of ecstasy or mystic absorption so intense as to cause a temporary loss of consciousness at the earthly level," and a modern use, "a type of electronic dance music with repetitive rhythms, aiming at a hypnotic effect."

As you can see, the term "trance" covers a wide variety of physical and mental symptoms and is often equated with another altered consciousness term, "ecstasy."[9] The two words are not the same, however. According to Collins, ecstasy implies either "a state of exalted delight, joy, etc.; rapture," an "intense emotion of any kind" (as in an "ecstasy of rage"), "a state of prophetic inspiration" (as in the Hebrew prophets), or slang for "3,4-methylenedioxymethamphetamine; MDMA: a powerful drug that acts as a stimulant and can produce

---

8   David Aldridge and Jörg Fachner, *Music and Altered States*, 13.

9   "Ecstasy" is derived from the Greek *ekstasis*, "displacement, trance," from *existana*, "to displace": from *ex-* ("out") and *histanai* ("to cause to stand").

hallucinations." The *Encyclopedia Britannica* also associates ecstasy with Middle Eastern dervishes, defining Sufism as a "mystical Islamic belief and practice in which Muslims seek to find the truth of divine love and knowledge through direct personal experience of God." Those who practice mysticism often understand ecstasy as the experience of the divine or a union with the Creator. Ultimately, both terms describe altered states, but ecstasy involves heightened emotions, whereas trance may be induced by calming emotions (meditation). Nevertheless, both conditions share a common trait—narrowly focused attention. The more intense the concentration, the deeper the state.

Enough definitions. They only outline external symptoms anyway. To truly differentiate normal from altered consciousness, you will need far more than dictionary descriptions. But before I go any further, I need to narrow our scope a bit, to only one (large) branch of the trance tree.

Static Meditation vs. Kinetic Trance

Trance is divided into two general categories according to how it is induced: static and kinetic. In other words, immobile versus moving (sitting quietly, versus dancing to loud music), or understimulation versus overstimulation of the brain. As Gilbert Rouget, the twentieth century's trance expert, explained, meditation is practiced in solitude, stillness, and silence while kinetic trance is usually practiced within a communal framework, with music and strenuous activity. Institutionalized religious trance includes sensual overstimulation by bombarding the trancer with sound. Meditation, on the other hand, seeks to still the barrage of sensory input. Kinetic trance is emotional while meditation seeks to transcend emotion.[10]

In sum, kinetic trance is ideal for people who hate to sit still. It occupies the senses: hearing, vision, balance, muscle coordination—and smell, if you use incense. It accelerates heartbeat, blood flow, oxygenation (oxygen uptake), metabolism, and fluid extraction (in direct opposition to static meditation). It resynchronizes the brain's electrical impulses to an external source (music) and interrupts cognitive loops by partially shutting down upper brain functions. Psychologically, it arouses emotions while reducing shyness and inhibitions. It releases physical blocks, daily tensions, and fixed expectations. It promotes

---

10   *Music and Trance*, 6–12.

selflessness, quiets inner dialogue, and enables the body to withstand pain and fatigue. That's a lot of pluses!

Actually, many of these benefits simply come from prolonged physical exercise. And since science has already proven why exercise is good for you, I won't belabor the point. What I want to look at is why exercise can cause trance. In fact, most forms of strenuous, monotonous, or improvised physical activity alter consciousness if continued long enough. Long-distance running and dancing all night (drugs and alcohol aside) are only two examples. Fatigue disappears into a "second wind" and the mind floats into "the zone." That zone is trance. Fire spinners, jugglers, and hoop dancers also have a zone, but they call it "flow." This, too, is trance—when the autonomic nervous system takes over and does things you never thought possible. And if you consciously try to recreate those fancy moves, flow disappears and you can't. In general, someone who has just been exercising will respond more strongly to sexual stimuli or listening to music than someone who has just risen from sleep. As ethnomusicologist Judith Becker writes, "Arousal is fundamental to the triggering of trancing," particularly emotional arousal, such as joy, fear, or rage. Kinetic trance requires high energy arousal.[11]

Static meditation, on the other hand, is the realm of Buddhist monks and Zen practitioners. Countless books have been written about sedentary trance induction, so I won't cover it here, but an excellent in-depth scientific analysis can be found in James Austin's *Zen-Brain Reflections*.

As a dancer, I liked the idea of combining meditation with physical activity. Unfortunately, yoga and Tai Chi moved too slowly for me. But I found what I was looking for in Sufi manuals—a wealth of information about kinetic trance (for men). As I mentioned, Sufism is the mystic branch of Islam, whose followers have turned praying in motion into an art form. About a hundred and fifty years after the Prophet Muhammad's death (over 1,200 years ago), Sufi dervishes, particularly a man named Al-Ghazali, began to adapt ancient shamanic practices into effective ecstasy-inducing rituals. In fact, the methods they borrowed predated civilization. Long before Islam, or Christianity, or Judaism, long before *Homo sapiens* believed in One God, or many gods, or no god (atheism), even before religion was even conceived of, humans used these techniques to conjure faces in the flames.

---

11   *Deep Listeners*, 52.

But before we explore the past, here is a little homework to begin preparing you for a journey into the realm of the Invisibles.

Homework: Dancing with Fire

Please obtain the following items:

- **Trance Dance Journal**—Throughout the book I will be asking you to write things down. This is because the fleeting images and thoughts that occur during trance remain only a minute or two in short-term memory and then are lost forever—unless you write them down. Keeping everything in one place also makes it easier to interpret messages later.

- **Rug**—A colorful dance surface serves several purposes. Obviously, it's easier on your feet, but it also delineates your dance space when your eyes are closed. And when your eyes are open it helps stimulate visions.

- **Anchors**—The deeper into trance you go, the more you will need things to help you resurface afterwards. I will talk more about this in Part Three, but for now, find a small object that makes you feel happy and safe, your "happy thought," and keep it in sight when you dance, just in case you feel "blue" and need to put a smile on your face.

- **Candles and incense**—Light a scented candle, or your favorite incense and an unscented candle.

Put on 15–30 minutes of continuous (no silences between tracks) fast rhythmic music and dance in the dark as you focus on the flame. After the music stops, immediately write down what you thought or felt. Twenty-four hours later reread what you wrote (after a night's sleep). Is the meaning clearer? Don't be discouraged if it isn't. Sometimes things take days or weeks to be explained.

2

....

Trance History

The famous legend below is one of ancient Egypt's earliest written references to spirit possession. The sandstone tablet ("stele") it was carved on was discovered in a small Greco-Roman shrine next to Khonsu's temple at Karnak, the monumental home of Upper Egypt's New Kingdom gods. The story supposedly takes place during the Nineteenth Dynasty reign of Ramses II (1279–1213 BCE), but it was actually recorded eight hundred years later, around 400 BCE, after the Persians conquered Egypt.

The Princess of Bekhten[12]

They came from far and wide to pay him tribute, each vying to outdo the other with their magnificent gifts. The northern chiefs would not be put to shame before the great pharaoh Ramses II. One after the other they presented him with gold, lapis-lazuli, malachite, and precious woods. When it came the turn of the Prince of Bekhten, he placed his eldest daughter before his other offerings. She was exceedingly beautiful, and as he expected, delighted the pharaoh beyond all else. His Majesty gave her the name Nefrure, "Beauty of Re," the title of "Chief Royal Wife," and when they returned to Egypt, the duties of the Queen of Egypt.

---

12   E. A. Wallis Budge's translations of the stele can be found in *The Gods of the Egyptians* and *Legends of the Gods*, and S. Birch's translation can be found in *Records of the Past*, Vol. 4, pages 53–60. This version is my own rendition from various sources.

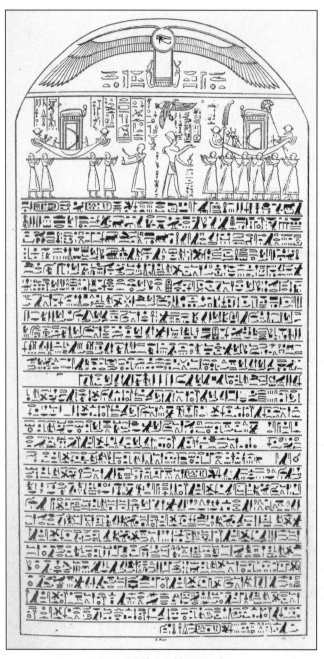

Figure 1: The Bekhten Stele

Twenty-three years into his reign, Ramses II was in Thebes celebrating the Southern Opet festival[13] when an ambassador from the Prince of Bekhten arrived bearing gifts for the Royal Wife. The messenger kissed the ground before the king and announced, "I have come on behalf of the Queen's little sister, Bent-Reshet, 'Daughter of Joy.' An evil movement has penetrated her limbs. Would Your Majesty send a sacred scribe knowledgeable in magic and medicine to see her?"

"Bring the scribes from the House of Life," His Majesty ordered, "and those acquainted with the mysteries of the Inner Palace. Have them choose one from among them who is intelligent in his heart and skilled with his fingers."

They did as he commanded and chose the royal scribe Tehuti-em-heb to accompany the envoy back north.

When Tehuti-em-heb arrived in Bekhten, he was unable to exorcise the spirit that possessed Bent-Reshet. Frustrated and deeply disappointed, the Prince of Bekhten sent Tehuti-em-heb back with a request to send a god instead. The scribe returned to Thebes during the festival of Amun, in the 26th year of His Majesty's reign. When Ramses II heard the prince's request, he went to the great temple of Khonsu "Nefer-hetep" and addressed the god.

"My good Lord Khonsu, I am again before you on behalf of the Princess of Bekhten." The pharaoh had the god's idol brought before another of its images and asked, "Would you turn your face to this Khonsu, Giver-of-Oracles, this 'Driver Out of the evil spirits that attack men'?" The statue violently nodded its head in agreement. "As a great favor, will you protect this Khonsu on his journey to Bekhten to save their princess?"[14]

The statue nodded again, and the god instilled its power into Khonsu, Giver-of-Oracles.

---

13 In the Egyptian Holy cities of Karnak and Thebes, the annual Opet (fertility) festival was considered the holiest event of the year. Every spring, a flotilla of boats escorted the effigy of the "Unseen One," Amun (later Amun-Re or Amun-Min), up the Nile for a conjugal visit with his consort Mut, who resided with their son Khonsu in Luxor Temple, also known as the "Harem of the South." It was a time of considerable public "debauchery" as everyone celebrated the renewal of life.

14 Meaning, would the god transmit his power to the other statue?

Figure 2: Khonsu

The newly empowered Khonsu-Giver-of-Oracles was carried to Bekht-en on a great ship, accompanied by five transport boats, numerous chariots and horses, and a priest-interpreter.

It took seventeen months to reach their destination and when they finally appeared, the prince, his chiefs, and his soldiers all threw themselves onto their bellies in greeting. They took the god straight to Bent-Reshet, where the priest performed Khonsu's protection ritual over her. She was cured immediately.

"You have come in peace, O Great God," the spirit who had possessed Bent-Reshet said to Khonsu after relinquishing control over the princess. "O Driver Away of Possessors and spirits who attack men, Bekhten is your city; its men and I are your slaves. I will return to whence I came, but first let the Prince of Bekhten perform a great sacrifice for us, O Giver-of-Oracles, that we should spend the day in celebration." And after this was done, the spirit kept its promise and left in peace.

The prince and the people of Bekhten were overjoyed, so much so that the prince decided not to return the idol, but to keep it in Bekhten. It remained with the prince for three years, four months, and five days—until one day Khonsu came to the prince in a dream. A gold hawk flew from the god's shrine and soared high into the air back to Egypt. Terrified, the Prince of Bekhten told Khonsu's priest-interpreter to return to Egypt at once. He loaded the god's chariot with gifts and had his troupes escort the divine delegation back to Thebes.

When Khonsu-Giver-of-Oracles returned home, the priest-interpreter took all the idol's gifts to the Great Temple of Khonsu Nefer-hetep in gratitude for the power bestowed upon it, and it reentered its temple after a long six-year absence.

Although this legend is based on actual people, and Eighteenth Dynasty Amarna records indicate gods and goddesses were occasionally sent on healing missions between Egypt and Mitanni (southern Anatolia and the Hittite Empire),[15] the stele's authors got many details wrong.[16]

---

15 The Amarna Letters, quoted in Henry Breasted, *Ancient Records of Egypt*, Vol. 3, 188.

16 Ramses II did marry a Hittite princess later in life, the Great Royal Wife Matnefrure (corrupted into Nefrure), but during the 34th year of his reign (at age 52), not before. Furthermore, he did not go north to collect tribute, but, according to the Marriage Stele, hosted the Hittite chief and his daughter in Egypt.

This just goes to show how corrupted facts turn into legends—and why pinpointing the origin of something as ancient as spirit possession or trance dancing is almost impossible. Intuitively, it's easy to imagine how dancing accompanied the Paleolithic invention of music, and how altered consciousness could have occurred during prolonged periods of frenzied movement, hyperventilation, and/or sensory deprivation in caves. But how do you prove this? Exaggerated dawn-of-time fairy tales are hardly evidence… yet they are a good place to start. They show that humans sought to communicate with the spirit world early on, and that these encounters were important enough to document in words, pictures, and artifacts.

Dancing, Illness, and Ancient Middle Eastern Spirits

Attitudes toward spirits varied throughout the ancient world. Despite the above (relatively late) story, spirit possession was not a common subject in early Egyptian literature, compared to the Mesopotamian texts of the time. Dancing was mentioned far more often. For example, the Middle Kingdom story collection *King Kheops and the Magicians* (1700 BCE)[17] tells the tale of three goddesses disguised as *khener*, Hathor's itinerant dancing girls/midwives, sent to help deliver royal Fourth Dynasty triplets. Early images of dancers were common. A number of the Old Kingdom tombs in Egypt's Saqqara burial ground display troupes of dancers (2400 BCE),[18] while older predynastic pottery and statuettes immortalize the raised arms, pear shapes, rattles (*sistra*), and clappers (finger cymbal precursors) (3400 BCE) of ancient female performers.[19]

---

17 This is from the Westcar Papyrus (18th–16th centuries BCE). *King Kheops and the Magicians* and *The Princess of Bekhten* were both written in hieroglyphic script, the early pictorial notation system of the Nile Valley in which a sound or an idea was associated with the image of an object or person (such as a dancing man at the end of a word to denote the act of dancing).

18 Particularly Fifth and Sixth Dynasty tombs (2400–2300 BCE) near Saqqara's step pyramid, which is a thirty-minute drive from Giza's famous Fourth Dynasty pyramids. See figure 3.

19 Some of the best examples of these are the predynastic painted terracotta statuettes of the Naqada IIa Period (ca. 3500–3400 BCE), reportedly from Ma'mariya, Egypt, in the Brooklyn Museum Ancient Egypt collection. See figure 4.

Figure 3: Dancers on the tomb of Mereruka, a Sixth Dynasty vizier

Ancient images of dancing can be found throughout the Middle East. The region's oldest, so far, is a wall painting of trance-dancing men (some headless, others with drums) in Catal Hoyuk (5700 BCE), a proto-city located in Anatolia (present-day Turkey).[20] And artifacts found in Israel imply dancers and their percussion instruments were in the region as far back as Palestine's Natufian era (13,000–9800 BCE). The female pelvic bones of a skeleton unearthed near Mount Carmel, Israel, were adorned with "dance" jewelry—a fox-tooth rattle belt (see figure 5).[21] Elsewhere, in a cave near Jerusalem, archeologists discovered hundreds of paired bone "castanet" pendants. Note the common theme of dancers with percussion instruments.

In *Music in Ancient Israel/Palestine*, Israeli musicologist Joachim Braun described the discovery, in the

Figure 4: Terracotta dancer in Hathor's "horned" position

20 Catal Hoyuk was one of humanity's first proto-cities, along with Jericho.

21 Found in the Yonim Cave/Mugaret el-Hamam on Mt. Carmel (11,000–9,000 BCE). Braun, *Music in Ancient Israel/Palestine*, 51–52.

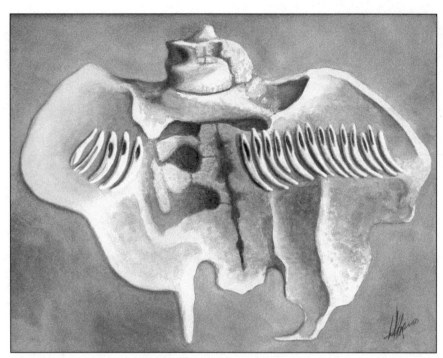

Figure 5: Fox-tooth rattle belt

HaYonim Cave in Upper Galilee, of hundreds of finely polished bone pendants "ranging from oval to rectangular to breast or castanet-shaped," in excellently crafted pairs. "These pairings," Braun wrote, "along with the identical size and flat interior sides, suggest they were ideal for striking against one another... The castanet form seems particularly suitable for such clapping sounds, since their lower parts are somewhat thicker and thus quite resonant." When Braun tried playing "these Stone Age castanets," he discovered they "were capable of producing a pure, transparent, but pitchless sound."[22]

But to return to possession, the Sumerians and Babylonians, contrary to the Egyptians, frequently discussed spirit possession in their literature—as illustrated by this early "demon banishment" charm (from approximately 1700 BCE): [23]

---

22 *Music in Ancient Israel/Palestine*, 52-53.

23 Charms are vocal incantations recited to banish or attract spirits. Many *Pyramid Text* verses are charms.

TABLET 2: From the burning spirit of the entrails which devours the man,
From the spirit of the entrails which works evil,
May the king of heaven preserve,
May the king of earth preserve....

TABLET 4: From sickness of the entrails,
From sickness of the heart,
From the palpitation of a sick heart,
From sickness of bile,
From sickness of the head,
From noxious colic,
From the agitation of terror
From flatulency of the entrails,
From noxious illness,
From lingering sickness,
From nightmare,
May the king of heaven preserve,
May the king of earth preserve....

TABLET 6: From the cruel spirit of the head,
From the strong spirit of the head,
From the head-spirit that departs not,
From the head-spirit that goes not forth,
From the head-spirit that will not go,
From the noxious head-spirit
May the king of heaven preserve,
May the king of earth preserve.[24]

---

24   From A. H. Sayce, "Babylonian Exorcisms," *Records of the Past*, Vol 1, pages 131–35. (Translations
from a nineteenth-century journal of English translations of the cuneiform and hieroglyphic
inscriptions held by the British Museum and elsewhere, published in their original languages and
scripts by Henry Rawlinson [1810–1895] in *Cuneiform Inscriptions of Western Asia*, Vol. II, plates
17 and 18.)

Similar to the Jews, the Babylonians and the Assyrians held that "the world was swarming with noxious spirits who produced the various diseases to which man is liable, and might be swallowed with the food and the drink that support life." Furthermore, "they counted no less than 300 spirits of heaven and 600 spirits of earth. All this, with the rest of their mythology, was borrowed by the Assyrians from the [Babylonians]."[25]

Babylonian spirits were shapeless entities that assumed animal or human appearance at will, inhabited desolate places, and preferred blood for food. Females were the most dangerous, particularly night demons like Lilu, Lilitu, and Ardat Lili, who attacked men. For good reason, the Quran mentions Babylon as the birthplace of magic.[26] The region, Mesopotamia (the "Land Between Two Rivers," the Tigris and the Euphrates), retained vestiges of these early beliefs into the Prophet Muhammad's lifetime (600s CE)—which was what prompted his monotheistic teachings.

The Egyptians, too, believed in airborne and underground spirits and developed symbiotic relationships with some of them—particularly the six varieties that cohabited their bodies. Arabic *afreet* (from the Quran) and *qarin* (human spirit doubles that live underground) are holdovers from these ancient beliefs. On the other end of the spectrum, the ancient Egyptians also believed that powerful inhabitants of the night sky's northern circumpolar region governed the world as they knew it.

The Egyptians agreed with the Babylonians that spirits caused illnesses, either by invading bodies or by piercing them with "arrows." As Halioua and Ziskind point out in *Medicine in the Days of the Pharaohs*,[27] even though Egypt's ancient medical papyri show advanced knowledge of human organs, some diseases, and plant remedies, the treatments they prescribed relied heavily on amulets, magic spells, and charms. Nevertheless, by Homer's time, the late Bronze Age, Egyptian physicians had accumulated over a thousand years of experience and were world-renowned: "Every man is a physician [in Egypt], wise above human kind" (*The Odyssey*). Where these beliefs originated—Mesopotamia, Egypt, Africa or elsewhere—no one knows. According to Jeremy Naydler in *Shamanic Wisdom in the Pyramid Texts*, they developed from eons of prehistoric shamanic visions

---

25   Sayce, 131.

26   According to the story of Harut and Marut in the Quran, 2:102.

27   Pages 7 and 179.

and, perhaps, drug-induced near-death experiences. These shamans evolved into priests, and their roles of healer and Invisible middlemen became priestly duties. Perhaps this is why the Ebers Papyrus describes three types of priest-physicians: the traditional doctor (*swnw*), the *wab*-priests of arrow-shooting Sekhmet (the equivalent of modern healers), and the exorcists (*kherep*—priests) of the protective scorpion goddess Serqet.[28] Apparently, Serqet's venom wasn't ideal for curing Sekhmet's arrow wounds.

So far, I have mentioned three Egyptian deities associated with illness: Khonsu, Sekhmet, and Serqet. Khonsu's functions evolved over time, from bloodthirsty god-catcher in the *Pyramid Texts* to healer in the Bekhten stele; nevertheless, he was usually associated with the moon, measuring time, and fertility. It was the lioness archer Sekhmet, a bloodthirsty incarnation of Hathor, that was the most lethal of the three. And so we arrive at the deity we're really interested in: Hathor, the early Egyptian patroness of music, dance, and drunkenness—and by extrapolation, trance.

Figure 6: Sekhmet

To better explain who Hathor was, here is the first section of an ancient Egyptian legend, *The Book of the Heavenly Cow* (i.e., of Hathor). While several versions survive, the one below is based on different translations of the legend inscribed inside Seti I's funerary temple in the Valley of the Kings.

---

28   Halioua and Ziskind, *Medicine in the Days of the Pharaohs*, 10.

Figure 7: Hathor with cow ears

The Book of the Heavenly Cow [29]

It came to pass that His Majesty Ra, King of Mankind and the gods, discovered Mankind was plotting against him. It was the end of the Golden Age, when The Almighty lived among his creatures on Earth, and He was old. His bones had turned to silver, his flesh to gold and his hair to lapis lazuli. With sadness and resolve, He secretly summoned his all-seeing Eye, Hathor, to his palace, along with his faithful retinue, Nun, Shu, Tefnut, Geb, and Nut.

---

29   This version is my own rendition from various sources, notably E. A. Wallis Budge, *Legends of the Gods*, 14–25 and xxiii–xxxii. Also Adolf Erman, Henry Breasted, and Henry Rawlinson.

"I seek your counsel. The humans are plotting against me. Many have fled to the southern desert. They fear retaliation. I want your opinions before I slaughter them."

"They fear your Eye, Hathor," replied the primeval watery void of Nun. "Send her to smite the conspirators."

And so Ra sent Hathor in her ruthless form, Sekhmet, The Powerful One, to slay the humans in the desert. The sand turned red with their blood and Ra was pleased.

"As you live, Almighty Ra, I have overcome Mankind and it brought joy to my heart," Sekhmet reported. "But you have called me back too soon." And so the goddess returned to the South and blood ran like a river to the sea.

After a while, Ra missed his Eye and regretted the slaying of so many humans. He sent the god of the Earth, Geb, the son of Shu and Tefnut and the brother and husband of Nut, to bring her back. But his Terrible Eye refused to stop the slaughter. She had become addicted to blood.

"Send my messengers to fetch red ocher in great quantity," Ra ordered. "Grind it and add it to the barley my maidservants are crushing for beer." His retinue did as He asked. When the maidservants were done, the beer-mash looked like blood and they filled seven thousand jars with it. "Pour this onto her killing fields at night, so that when she awakes, famished, she will find it."

His retinue carried the jars to Sekhmet's lair and poured them onto near-by fields, flooding them three palms high with the draught. When the deity awoke and found the fields inundated with blood, she rejoiced and drank her fill. By nightfall she was so intoxicated she fell into a stupor and slept for days. When she finally came to, she did not recognize Mankind and her thirst for blood was gone. Ra welcomed back his favorite.

"Welcome in peace, O Golden One! You were sorely missed." To celebrate, Ra commanded his servants, "Let this sleeping draught be prepared for the Eye of Ra during the annual feasts of Inundation, when the Great River runs like blood. Entrust the maidservants with this sacred duty."

To this day, maidservants prepare sleeping draughts for the Feast of Hathor—to honor the Powerful One's return from addiction.

Hathor, the Heavenly Cow, wore many hats—or headdresses. Besides being the patron deity of the good things in life (including sex), she also oversaw birth and rebirth. Predynastic rock art shows dancers with her symbol, the *sistrum*,[30] and/or their arms raised overhead in her traditional "horned" cow dance posture. Hans Hickman, an expert on ancient Egyptian music, remarked, "the dance with lifted arms was ancient, found in Africa, Northern Europe, Pharaonic Egypt and elsewhere. It imitated or was a symbol of the horns of a cow."[31] Curt Sachs, a world dance specialist, gives an even better description: "Women dancers round their arms above their heads like handles, so that the tips of their fingers touch their shoulders."[32] A unique piece of predynastic pottery shows musicians playing clappers and female dancers with their arms in this "Hathor" position.[33] The pose was later modified to imitate Hathor's hieroglyphic symbol, cow horns surrounding Atum/Ra's solar disc, by pointing rounded arms skyward. Guillaume-Andre Villoteau mentioned this position in his early nineteenth-century description of *ghawazee* street dancers in Egypt.[34] Belly dancers from the 1930s used it in old Egyptian films, and modern belly dancers around the world consider it a standard arm placement.

Hathor had many epithets: Celestial Cow, Golden One, and Eye of Ra were the most popular, although Lady of Drunkenness was not far behind. You could also say she was Mistress of Altered Consciousness as well! At times she was a nurturing figure, as the Afterlife mother of all dead kings, and linked to birth through her association with Inundation. The annual flooding fertilized the Nile's banks, which helped seeds to sprout. Hathor's centers of worship were Giza, Memphis, and Denderah, and her portion of the circumpolar sky was called the Mansion of Horus (*Hat-hor*). By the Sixth Dynasty her priestesses included the eldest daughters of pharaohs[35] and her initiates

---

30 A handheld rattle with moving metal disks on wires. See figure 11 for an example.

31 *Catalogue Generale des Antiquites Egyptiennes*, 116. My translation from the author's French.

32 *World History of the Dance*, 85.

33 D. Randall-MacIver and A. C. Mace, *El-Amrah and Abydos*, plate xiv, D46.

34 Book 13 of *Description de l'Egypte*, 497.

35 The eldest daughter of King Teti was a priestess of Hathor and married to Mereruka. Her portion of her husband's mastaba (flat-roofed) tomb in Saqqara, still visible today, is decorated with reliefs of dancers and musicians. See figure 3.

roamed the country as *khener,* troupes of professional singers, musicians, dancers, and midwives who facilitated birth, entertained the living, mourned the dead, and aroused procreative instincts at funerals. Sexual passion and energy were necessary precursors for birth and therefore rebirth into the Afterlife. In a nutshell, then, Hathor bestowed life on Earth and in the Afterworld, but as Sekhmet, she took it away.

Figure 8: Nebamun dancers, or *khener,* from wall painting [36]

---

36 Nebamun was a Theban grain scribe who worked in the Amun temple at Karnak during the reign of Amenhotep III (c. 1390–1352 BCE). Fragments of his tomb-chapel wall paintings were purchased by the British Museum in the 1820s. They include some of the most well-known images of ancient Egyptian dancers and musicians in the world.

Figure 9: Hathor, the Heavenly Cow

As patron deity of music and trance, percussion was important to Hathor. Her initiates wore rattles (*menat* collars and dance belts[37]), shook sistra, and played clappers. Rhythm restored *maat*—balance and order—and these sounds reminded ancient Egyptians of rushes rustling as the Celestial Cow wandered through *Aaru*, the Field of Reeds—Egyptian heaven. Rattling also helped navigate the vortexes of altered consciousness and death. The most famous illustrations of khener playing percussion instruments are in the British Museum, where fragments from the tomb chapel of Nebamun, an Eighteenth Dynasty New Kingdom scribe under Amenophis III (1388–1351 BCE), are displayed in a dedicated room. A banquet scene shows young women and male servants waiting on guests and performing for the deceased and his wife. Wearing nothing but floral wreaths, jewelry, and dance belts, two khener dance and snap their fingers while two others, seated and clothed, stare straight at the viewer—a highly unusual break from ancient Egyptian artistic convention. These women are musicians: an aulos player (a double reed flute from Anatolia) and a (clapping) percussionist. They are accompanied by two more clapping women, who probably also sang, since lyrics are written above their heads. To the right, in a different fragment but from the same wall, five more clothed musicians also play for the dancers and guests: two lute players, another clapper, a second aulos player, and what appears to be a percussionist striking a rectangular frame drum. They all wear floral wreath crowns, except the two facing front with disheveled hair.

I believe these two musicians were painted differently to highlight their wild eyes and hair—both symbols of altered consciousness. While "head tossing" and its resulting trance could have been native to Egypt, it might also have been imported into New Kingdom harems by enslaved Cybele worshippers sent to Egypt as tribute (Cybele was the Bronze Age incarnation of Anatolia's Neolithic Great Mother). Thutmose III, the "Egyptian Napoleon" (1458–1425 BCE), had conquered Syria and Mitanni, part of Cybele's home turf, only a few generations before this tomb was painted. Since Cybele's initiates are credited with inventing the aulos and were known to drink copious amounts of wine (a trance induction aid), it is possible the tradition of drunken ecstatic

---

37 Dance belts or "girdles" were originally made with cowry shells filled with coarse sand and pebbles so that they rattled when a dancer moved her hips. The Metropolitan Museum of Art has beautiful Middle Kingdom examples on display made from gold and silver.

worship made its way from Anatolia to Egypt at this time. The presence of alcohol is emphasized in Nebamun's banquet scenes and vineyard depiction, which, with the help of magic, ensured an unlimited supply of wine in the Afterlife.

According to the Book of the Heavenly Cow, drunken revelry was an essential part of Hathorian ritual long before the New Kingdom, but the ancient Greek historian Herodotus's later description of Hathor's annual celebrations paints the clearest picture. By his visit (440 BCE, slightly before the Bekhten Stele), Hathor's more benevolent cat form, Bastet (later associated with the Greek Diana), had replaced the lioness Sekhmet as her incarnation of honor.

Figure 10: Nebamun dancers (entire fragment of tomb-chapel
wall painting), with musicians and possible Cybele trance dancers

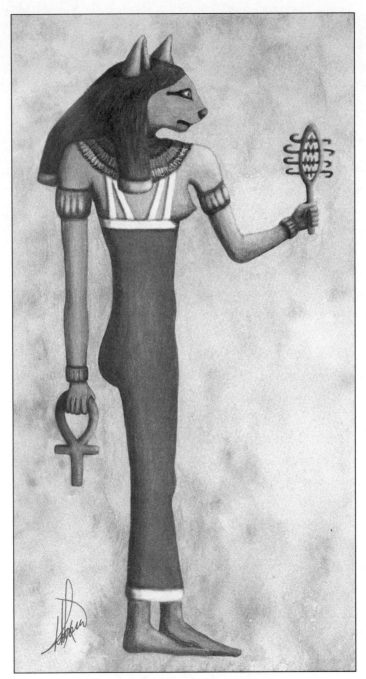

Figure 11: Bastet holding an ankh in her
right hand and a sistrum in her left

Herodotus noted that "the Egyptians were also the first to introduce solemn assemblies, processions, and litanies to the gods; … which the Greeks were taught the use [of] by them.… The Egyptians do not hold a single solemn assembly, but several in the course of the year. Of these the chief, which is better attended than any other, is held at the city of Bubastis, in honour of Diana." He then went on to describe the festivities at Bubastis:

> Men and women come sailing all together, vast numbers in each boat, many of the women with castanets, which they strike, while some of the men pipe during the whole time of the voyage; the remainder of the voyagers, male and female, sing the while, and make a clapping with their hands. When they arrive opposite any of the towns … they approach the shore, and, while some of the women continue to play and sing, others call aloud to the females of the place and load them with abuse, while a certain number dance, and some standing up uncover [their private parts]. After proceeding this way all along the river-course, they reach Bubastis, where they celebrate the feast with abundant sacrifices. More grape-wine is consumed at this festival than in all the rest of the year besides. The number of those who attend, counting only the men and women, and omitting the children, amounts, according to the native reports, to seven hundred thousand.[38]

Cybele, Maenads, and the Great Minds of Greece

Let's now leave Egypt and explore Anatolia (Asia Minor), homeland to the Great Mother. Humans have gathered on its mountainous steppes and in its valleys since the Mesolithic era, long before the first pharaoh united Upper and Lower Egypt. Humanity's oldest known temple, Gobekli Tepe, sits on a plateau overlooking the northern edge of the Fertile Crescent in present-day Turkey. Over 11,500 years old, it predates the invention of agriculture—in which it is now thought to have played a crucial role. Although archeologists are uncertain of what, who, or how people worshipped among the temple's concentric rings, genetic evidence implies that enough hungry mouths gathered there on a regular basis to spur the domestication of local wheat. And even though the site

---

38 *History of Herodotus*, Vol. II, trans. G. Rawlinson, 100–104.

was filled in and abandoned 1,500 years later, the region continued to foster belief in the sacred. Between 7500 and 5700 BCE, the Neolithic proto-city Catal Hoyuk sprouted in the Konya plain, 450 miles to the west, at roughly the same time as Jericho and Ein Ghazal in the Jordanian Valley and Abu Hureya in Mesopotamia. Although Jericho is much older, Catal Hoyuk is more important to trance dancing because of its wall paintings and how one of its deities—the Great Mother—is an earth goddess eerily similar in appearance to Europe's carved Paleolithic Venuses, although she was often depicted seated on a throne rather than as a solitary, faceless figure with large breasts and hips.

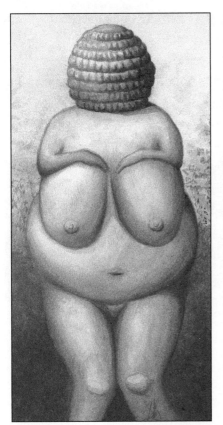

Figure 12: Goddess statues: the Paleolithic Willendorf
Venus (left) and Catal Hoyuk's Great Mother (right)

Now let's fast-forward five thousand years, past the Hittite Empire, to the era of Phrygia (its southern border included Catal Hoyuk)—when, again according to Herodotus, the Thracians founded the city of Gordium (now Yazilikaya).

Although the country did not produce much literature, it became famous for its legendary kings Midas and Gordias (of "the Golden Touch" and Gordian Knot fame), its music, and its ecstatic orgiastic rituals honoring Cybele (also Kybele, or Rhea-Kybele), the Great Mother's Bronze Age descendant. Worshippers, spurred on by self-castrated priests called Gallai or Corybantes, achieved wild frenzied states with occasional bloody consequences.

By the eighth century BCE, Cybele's cult, centered in Pessinus and Pergamum, extended from the southern Balkan Mountains to neighboring Assyria, the Aegean coast, and the Greek islands. And although Phrygia was eventually swallowed into Cyrus's Persian Empire in 690 BCE, the goddess continued to thrive throughout the region until the Greeks combined her with Rhea, Zeus's mother, and Dionysus won out as the ultimate deity of wine, revelry, and ecstatic release.

Figure 13: Maenads dancing with Dionysus

Figure 14: Cybele, in the style of Greco-Roman statues from the first century BCE

And so we return, once again, to the era of the Bekhten stele, when belief in spirit possession extended around the Mediterranean and Greece's age of reason gave birth to the great thinkers Pythagoras, Herodotus, and Plato. Ecstatic dancing and mystery rites were an essential part of the religious landscape, and Phrygia's "foreign deities" Dionysus and Cybele were firmly transplanted onto Greek soil—as these lines, uttered by Dionysus in *The Bacchae*,[39] show:

Figure 15: Maenad with thyrsus
staff, tossing her head

To this city, the first of Greece,
I come, here lead my dance, my mystic rites
Establish here, that mortals may confess
The manifest god. Of all realms of Greece
In Thebes I first have raised my shouts …

…

But should the Theban state
In rage attempt with hostile arms to drive
My Bacchae from their confines, I will head
My Maenades, and lead them to the fight.

…

But you, my frolic train, who left the heights
Of Tmolos, Lydian Mount, ye female troop,
Whom from barbaric coasts I led with me
Associates, and attendants on my march,
Resume your Phrygian timbrels framed by me
And mother Rhea.[40]

---

39 *The Bacchae* is a tragedy, written by the Greek playwright Euripides, featuring the god Dionysus (Bacchus). It was first performed in 405 BCE, shortly after the playwright's death.

40 Euripides, *The Bacchae*, from *Euripides*, Vol I, trans. R. Potter, lines 23–27, 58–61, and 64–69.

Figure 16: Bacchae carrying thyrsus staffs, an aulos, and a hand drum

Although Dionysus is considered the poster boy for ecstatic worship, the actual dancing was done by his "female troop." Clad in fawn skins, they ran through the woods calling his name, tossing their heads, and rattling thyrsus sticks, long staffs with pinecones attached to one end.[41] When entranced, they prophesied, were fearless in battle (because of the extraordinary strength and analgesic effects of deep trance), safely handled snakes, ripped apart live animals, and ate raw flesh.

As Dionysus's worship evolved, Greece's finest minds scrutinized the proceedings. Plato, in particular, wrote extensively about altered states, or "manias," which he described as "enthusiasm"; literally, "being engodded." He concluded there were different types of trance and not all were beneficial, especially those caused by disease.

---

41 Barbara Ehrenreich, *Dancing in the Streets*, 35.

Figure 17: A head-tossing maenad carrying the carcass of an animal

In *Phaedrus*, he divided the desirable "*theia mania*" (divine madness) into four categories: mantic, a prophetic state inspired by Apollo; telestic, the possession realm of Dionysus that resembled madness; poetic, the artistic gift of the Muses; and erotic, the passionate obsession generated by Eros and Aphrodite to encourage reproduction of the species.

Plato believed trance was linked to music—melody, not rhythm—and in particular, to pieces composed in the Phrygian mode, to the dithyramb meter. Plus, the music had to be played on an aulos. Even though percussion instruments (frame drums, kettledrums, castanets, and cymbals) accompanied the melodies, Plato did not believe their sound caused trance or influenced it in any way.[42] Gilbert Rouget devoted an entire chapter of his comprehensive study, *Music and Trance*, to the Greeks, and included a list of *maenad* movements from first-hand literary sources, images on pottery, and stone carvings: wild spinning, wide swinging arms, head tosses to the point of Pindar's "neck dislocation," violent full-bodied arching, absent or pained expressions, line and circle dances, and dancing while playing clappers.[43] We will revisit this list in Part Three, but it certainly fleshes out these uninhibited wilderness escapades!

Besides gods and goddesses, lesser entities also influenced Greek and Roman daily life. Known as "tutelary," these guardian deities or nature spirits protected specific places, people, cultures, and occupations. In Greece, they were called *daemons*; in Rome, *genii* (singular *genius*). Human daemons accompanied their charges from birth (for example, Socrates's inner voice), much like the familiar spirits of shamans and the qarin of modern Egypt. Later, these entities gave rise to modern demons and jinn—but their initial appearance probably occurred at the dawn of *Homo sapiens* evolution.

Before I start digging into our prehistoric roots to explain why I think this, however, there is one more Bronze Age possession trance source I would like to mention—history's most well-read book, the Old Testament.

---

42   Rouget, *Music and Trance*, 80.
43   Ibid., 181.

Mantic Trance: Prophesy and the Old Testament

Believe it or not, the Old Testament describes multiple possessions and exorcisms. Back when its books were written, the Jews believed that demons were the winged children of Adam and his first wife, Lilith, a shapeshifting man-seducer and childbirth demon.[44] My favorite banishment story is in *The Book of Tobias,* where a young man expels a violent Persian demon ("*aeshma daeva*," or "Asmodeus") from his bride on his wedding night. The entity had murdered her seven previous grooms, but with help from the angel Raphael and pungent, disagreeable incense, the young man exorcised the spirit and avoided becoming dead husband number eight.

The Old Testament also gives many examples of prophetic trance (Plato's "*mantic mania*"). Its entire second section, from the death of Moses (c. 1200 BCE) to the Hebrew return from Babylonian exile (515 BCE), is called "Prophets," or "*Nevi'im*," and is filled with divine predictions and altered states. One concerns Saul, Israel's first king, and his successor David, "the giant slayer." Around 1050 BCE, the prophet Samuel poured a vial of sacred oil over Saul's head, kissed him, and prophesied:

> [T]hou shalt come to the hill of God, where is the garrison of the Philistines: and it shall come to pass, when thou art come thither to the city, that thou shalt meet a company of prophets coming down from the high place with a psaltery, and a tabret, and a pipe, and a harp, before them; and they shall prophesy:
>
> And the Spirit of the Lord will come upon thee, and thou shalt prophesy with them, and shalt be turned into another man.
>
> …
>
> And when they came thither to the hill, behold, a company of prophets met him; and the Spirit of God came upon him, and he prophesied among them.[45]

But Saul did not remain on good terms with God. Many years later, when Saul attempted to kill David, David took shelter with Samuel. Together they went to Naioth, where Samuel guided a community of prophets…

---

44   Gerda Sengers, *Women and Demons,* 32.

45   1 Samuel 10:5–6, 10 (King James Version).

And it was told Saul, saying, Behold, David is at Naioth in Ramah.

And Saul sent messengers to take David: and when they saw the company of the prophets prophesying, and Samuel standing as appointed over them, the Spirit of God was upon the messengers of Saul, and they also prophesied.

And when it was told Saul, he sent other messengers, and they prophesied likewise. And Saul sent messengers again the third time, and they prophesied also.

Then went he also to Ramah, and came to a great well that is in Sechu: and he asked and said, Where are Samuel and David? And one said, Behold, they be at Naioth in Ramah.

And he went thither to Naioth in Ramah: and the Spirit of God was upon him also, and he went on, and prophesied, until he came to Naioth in Ramah.

And he stripped off his clothes also, and prophesied before Samuel in like manner, and lay down naked all that day and all that night. Wherefore they say, Is Saul also among the prophets? [46]

For me, these stories inspire burning questions. First of all, did the king of Israel really roll around, foaming at the mouth, eyes reversed, telling fortunes for twenty-four hours? I guess that depends on what the verb "to prophesy" means—to convey God's words or predict the future. And where did the information come from—God, the Invisibles, a ripple in time, hallucination? Even more difficult, how was this knowledge transmitted? According to the descriptions, it came during altered states of consciousness. Why? What is it about trance that allows communication between the realms? I also have a problem with what prophesy implies. Were the speakers truly clairvoyant or simply manipulating the people around them with auto-suggestion? How many verifiable episodes were required to eliminate chance and prove an otherworldly connection? And what were these prophets connected to? A sixth sense? Other life forms telling them what they thought would happen? Souls traveling through time? God Himself (or his envoys) communicating what He wanted them to know?

I believe the answers to these conundrums are connected to choice—the ability to sift through a stream of ideas, compare them to memories or accumulated knowledge,

---

46   1 Samuel 19:19–24 (King James Version).

imagine possible outcomes, and then decide on a course of action. Indeed, many of the world's religions believe God's ultimate gift to humanity (and to the jinn, according to the Quran) is choice. If this is true, though, how can the future be "readable"—i.e., predetermined—if our actions are unknown until we make them? Or, on a larger scale, how can universal events be predicted if they originate from random electrical impulses and chemical reactions? There is, of course, a middle ground: predictions based on a current trajectory and past choices. But if choices were predetermined—for example, through thought manipulation—this influence would have to have been made at the atomic level, through gravitational, electric, magnetic, or other unknown forces. Personally, I don't know whether a force, an entity, or multiple entities influence my thoughts. I do know, though, that I have chosen to believe Invisibles exist. I also know that, in my experience, meaningful answers often hinge on asking the right questions.

Leaving these great existential riddles aside, the points I am trying to make are that (1) during Biblical times, people believed chosen individuals were permitted to glimpse the future, albeit through blurry glasses, and (2) these enlightened seers were not in a normal waking state of consciousness when "the Spirit of God fell upon them." They were in trance. Somehow the altered functions of deep ecstasy allowed their brains to perceive, recognize, and interpret information from the Invisible world and/or the future.

Let's return to what the Old Testament meant by "prophecy" and "prophesying." The original text was written in Hebrew before the Greeks translated it. Their main root for "prophet" was similar to the Arabic *nabi* (or *navi*), a "spokesperson for God." This was derived from the Hebrew term *niv sefatayim*, "fruit of the lips." Scholars disagree, though. Some claim the word was derived from the Akkadian verb "to call." Others think it evolved from another Hebrew root meaning "to bubble up" or "to boil" (possibly referring to epilepsy or the ecstatic state). At any rate, prophets were common back then, transmitting ordinary messages to ordinary people. Yet only fifty-five men and women were actually named in the Old Testament—including Sarah, who was said to have had a greater prophetic ability than Abraham.

The great Jewish philosopher Maimonides was also curious about prophesy and developed Plato's mantic mania in his *Guide for the Perplexed*.[47] He suggested there were

---

47 *The Guide for the Perplexed*, trans. M. Freidlander, part II, chapter XLV, 241–45. Available at http://www.sacred-texts.com/jud/gfp.

multiple levels of prophesy and listed them: inspired actions; inspired words; symbolic dream revelations; auditory dream revelations; audiovisual dream revelations by either a human speaker, an angelic speaker, or God; symbolic waking visions; auditory waking revelations; audiovisual waking revelations by either human or angelic speakers or God Himself, specifically in the case of Moses. Curiously, these ecstatic levels mirror the progressive degrees of hallucination articulated by the neurologist Oliver Sacks.[48] And this brings up another hard question: what fine line divides divine stimulation from physical malfunction?

Is prophesy, or trance in general, nothing but malfunction, or did humans evolve ethereal communication conduits because they were somehow advantageous? Or is trance merely a byproduct of other useful processes, like sleep, as David Lewis-Williams, a leading expert on trance and prehistoric religion, contends? Dreaming and trance are global *Homo sapiens* traits, like speech, so they must have evolved before our ancestors migrated out of Africa—for a good reason.

The Paleolithic Era

To address these questions, we must return to the Paleolithic era—when tool-making was discovered, fire was tamed, and art was born. Logically, it makes sense that trance dancing developed during the Upper Paleolithic, when *Homo sapiens* invented musical instruments and recreated shamanic visions on the walls and ceilings of European caves. But I believe altered states began to surface much earlier, because of a far more important discovery—the taming of fire—or "permanent fire control," as Richard Wrangham dubs this evolutionary milestone in his book *Catching Fire*.

Wrangham contends that sometime around 1.8 million years ago in Africa, our early ancestor, *Homo erectus,* captured coals from a lightning strike or a spark from a flint tool and coaxed flames into a controlled burn.[49] Suddenly they could cook, scare away predators, see at night, and stay warm throughout the winter. And according to

---

48   Oliver Sacks was a professor at the NYU School of Medicine. He wrote many books (*Hallucinations* [2012], *Musicophilia* [2010], and *Awakenings* [1973], among others) about the myriad experiences of the human brain.

49   *Catching Fire*, 190–91; and Jennie Cohen, "Human Ancestors Tamed Fire Earlier Than Thought," History.com, April 2, 2012.

Wrangham's theory, cooked food fueled the evolutionary changes that made us the species we are today. Yet taming fire might have also had another, less obvious consequence: staring at campfires can induce trance. Dancing plasma flares are hypnotic. It doesn't take long for shapes and faces to appear in them. However, Lewis-Williams and others have hypothesized that *Homo erectus* did not have a large enough brain to see faces where there were none or conceive of ethereal life. That would require another million years or so, and the evolution of the *Homo sapiens* prefrontal cortex with its abstract thinking, planning, innovation, creativity, and symbolic behaviors.[50]

Let's look back in history to see if we can guess when humans conceived the possibility of non-corporeal life and hence the belief in spirits.[51] Below is a rough timeline of hominoid development and achievements I have gathered from various sources. All dates are approximate.

Date	Notes
3.3 million BCE	Primitive stone tools found near Lake Turkana, Kenya.
3.18 million BCE	Lucy—*Australopithecus afarensis,* found near Hadar, Ethiopia—a World Heritage Site.
3 million–130,000 BCE	The **Lower Paleolithic** began in Africa with tool-making hominids, including *Homo erectus, habilis,* and *naledi. Homo erectus* tamed fire.
2.8 million BCE	Appearance of *Homo* genus. Age of *Homo* jaw found in Ethiopia.

---

50   Lewis-Williams, *The Mind in the Cave*, 96.
51   Ibid., 38; and Wrangham, *Catching Fire*, 85–89.

2.8 million–? BCE	*Homo naledi*, near Johannesburg, left 15 of their dead in a remote-access cave.
1.8 million–143,000 BCE	*Homo erectus* walked the Earth—our direct ancestor evolved a larger brain, a smaller gut, and walked upright from eating cooked food. The first hominid to colonize Europe and Asia.
1.5 million BCE	The earliest evidence of controlled fire, discovered in South Africa's Wonderwerk Cave in 2012.
800,000–250,000 BCE	*Homo heidelbergensis* evolved—the last common ancestor of both Neanderthals and *Homo sapiens*.
790,000 BCE	Gesher Benot Ya'aqov (on Israel's side of the Jordan River), until 2012 the oldest reliable evidence of fire control.
400,000 BCE	Controlled fire campsite found in Schoningen, Germany.
300,000–160,000 BCE	*Homo sapiens*, or "anatomically modern humans" (AMH), evolved in East Africa/Ethiopia.

220,000–45,000 BCE	The **Middle Paleolithic** and *Homo neanderthalis*. Unlike *Homo sapiens*, the Neanderthals did not make art (according to Lewis-Williams), made simpler tools, and did not plan hunts. Yet in a French Neanderthal burial site, the rock slab covering the grave had "cupules" carved underneath and other markings nearby.
195,000–160,000 BCE	The age of the oldest *Homo sapiens* skulls, from Ethiopia.
160,000–135,000 BCE	*Homo sapiens* spread throughout Africa.
150,000–40,000 BCE	Neanderthals in Europe.
140,000 BCE	Long-distance exchange/trading and shell fishing.
100,000 BCE	Bone tools and mining.
90,000–60,000 BCE	*Homo sapiens* in Israel—fully modern skeletons from Qafzeh and Skhul. *Homo sapiens* perhaps traveled from Ethiopia across the mouths of the Red Sea and the Persian Gulf to Iran, and then around the Indian Ocean to Indonesia and Australia.

77,000 BCE	Oldest reliably dated art in the world (so far); a piece of ocher engraved with hatched cross marks from South Africa.
74,000 BCE	Mount Toba in Sumatra exploded, killing many of the world's *Homo sapiens* during a suspected 6–10 year winter—the DNA "bottleneck."
60,000 BCE	Aborigine in Australia. European interbreeding with Neanderthals that left traces in all modern *Homo sapiens* DNA outside of Africa.
52,000–45,000 BCE	*Homo sapiens* migrated from Iran through Anatolia and Germany into Europe.
50,000 BCE	Ostrich-egg shell bead making started.
45,000–35,000 BCE	**The Middle to Upper Paleolithic Transition**/Revolution. During this creative explosion, Neanderthals gave way to *Homo sapiens* in Europe. Modern skeletons, behavior, and art suddenly appeared in Western Europe.

45,000–10,000 BCE	The Upper Paleolithic
41,000 BCE	Bone flutes found in the Danube River valley.
40,000 BCE	Spanish Paleolithic cave art—El Castillo in northern Spain, Nerja Cave in the south near Malaga.
40,000 BCE	The last traces of Neanderthals in Europe (Northern Spain).
36,000 BCE	Chauvet Cave, France and Coliboaia Cave, Romania.
35,000–9,000 BCE	Venus statuettes throughout Europe, the oldest from Germany and Austria.
20,000–15,000 BCE	*Homo sapiens* crossed the Bering Straight into North America.
18,000–14,000 BCE	Altamira Cave in Northern Spain.
15,000 BCE	Lascaux Cave in the Dordogne region of France.
15,000–10,000 BCE	**The Magdalenian**—end of European Ice Age. Major cave art in France, Spain, and England.

13,000–10,000 BCE	Decline of cave art. Las Monedas cave in Spain.
12,500–9,500 BCE	Natufian era in the Levant
11,000 BCE*	Britain's Creswell Crags.
12,000–7,000 BCE	**The Mesolithic**—a period of climactic instability when humans domesticated plants and animals. First large-scale inter-human fighting over resources.
10,000–3,000 BCE	**The Neolithic**—depending on the region, with the Levant and Natufian culture as point of origin. It begins with plant domestication (farming) and ends with large-scale metal tool production.
9,100–7,500 BCE	Gobekli Tepe temple in use.
9,000 BCE	Jericho founded by the Natufians.
7,500–5,700 BCE	Catal Hoyuk founded. Plastered human and auroch (pre-domesticated cattle) skulls, shamanistic trance dancers painted on a habitation wall, and Great Mother statues.

*Britain was late to the Mesolithic Era, which started earlier in the Middle East.

Figure 18: Dancers as painted in Catal Hoyuk

And so we arrive at Catal Hoyuk, the Great Mother, and Mesolithic evidence of trance dancing (images painted in a style similar to Paleolithic caves, and also to modern San/Bushmen rock drawings). As for the dawn of religion, European evidence points to the Upper Paleolithic period, with its Venus figurines (one of them, discovered in Galgenberg, close to Stratzing, Austria—not far from the site of the Venus of Willendorf—appears to be dancing!) and cave wall paintings. Yet the *Homo sapiens'* "anatomically modern" brain could have discovered trance, music, and dance at any time after 300,000 BCE. They had voices to sing with, hands to clap, feet to stomp, and fire to induce trance.

In a nutshell, then: after *Homo erectus* tamed fire, diet and nutrition levels changed—prompting the evolution of a larger and more efficient, but energy-hungry, cortex. The warmth and protection of "controlled combustion" also allowed safe travel to new hunting grounds—the continents of Eurasia and Africa for *Homo erectus*, and throughout the planet for *Homo sapiens*. Fire also protected them while they slept. This was crucial since the body is paralyzed during REM sleep, i.e., dreaming. Nighttime illumination also allowed *Homo erectus* and his descendants to remain awake longer, which changed their sleeping patterns. Staring at flickering flames under low-light conditions could have also altered their consciousness while awake. But although rare objects might imply that *Homo erectus* or Neanderthals had artistic capabilities and hence the potential for creative and conceptual thinking, scientists

Figure 19: Dancing Venus of Galgenberg

believe only the *Homo sapiens* cortex was able to conceive of life outside a physical body. And yet … *Homo naledi* and Neanderthals gave their dead special care. Does this mean they believed in life after death and an invisible soul? Perhaps they simply didn't want scavengers prowling their camps or couldn't bear to see (or smell) a loved one rot. Family love is a mammalian trait.

Even if the European Middle to Upper Paleolithic transition seems to have been a turning point for human artistic development, the oldest flutes were found in the Danube Valley corridor. This implies they were invented before humans arrived in Europe. And although most early artistic evidence is Euro-centered and created after *Homo sapiens* interbred with Neanderthals, my hypothesis is that *Homo sapiens* conceived of ethereal beings at the dawn of their existence in East Africa and Ethiopia around 300,000 years ago, long before they emigrated anywhere. If this is true, then the native trance dances and possession cults discussed in this book—the eastern Ethiopian zar and Sudanese *tumboura*, the western Nigerian bori and orisha, and the southern San/ Bushmen trance dancing—could be vestiges of the same original religion.

Let me tell you why I think this. The oldest *Homo sapiens* fossils found so far (195,000 BCE) were unearthed near the southern Ethiopian town of Kibish, close to the South Sudan border.[52] Another set, from around 160,000 BCE, was discovered near Hadar in Herto, Ethiopia, to the east, in the Awash valley of the Afar Depression, the region rich in humanoid fossils where "Lucy" was found.[53] The Herto skulls (three were found together, two adults and a child, without skeletons) are remarkable not only for their age but because they had cut marks indicating they had been ritually de-fleshed (as a mortuary practice). Their polish and markings suggest that, rather than simple cannibalism, they were ritually skinned, similar to the plastered skulls found in Catal Hoyuk and Jericho and the ancestor skulls venerated by a few modern New Guinea

---

52 Richard Leakey discovered the remains of two hominids there, one distinctly *Homo sapiens*, in 1967. Originally thought to be 130,000 years old, their age was later reevaluated to 195,000 BCE. Hopkin, "Ethiopia Is Top Choice for Cradle of *Homo sapiens*."

53 The Herto discovery was made in 1997 and published by Tim D. White et al., "Pleistocene *Homo sapiens* from Middle Awash, Ethiopia," 742–747.

tribes. This implies that the Herto skulls could be the earliest known evidence of human conceptual thinking, religious behavior, and perhaps … belief in spirits.[54]

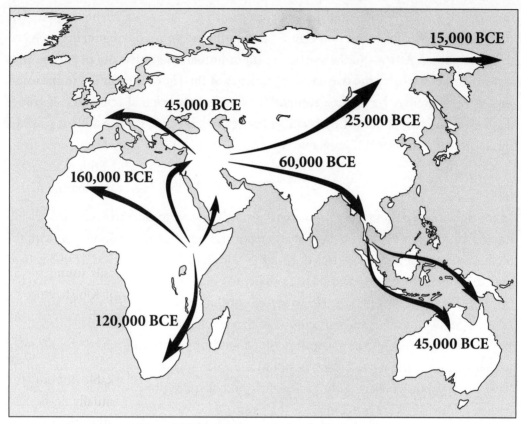

Figure 20: The global spread of early *Homo sapiens*

Unfortunately, other evidence from this time period has yet to surface. Nevertheless, mitochondrial DNA studies indicate that three separate *Homo sapiens* groups left East Africa to populate the rest of the continent at about this time. One traveled into the steppes and savannahs of the Sahara and Sahel (including present-day Niger and upper Nigeria), the second found its way to the tropics of West Africa, and the third

---

54 Robert Sanders, "160,000-Year-Old Fossilized Skulls Uncovered in Ethiopia Are Oldest Anatomically Modern Humans."

ended up in the south, according to a 2009 study[55] of African genetics. Each branch developed different—yet similar—spirit possession traditions that all involved some form of trance dancing, judging from present-day practices. The San/Bushmen, famous for their trance dance traditions and ancient rock paintings,[56] are an excellent example. The study links the San/Bushmen homeland—the southwestern coastal region between Namibia and South Africa—to the starting point of human migration out of Africa. Tests show that the San carry the two earliest branches of the *Homo sapiens* Y-chromosome, suggesting they may be direct decedents of humanity's original ancestors. If trance dancing is an integral part of their current religious practices, it is possible it played a similar role for our original progenitors.

———————

In conclusion, even though the first actual "proof" of dancing dates to a Neolithic dwelling wall in modern Turkey, I believe shamanism and trance dancing developed with the birth of our species in East Africa during the Middle Paleolithic period. If this is true, then our link to the spirit world and our ability to perceive and communicate with it has been "selected for" throughout *Homo sapiens* evolution. Or, in other words, since our relationship with fire began—since none of this would have been possible without it.

And there you have it, the uncomfortable conundrum our species has been confronted with from the beginning: to believe or not to believe in spirits. Up till now, *Homo sapiens* have leaned toward believing. But scientific minds require proof—which is difficult to come by if Invisibles are as nebulous as the plasma flares of a bonfire. Besides, spirits may not all be capable of manipulating solid matter. One, however, is capable, according to general consensus, on a universal level in countless dimensions: the Creator. But whether this Being chooses to manifest on our insignificant plane when we ask it to is the subject of modern religion and beyond the scope of a trance dance manual.

———————

55　Sarah A. Tishkoff et al., "The Genetic Structure and History of Africans and African Americans," 1035–44. The study compared DNA from over 3,000 individuals—121 African groups, 4 African-American groups, and 60 non-African populations—to trace the genetic structure of Africans to 14 ancestral population clusters.

56　The oldest San paintings in Namibia are thought to be 26,000 years old; not as old as some of Europe's painted caves, but old nonetheless.

What I would like to explore, though—before we move on to Middle Eastern spirits—is what trance actually *feels* like and the biological mechanisms behind it. Understanding the physical causes behind altered consciousness will make surrendering to it easier. Surrender is key; without it, induction requires drugs. But most drugs (including alcohol) tend to dull the senses and scramble signals, so it's best not to rely on them for long-term communication (even if the ancients had no such scruples!). With that said, let's move on. But first, please do the homework.

Homework: Your Ancestors and Their Music

Research your ancestors, the sources for your DNA River of Blood. What sacred dance forms did they do? Listen to examples (slow and fast) of their music. Does any of it appeal to you?

3

·········

Trance the Experience

The best way to preface this chapter is to continue my description of an Egyptian zar hadra from chapter 1. Do you remember, when I left off, the Harim Masri band had arrived and the ritual was about to begin ...

Dancing with Genies—A Zar Hadra

One of the Harim Masri musicians, clutching a burner in her red-hennaed fingers, went to fetch live coals from the kitchen. As she sprinkled bakhour on the glowing red embers, the heavy scent of frankincense and sandalwood wafted through the apartment. Basin in hand, she made her way around the living room, pausing as guests fanned the fragrant smoke towards their faces. Muttering a prayer, she lifted right arms, then left, then shirts or galabeyas, over the coals for the aromatic plumes to infiltrate the intimate spaces beneath. She completed her sacred mission—creating scented barriers against uninvited spirits—by fumigating the soles of their feet. When she was finished, participants dutifully dropped money into the basin, grateful for the sweet-smelling armor.

The First Band:
Harim Masri (the "Egyptian Women"), also called the Firqa Saidi

Someone lit the altar candles and the musicians picked up their percussion instruments.[57] A hypnotic, syncopated heartbeat of a rhythm reverberated off the walls. The women on frame drums[58] kept beat while the tabla drum player layered riffs on top. Eventually, the musicians began to sing, their voices harsh and rasping over the percussion. First they praised the Prophet Muhammad, then they switched to a chant summoning Abou Danfa, a spirit from the Saidi region of Upper Egypt.

A large middle-aged woman in a black cover-up with a black *tarha*[59]—a scarf—draped over her face began to dance. Her torso rocked forward and back as she bounced double-time to the beat. It wasn't long before the scarf slipped, though, revealing eyes rolled toward the ceiling. Seeing this, the musicians quickened their pace, faster and louder, until, with a loud bang on the drums, they reached a climax. As if on cue, the woman collapsed to the floor unconscious, her fall softened by a spotter—after only two minutes of dancing. Other female guests propped her up, rubbing her arms and back to revive her. Someone sprinkled rose water on her. Another gave her bottled water to drink. Within minutes the fallen woman rubbed her eyes, dazed. Her head sank into in her hands, her energy spent. The others respected her privacy.

A song similar to a dirge followed. Another middle-aged woman, with a gold tarha, got up. She, too, moved mainly her torso, pulsed double-time to the beat and took only minutes to collapse into trance. A different spotter caught her on the way down.

---

57   Please see appendix 2 for a list and description of zar instruments.

58   Frame drums are (generally) acceptable to Islam, so their use is less controversial than other instruments.

59   Dancers put veils over their heads and faces to help them concentrate on the music and separate them from the audience. There is no prescribed color, but black is less see-through.

Next, the musicians sang praise for Rumi Nagdy, a spirit soldier, and his beautiful sister. A third woman, with a pink tarha, in her early forties rose. Vigorously tossing her head forward and back, she loosely swung her arms until they flailed in front of her, like a stranded alpinist desperately climbing a rope. Seconds later she, too, keeled over backwards, oblivious to the world.

The group ended their set with "*Benat al-Handasa*," a favorite about schoolgirls and their dolls, in honor of the child spirit Rouqash. A familiar face took the floor: the first dancer, who had removed her black cover-up in the stifling heat. A black tarha still covered her head, but no longer hid her face. Smiling, half in trance, she bounced to the music and played peek-a-boo with the scarf. Switching to a folkloric hop step, she jiggled her hips in belly dance fashion, her elbows flapping like chicken wings. She quickly tired of this, though, and returned to her veil. The woman with the pink tarha joined her. Soon, both were bouncing and swaying in unison, until, several measures later, the first woman collapsed to the floor—after only a minute of dancing.

The woman with the pink tarha continued without her, waving her arms and pointing to her forehead in typical folkloric style. Smiling, eyes shut, her head tilted back, she waved away the candy dish one of the singers offered her from the altar. Then, stumbling as if drunk, her expression changed. Her lips parted in a frozen smile; her vacant eyes fixed on the ceiling. The tempo quickened. She writhed forward and back, faster and faster, until, in ultimate surrender, she too collapsed to the floor.

It was time to switch musical groups. During the intermission, family and neighbors filed into the apartment until all the chairs were taken and onlookers, finding standing room scarce, spilled down the hallway into the kitchen.

The Second Band:
Tumboura (the Sudani Group)

After a ten-minute break, the male duo who had arrived with the Harim Masri took over: a *sunjuk* (or *tumboura* player) and a percussionist. The *tumboura*, a six-string lyre, is a favorite of zar ceremonies, with its circular, banjo-like sounding board and rudimentary harp frame. Its owner—a young man from a long line of zar musicians—sat on the floor, his back against a wall with the lyre propped upright next to him. Its navy blue frame, intricately decorated with white string and cowry shells, towered over his head. His left arm, draped behind it, plucked or muted the strings at the top while his right hand, holding a pick, strummed them from the bottom. He improvised while the percussionist donned a goat- or sheep-hoof belt called a *mangour*, picked up the incense basin, and passed it among the crowd.

Two Harim Masri percussionists joined the duo and struck up a driving rhythm on a couple of small, thick-framed drums called *tabla sudani*. With a short curved stick and an open palm, they banged out a decidedly African beat. The mangour player joined them, a rattle in hand. Rolling his wrist, he layered a continuous clatter over the rhythmic two-count swish of his twisting hips. Once the beat steadied, the tumboura player began to sing. A third female musician joined him, repeating the verses in chorus style. It was a quick, lively melody, especially when the others clapped syncopation.

Many got up to dance. One young woman did a lively jig, her arms flapping like chicken wings while her shoulders shrugged double-time to the beat. Another did a two-step, leaning forward, arms swinging like a power walker, until she clasped her hands behind her back, Brazilian Umbanda style. A third wove her torso in wide figure eights, her head dipping and rolling precariously. Eventually, she and the others lost their crispness and staggered around with serious, far-away expressions on their faces—yet no one lost control. After five minutes they sat down, looking disorientated and nauseous.

Figure 21: Tumboura lyre

The Rattler—i.e., the mangour player—pulled another woman up to dance, the younger sister of the first dancer, who quickly went into a semi-trance. Supported under the arms from behind, the woman leaned her head on her sister's shoulder as her sibling whispered in her ear. Not long after, she collapsed onto the floor. Again, several women hurried to care for her, along with her sister and the Rattler.

Ten more minutes of music followed. Women rose to dance, then fell into a trance. Smiles morphed into anguished grimaces, eyes rolled into heads, and bodies sank to the ground, dazed or unconscious. Finally, the tumboura was put away and, after another intermission, the last group of the evening took its place.

Figure 22: Mangour player in the 1880s

The Third Band:
Abou al-Ghreit

This group, named after an Islamic sheikh, was composed of four male singers (who also arrived before the ritual began) and their instruments: a *tabla* (a goblet drum), a *mazhar* (a large, thick-framed tambourine), a *nay* (a reed flute), and *toura* (large, flat-rimmed finger cymbals). None of the Harim Masri joined them. As they set up, the toura player offered incense one last time.

They played only two songs, *"Saly ala Muhammad"* and their namesake, *"Abou al-Ghreit,"* for ten minutes each. The flute's haunting melody brought a hush over the room, while the toura chimed like otherworldly church bells summoning the faithful to prayer. I understood why this group went last. Their music affected everyone.

Even the women sitting quietly in a corner (who had refused to dance) had tears streaming down their cheeks. Those who had danced, danced again. Even the family's disabled eighty-five-year-old matriarch could hardly contain herself. She twisted so violently in her chair they had to help her onto the dance floor—and eventually reseat her next to the musicians.

And then the hadra was over. The musicians put away their instruments and the guests filed slowly out the door. One of the Harim Masri uncovered the tub of popcorn and distributed its contents. The candles were blown out and given to those most in need of good luck. I received the remaining incense. In the end, none of the neighbors complained. How could they? They had all been there, trance dancing with the jinn.

Figure 23: From left to right: large toura,
bell-shaped sagat, small toura, flat-rimmed sagat

Introduction to Induction

So, what happened to these women as they collapsed to the floor? Did their souls join the Almighty while their bodies hosted disgruntled, bloodthirsty spirits? Or were their visions lucid and personal, of vented frustrations and forbidden desires in the personae of handsome ethereal soldiers or naïve little girls?

To begin with, Oliver Sacks made an important distinction between temporary states of altered consciousness:

> There is, of course, a world of difference between the long-lasting
> pathological state we call hysteria and the brief trance states which
> can be induced by a hypnotist (or by oneself) ... The commonest [and]
> most "normal" of [these] exceptional mental states is that of a spiritually
> attuned consciousness, in which the supernatural, the divine, is experi-
> enced as material and real.[60]

---

60   *Hallucinations*, 247–48.

There are a few things you should know about trance, though, before we discuss what happened to these women, or, better yet, I teach you how to reach a similar state yourself. The first and most important point is that trance is a common, healthy, genetically transmitted human trait—a fact determined in 1963 by a National Institutes of Health (NIH) funded study. That's right, science proved over fifty years ago that "ecstasy did not represent any pathology."[61] However, even though all humans are born with this ability, some are better at it than others.

Secondly, deep trance rarely manifests on its own without provocation. It requires considerable mental preparation and unwavering intention, as well as physical stimulation. In other words, it must be triggered, which is the reason for initiation ceremonies—to teach novices how to enter it on cue. Accidental onsets do occur, though. Non-Western societies consider such incidents signs of Invisible pre-selection. Westerners, on the other hand, consider these to be symptomatic of pathological conditions, particularly scientists who do not believe in non-corporeal entities. True, science's physical cause-and-effect approach has brought us far, but much still needs to be explained about our universe, particularly in relation to divine, supernatural, or paranormal phenomena. Open minds would benefit everyone.

So, if trance is rarely spontaneous, is it hard to induce? Is the process painless? And if you succeed, is it like riding a bicycle—once you learn, you never forget? My goal is that by the end of this book you can answer these questions for yourself, from personal experience. For now, though, know that shamans and other spiritual practitioners develop their skills through years of training. Even gifted "seers" predisposed to trance benefit from guidance. Prophetic states can be difficult to bear or control without it.

In the same vein, zar participants don't automatically collapse into trance during their first ritual. The healer, or *sheikha*, and perhaps the patients' families and friends, coach them first about "good behavior." Novices to Umbanda—an Afro-Brazilian religion that combines ancestral African entities with Brazilian ancestor spirits, Spiritualism, and Catholicism—go through long periods of apprenticeship, as do the "whirling dervishes" of the Mevlevi Sufis, who undergo years of instruction. That being said, severe shock such as death, marriage at a young age, or radical family, political, or social

---

61   Felicitas Goodman, *How About Demons?*, 5.

change (for example, slavery) can force supernatural abilities to surface spontaneously. Examples can be found among New World slaves, the severely repressed or abused, and monks, nuns, and dervishes who practice long-term fasting and isolation. While all humans are wired for trance, a jolt and instructions help flip the switch.

Participants also need to practice. Entering trance on cue, particularly a trance that conforms to cultural expectations, is a learned process. So please, don't feel frustrated or give up if you don't succeed the first time. Be patient. The key is to enjoy the process— the dancing—and to consider trance as an added bonus if or when it occurs.

There are many ways to enter trance besides kinetic induction. Perhaps the best known of these is sensory deprivation. The brain not only needs constant input, but constant change. Even a lack of variety can push the mind to create new stimuli, i.e., hallucinations.[62] This is why Europe's pitch-black caves were ideal for prehistoric vision quests, and one reason closing the eyes or gazing at crystal balls and scrying bowls produces visions.[63]

Auditory driving, or rhythmic entrainment, is another popular method. Fondly referred to as "drumming till you drop," it exploits bottlenecks in the auditory nerve and the ability of loud percussion to overpower and synchronize the body's internal rhythms (breathing, heartbeat, and brainwaves) to its own.[64] Chanting, storytelling, overtone singing, or loud melodic music work as well, but take longer. For example, Dr. Felicitas Goodman, the author of *How About Demons?*, a pivotal book on religious trance, based her induction techniques on fifteen minutes of continuous rattling at 220 beats per minute; in other words, monotony and rhythmic entrainment. Kinetic trance's head tossing and spinning, or "equilibrium disruption," also falls in this category, but it targets the balance portion of the nerve, rather than its hearing functions. I will talk more about this in chapter 4.

---

62 See Oliver Sacks's discussion of Charles Bonnet syndrome, the production of visual hallucinations by the visually impaired, on TED: http://www.ted.com/talks/oliver _sacks_what_hallucination_reveals_about_our_minds.

63 Sacks, *Hallucinations*, 34.

64 Research has found that excessive synchronization overloads the consciousness-processing regions of the brain, which prevents them from treating incoming information and eventually causes loss of consciousness. Arthuis et al., "Impaired Consciousness," 2091–2101.

Another effective method, used by Native American shamans, is sleep deprivation, which is notorious for provoking hallucinations.[65] Breath regulation or hyperventilation is also popular, particularly pranayama, specialized breathing exercises, and the heavy chanting used for zikr rituals. Even sexual orgasm with its prolonged panting can induce trance, although the effects quickly fade. Other sensory overload techniques include excessive heat (Native American sweat lodge rituals); olfactory saturation (via perfume, pheromones, incense, flowers, or any odor with a memory of trance attached to it); ingestion—or its lack (fasting, thirsting)—which includes drug consumption (marijuana, LSD, ayahuasca, ibogaine, peyote, psilocybin mushrooms, or MDMA, to name a few); trauma; nitrogen narcosis (deep diving); fever; brainwave manipulation through hypnosis; and meditation or prayer work without involving the senses.

Once you decide on an induction method, the next step is to learn how to monitor your descent. Lucidity is a key indicator. Are you awake or not? Do you know what's going on around you or not? Kinetic trance follows a sliding scale, which begins with mild to ecstatic lucidity, much like the meditative states produced by prayer or yoga. Dancers remain vaguely aware of their surroundings and can resurface at any time, albeit slowly. This description also applies to lucid anesthesia, "interrupted pain perception," which is the next stage (the dervishes eating live coals in chapter 8 are perfect examples of lucid anesthesia, although I don't recommend you test yourself that way). After that, beginning with amnesiac possession, lucidity diminishes until hosts no longer control or remember their actions. During Umbanda rituals, for example, roughly 20 percent of mediums are fully unconscious with complete amnesia. The rest feel the presence of a foreign will beyond their control but remain vaguely aware of their surroundings, even though they quickly forget what transpired once they resurface. Various stages of obscurity ensue, culminating in profound, cataleptic rigidity, where muscles stiffen and the mind goes dark (a symptom often taken advantage of by side-show hypnotists).

Experiences can fall anywhere along this sliding scale, although descent beyond mild lucidity requires a great deal of practice. And experience makes a difference. People new to ecstasy find their first encounters are much stronger, with effects that linger,

---

65   Sacks, *Hallucinations*, 42.

compared to sessions they experience after habituation.[66] This is one reason why in Part Three, I only include techniques for lucid trance. While this book offers descriptions of possession states, I don't teach how to obtain them. They are not something you want to undergo without a spotter. It's one thing to observe spirits as they control your autonomic nervous system. It's entirely different to let them crash through the china shop unsupervised.

What Does Trance Feel Like?

No matter the method, successful induction hinges on how well you surrender to the process. This is why understanding what might happen to you is helpful. It is important to know that trance is not something to fear, but rather can be quite beneficial (even so, **please see pages 249–250 for a list of medical contraindications** for kinetic induction). To this end, I have gathered firsthand descriptions, from scholars and others around the world, of both lucid trance and complete possession. Of course, there are many types of altered states, and no two humans experience them exactly the same way—much like female orgasm. Both result from neural stimulation routed along highly variable, emotionally susceptible pathways.[67] But don't take my word for it, see for yourself!

Lucid Trance

Terpsichore Trance Therapy (or TTT, a therapeutic adaptation of Brazilian trance dance practices designed to help patients integrate traumatic experiences): "Dancers remain lucid without always experiencing amnesia afterward. Participants feel their bodies are uncontrolled and their movements generated from within—without mental guidance or forethought. Yet the mind still functions. They know where they are, who is near them and what their bodies are doing, but without inhibition."[68]

---

66 Goodman, *How About Demons?*, 55.

67 For information about female pelvic nerve variations see *Vagina: A Biography* by Naomi Wolf.

68 David Akstein, *Un Voyage a Travers la Transe,* 140. My translation from the original French text.

Rave culture (global youth): "I feel like, for me, another force takes over and I let go and my body just starts doing this dance, which is more intricate and patterned and fractalized than anything I could possibly come up with if I was actually trying to do it with my head. So my mind lets go and I'm watching myself, possibly even from a space slightly outside of myself."[69]

Umbanda (Brazil): Two elders from the Washington, DC, temple described their first spirit encounters to me. One told me, "In the beginning, for two years or so, I just spun. I couldn't find anything, like my antenna wasn't tuning in to the right thing! I don't remember the exact moment it happened. I know the first entity I actually encorporated was a *preto velho*… Drumming and dancing are essential for us. Experienced members can bring an entity without dancing, singing, clapping, or drumming, but when you start you definitely need these things. They help you lose your consciousness and step into another dimension. Our drumming is very… purposeful. When you connect with the drum you HAVE to get out of your head. You no longer listen to the words. You just hear the beat. You don't DO anything or try this or that. You move aside and connect to the beat. It's primal, like someone throws you a rope. The rope is that drum. Obviously you're moving, you're dancing, and suddenly the movements are no longer yours. They're influenced by an entity. When that happens, we call that an 'approximation.' It's not encorporation yet, but a moment of connection. I don't think I had an approximation, initially. I was so disconnected. I had nothing, nothing, nothing, nothing, nothing and then *there*. That's how it felt, a couple of years of nothing and then there it was."

Another elder added, "For me… since I came from a Native American tradition with a lot of drumming, I took about a year, because I was used to the feeling. Have you ever fainted? You know right before you faint there's that *whooosh* feeling?" (She spread her fingers on top

---

69   Qtd. in Robin Sylvan, *Trance Formation*, 91.

of her head, then pulled them up and together as if pulling something out of her skull.) "Like it all comes to a pinpoint?" (She loudly sucked in air.) "That's what it feels like, that moment."[70]

Possession Trance

Pentecostal worshippers: The soul "dwindles into nothingness" when the Holy Spirit takes over a person's body. A congregant recalled, "'my lips began to move and the sounds came tumbling out, and there was light all about and I knew nothing more.'"[71]

Ethiopian zar: "A zar marks its entrance or descent by the *gurri*, a form of trance dancing, accompanied by a sort of roaring and a choppy recitation of the spirit's name (*fukkara*). This is generally preceded by yawning and stretching, a feeling of oppression, of being weighed down or squashed, invaded by bees, struck by a lance or by pain in the shoulders or ribs. What patients feel during the gurri itself varies.

The healer first tries to provoke a trance by lightly pushing the patient or turning her head with a whip passed around her neck. Eventually, the trances become spontaneous and organized, except when bad spirits intrude unexpectedly."[72]

"The healer's role consists in part of educating the new zar entity, teaching the patient, considered the zar's horse, how to correctly execute the gurri, to dance or move without excessive vehemence so as not to hurt themselves and to generally show docility toward their spirit … The neophyte attending a *wadaga* for the first time (a night zar ritual) rarely does the gurri spontaneously. The healer must bring it … an apprenticeship that often requires several sessions. Other

---

70   My interview with Washington, DC, Umbanda Templo Guaracy elders, May 2013. The organization's website is www.tgwashington.org.

71   Goodman, *How About Demons?*, 3.

72   Michel Leiris, *La Possession et ses aspects théâtraux chez les Éthiopiens de Gondar*, 21–22. My translation from the French.

adepts may show neophytes what to do by executing the gurri in front of them, as if to teach by contagion."[73]

Sudan: "One must learn how not to resist a spirit's attempts to enter" the body, but a spirit should not enter a woman before she is married, while she is still a virgin, or menstruating. "Because it must conform to prescribed patterns of 'spiritness,' trance performance requires skill and considerable control. . . . The few women who do enter trance spontaneously . . . are long-term adepts of the zar who . . . have become progressively more skilled at alternating modes of consciousness and allowing the spirits to exhibit themselves through their bodies."[74]

Trance is experienced as a kind of out-of-body experience fueled by the rhythms of the drums. "When the spirit fords boundaries between the visible and invisible worlds . . . [the host] herself is transported to another domain. She transcends the visible world and 'sees with the eye of spirit' into the normally invisible parallel universe."[75]

North Sudan: "The dancers are protected [by spotters] from excessive behavior and from injuring themselves. They may dance to complete exhaustion and collapse, and become completely unaware of the surroundings and insensitive to pain."[76]

"Others respond to the spirits' chants from a kneeling position, bobbing up and down from the waist, torsos moving with impossible speed, tobs covering their heads like so many Halloween ghosts."[77]

South Sudan: The patient "would begin dancing in character and then fall on her knees and go into a set of convulsive isolations of the torso and head, until she would lie down exhausted."[78]

---

73   Michel Leiris, *La Possession et ses aspects théâtraux*, 40. My translation from the French.

74   Janice Boddy, *Wombs and Alien Spirits*, 134–35.

75   Ibid., 351.

76   I. M. Lewis et al., eds., *Women's Medicine*, 130.

77   Boddy, *Wombs and Alien Spirits*, 126.

78   Lewis et al., *Women's Medicine*, 158.

Nigeria: "Getting possessed is not always easy—many patients expect they will experience some more dramatic change in themselves than they actually do." One of them spent "29 days trying twice daily to get possessed." This "was not an unusual experience; others in the house and nearby had endured similar embarrassment." These patients "seemed to have similar personalities, sharing a certain bluffness, with jokes and laughter an important part of their character. As in hypnosis, people vary greatly in their suggestibility ... "

"Covered entirely with a blanket, the patient sits with legs straight out, hands in front, arms by the side, back straight. There is a bowl of burning incense at her feet, beneath the blanket; a rattle is shaken rhythmically beside her ear, the musician and his assistant seated close behind the patient. Thus the patient waits upon the sense of being possessed—which is expressed by making 'automatically' the movements of the particular spirit that the music is calling."[79]

Somalia: "The basic step was a kind of heavy skip; but people had their own variations." Patients danced with spotters or "went on hands and knees before the drums and shook their heads from side to side. Sometimes the dance ended with the patient's going into a trance; some did this very quickly, others took a long time. When in this state she might collapse on the floor, or run outside, or cling to the assistant or to someone else. Some made inarticulate noises or wept."[80]

Vodou possession (Haiti): "The participants, the future 'horses' of the deity" become "dazed, stiff, possibly [go] into convulsions."[81] With the onset of possession, "the devotee falls to the ground, rolling before the drums, or staggers blindly about the dancing space."[82] "The possessed person does not know whose horse he has become, and has no way

---

79   Lewis et al., *Women's Medicine*, 52–53.

80   Ibid., 170–71.

81   Goodman, *How About Demons?*, 13.

82   Melville Herskovits, qtd. in Goodman, *How About Demons?*, 13.

of speaking for himself.... In the course of a single ceremony, which often lasts all night, a person may even be possessed by a succession of deities, each exhibiting totally different behavior. Possession dissolves at the conclusion of the dance."[83]

Greece (400 BCE): Examples of possession trance from *The Bacchae*:

> She foamed with rage,
> Rolling her eyes askance, nor harbour'd thoughts
> She ought to harbour, frantic with the god.
> …
> To this royal house
> Agave speeds, rolling her furious eyes
> Askance.
> …
> I feel my sense return'd …
> All memory of my former words lost.[84]

There was no maximum age for trance, either:

> Some one will say I reverence not my age,
> Joining the dance, my head with ivy wreathed;
> But not distinctly did the god declare
> If the fresh youth should lead the dance, or those
> Of riper years; from every age he claims
> Those common honors.[85]

You can see that even though these examples depict a wide range of trance experiences, certain induction factors are common—particularly the attitudes or tendencies that block it. If the emotional current isn't flowing, the physical wiring won't work. Skepticism, irony, and derision make surrender impossible. Fear, lethargy, and stoicism

---

83 Goodman, *How About Demons?,* 13–14.
84 Euripides, *The Bacchae,* lines 1199–1201, 1245–47, 1346, 1349.
85 Ibid., lines 211–16.

also douse trance like a campfire in a deluge. Even too much thinking prevents altered consciousness. In other words, you must want and BELIEVE something will happen to you to cross the threshold (hence Jesus proclaimed, "Your faith has healed you" after his miraculous cures). Doubt ruins everything. It should come as no surprise, then, that kinetic trance responsiveness closely follows hypnosis susceptibility (static trance), for which there are charts.[86] But knowledge can be a two-edged sword. If you don't know the experts say you can't do something, you might succeed simply by persevering.

This brings me to expectations, another factor that affects all forms of induction. If you expect to fail, you will. If you expect to enter trance and find something valuable, you will. This is called "subconscious seeding." "Happy thoughts" work well, too. Another productive way to sow your mental oats is to challenge your subconscious with a quest before descending. But trance doesn't have to produce significant events to be beneficial. It can simply be an inner sanctuary for contemplating the day during exercise.

Fear, as mentioned, is also a major trance deterrent. People need to feel at ease before they will allow themselves to slip into a potentially vulnerable state. Safety enables relaxation, which leads to surrender. The flip side is that it is almost impossible to force people into trance against their will (except via drugs or extreme sleep deprivation, i.e., torture). So please remember, if you don't want to go, you can always say no.

Unfortunately, for whatever reason(s), some people have difficulty entering trance. Besides attitude, they may concentrate too hard or not move enough during induction, or slip into performance mode and try to execute complicated, showy dance steps, or even worse, choreography. Remember that thinking, i.e., prefrontal cortex activity, prevents descent. The idea is to get to know your subconscious through its spontaneous movements. Censorship defeats the purpose. *There is no right or wrong way to dance.* Just let go and trust the process.

Given the importance of mindset, trance ceremonies traditionally open with mood-enhancing activities. Like Pavlov's bell and salivating dog, they prompt the brain to respond on cue. But what works for some may not work for others, which is why you should develop your own pre-induction ritual. Only you know which relaxation techniques and

---

86   The most well known are the Harvard Group Scale of Hypnotic Susceptibility (HGSS) and the Stanford Hypnotic Susceptibility Scales (SHSS). Research them online if you are curious.

sacred triggers work best for you. I offer suggestions in chapter 9, but the choice is yours. In general though, the objective is to focus on the music—the here-and-now, not the future or the past—by clearing your mind of everyday concerns.

The Four Stages of Descent

Let's talk about the physical sensations of descent for a moment. Normally, kinetic induction passes through four levels, each with distinct sensory thresholds: dizziness, flow, objective observer, and disembodied soul.

> **Dizziness and Flow:** After setting up and stretching, induction begins by repeating chosen movements until the mind disengages and the autonomic nervous system, or "autopilot," takes over. This is "flow," free-form dancing or moving without thought. It generally follows dizziness, the first level, which you should dance through—**unless you encounter severe nausea or motion sickness, in which case you should stop.** This trance induction method is not for you. Typically, beginners take 15–20 minutes for autopilot to kick in, less with experience. Usually, the hardest part is recognizing the symptoms of success. Keep moving. The process may surprise you.

> **Objective Observer:** Phase three, passage through the ethereal threshold, begins with a shift in body awareness to "objective observer"—often via tunnel vision and "second wind" energy bursts (from minutes to hours). Music that triggers strong memories or emotions, good or bad, will intensify the experience. Whirling helps, too.

> **Disembodied Soul:** This last stage varies the most. For me, consciousness shifts outside and slightly above and behind my body, although other trance dancers describe a sinking sensation into the torso. As I said, everybody's different.

Now that you know how kinetic trance progresses, here's a chart you can use to gauge your descent:

Dizziness	Keep dancing (excluding the exceptions noted above). Go down on your hands and knees or sit if you think you will fall.
Flow	Completely relaxed muscles—dancing like a rag doll.
	Intense concentration focused on the music.
	Loss of inhibition.
	Disassociation of mind and body. Instantaneous improvisation. A feeling that someone else, far more experienced, is dancing for you.
	Prolonged bursts of energy.
	Distorted sense of time, space, or place.
Objective Observer	"Theta flares"—flashes of intuition and problem solving.
	Manic repetitive movements— head bobbing, spinning, or jumping.
	Dancing on the ground— kneeling, on all fours, sitting, or on the back.
	Unusual flexibility— upper or full body bends, forward and back.
	Altered body sensations— feeling light as a feather or heavy as a rock.
	Tunnel vision.
	Heightened audiovisual senses— colored lights, faces, and/or voices.

Disembodied Soul	Troubled sense of touch— anesthesia or thermal change (icy hands).
	Synesthesia, confusion of the senses— i.e., "feeling" or "seeing" music.
	Heightened emotions—crying as a cathartic release.
	Vocal energy release—grunts, groans, screams, cries, animal noises, or glossolalia (speaking in tongues).
	Memory issues—from forgetfulness to amnesia.
	Regression—childhood memories surface.
	Shaking—extended full body shivers, trembling or shuddering.
	Foaming at the mouth.
	Ocular inversion or revulsion— eyes rolling up or protruding with a fixed stare. Deep trance is indicated when only the whites of the eyes are visible.
	Swooning or collapse.

A major outcome of trance is that suppressed thoughts can seep into consciousness unfiltered—from the depths of your subconscious and the far reaches of the universe (I explain why in chapter 4). For now, the important point is that our brains process daily events using pattern recognition; i.e., by comparing new information to a constant stream of memories and learned behavior. This is why all thoughts are good *once*, but not all are worth dwelling on. Outrageous, off-the-wall ideas are a natural part of mental synthesis, but so is the ability to choose whether to pursue them or not. Don't ruin your trance experience by fixating on a negative channel. Switch stations and move on.

Other phenomena that surface are "theta or awakened mind flares"—flashes of insight seemingly from nowhere. These can be creative, solve problems, or illuminate banished traumatic memories. Unfortunately, they are notoriously fleeting, and like dreams, vanish as quickly as they appear—unless you write them down. Yet they are never totally forgotten. The subconscious remembers them, but will stop sending more if you consistently ignore them. On the other hand, if you value and act upon them, they will continue to erupt as faithfully as Yellowstone Park's famous geyser.[87]

Trance dancing stimulates memory to such a degree that some believers in reincarnation hold it even awakens past-life memories or those dormant in our DNA. Dredging up the past is fine if you have nothing to hide—i.e., you haven't repressed anything—but how many people can say that? This is where the healing aspect of trance comes in. Altered consciousness frees submerged skeletons so they can float up into the light of day; a cathartic liberation, certainly, but tricky without guidance. So as you navigate these potentially choppy waters, please remember the following suggestions.

Change is always possible: An event may be permanently written in stone, but how you react to it is not. Look for the silver lining around the thunderhead. Good things come from difficult circumstances; you just have to find them. And things could always be worse. Silver linings mean the sun is still there—and brighter days are not far away. This may be a tired cliché, but maintaining a positive attitude has many advantages. Besides, shining a bright light on shadowy demons diminishes their power. Even the ugliest monster is less scary in broad daylight.

Take time working through memories: Nothing has to be done immediately. Revisit issues only when you're ready. Often your subconscious will help you (when you least expect it) with dreams or free associations.

Almost everything can be healed: With time, and help if necessary, you can reintegrate even the most painful event. As I said, attitude is everything. Perseverance and a desire to heal WILL AFFECT the subconscious.

---

87   Anna Wise, *The High Performance Mind*, 166.

Sadly, some people are unaware they have repressed painful early events, or that their memories are only selected snippets of what really happened. Therefore, if during a session or shortly afterward you feel overwhelmed, stressed, afraid for no reason, depressed, or have persistent but illogical negative emotions about yourself or your projects, know that hidden traumas might be lurking beneath the surface, which could benefit from professional help.

Another trance highlight, and goal for many, is visions—from purple flashes, halos, three-dimensional landscapes, tunnels, and gothic faces to outright visitations. I have had the floor undulate in waves and fleeting wisps of smoke dart around a room full of faces (among many other experiences)—without drugs—after about thirty minutes of dancing. It depends on what you allow yourself to see.

Climax and Side Effects

While kinetic trance is beneficial at any level, a session's ultimate goal is climax, or neural overload, the trance dance equivalent of orgasm. While you dance, neural stimulation and physical energy build in waves (similar to sex) until they reach a "point of no return." Right before that, however, comes a "moment of truth," the last chance to back away. If you continue, your hyper-excited neural circuitry will overload and partially shut down (like blowing a fuse), either causing collapse or, short of that, a floating sensation and lucid dreaming, as if you were asleep. If you enter this state of limbo, stay as long as possible. It produces profound revelations. Eventually, though, and always too soon, once stimulation ceases (i.e., the music stops or you quit dancing), you will return to waking consciousness. Therefore, please allow for a buffer period before doing anything important (like driving) after a session.

Note that the deeper the trance, the longer recovery can take, sometimes an hour or more. You can speed up the process by taking rapid deep breaths, stretching, eating a small piece of candy (don't overdo it), turning your neck and head, and/or smelling pungent odors such as rose water or eucalyptus oil. Or you can take advantage of this delicious state and meditate.

Other post-trance side effects include itchiness, burping or hiccups, sensitivity to music, and aching muscles, especially in the neck and shoulders. Unexpected interruptions of the trance—"abrupt external terminations"—also result in decidedly unpleasant consequences. Besides leaving you sore, bewildered, and fuzzy for an hour or more, they can cause headaches and depression, depending how deep you were beforehand. Try to avoid these occurrences.

For many reasons, as you see, it's best to end sessions gradually. This is why I included cool-down suggestions in Part Three. Stretching after intense physical exercise is always good, but particularly after trance. Besides realigning the body and preventing soreness, it stimulates a return to waking consciousness. Ever stretch to wake up in the morning? These exercises have the same effect.

There can be psychological side effects from trance as well. David Akstein, the Brazilian psychiatrist who pioneered Terpsichore Trance Therapy, observed that patients were often introverted after sessions as they attempted to make sense of their experiences—the same patients who'd felt little when they began therapy. Others became extremely social and inquisitive, with intense surges of euphoria. And after a few weekly sessions, mid-week carryovers began to appear: flashbacks, vivid dreams, disorientation, and fatigue, or, alternately, elation, increased energy, and better sex. Critical material surfaces on its own time line, which can be disturbing if you are unprepared for surprises. This is normal, though, and will stop once your brain finishes processing whatever emerged. Talking helps, even if details are fuzzy. Writing things down and later rereading what you wrote also works, as does recreating images you may have seen—the subconscious (and the Invisibles) uses symbolism and/or metaphor to communicate.[88]

One especially peculiar post-trance oddity is regression behavior. Dancers occasionally act blissfully childlike when they resurface. But this, too, is normal, harmless, and actually quite therapeutic!

Adaptation, or "habituation," is another major side effect of long-term trance dancing; the more you do it, the less intense the "rush." As I explain in the next chapter, desensitization (including fewer emotional flare-ups) occurs because repetition stimulates neurons to thicken their conductive sheaths. In practical terms, this is why "aggressive" dancers transform into liberated movers. Participants who were once afraid of losing control, or who acted out, eventually abandon their wild movements for rhythmic, free-flowing dance. Yet

---

88   Akstein, *Un Voyage a Travers la Transe*, 50.

dance styles are like snowflakes—they vary immensely. During TTT, some cry, or just stop and swing their arms after fifteen minutes or so. Others cover ground, spin, or do wild, off-beat movements that require constant spotting. Yet after about thirty-five minutes, everyone ends up sweaty and exhausted on the floor, catharsis complete.[89]

As you can see, trance unleashes a broad spectrum of physical reactions and mental states, including some that foster spirit manifestations. The induction techniques in Part Three are designed for lucid trance, the easiest way to interact with the Invisibles. Possession trance, as experienced by zar, Candomblé, or Umbanda practitioners, is less predictable and should be approached gradually, under the tutelage of experienced practitioners.

Now I have a mission for you. As you visit the hidden recesses of your mind, try to bring back souvenirs or "keys": striking images, sensations, smells, sounds, etc., that instantly re-immerse you into your altered consciousness universe. The more vivid the recall, the easier your next descent will be.

Homework: Stress Reduction Techniques

Make a list of favorite stress reduction techniques in your trance journal. How do you calm down when you are angry, afraid, or upset? Are there special objects, memories, music, smells, etc., that take you to a "happy place"? How do you contact the sacred? If you pray, how do you prepare? What words do you use? Add these answers to your list. Later on, use this information to personalize your pre-trance ritual.

---

89   Akstein, *Un Voyage a Travers la Transe*, chap. 2.

4

....

Trance Science

So far, we have discussed trance history and trance symptoms, but not what actually causes trance. A NIH-funded study by Dr. Charles Limb, jazz saxophonist and well-known neurosurgeon, might shed some light on this. He and his colleagues, with volunteer musicians from the Johns Hopkins Peabody Institute, used functional magnetic resonance imaging to analyze brain activity associated with the musicians' creative improvisation. According to the university's news release, the research showed that "a region of the brain known as the dorsolateral prefrontal cortex…showed a slowdown in activity during improvisation." Notably,

> this area has been linked to planned actions and self-censoring, such as carefully deciding what words you might say at a job interview. Shutting down this area could lead to lowered inhibitions, Limb suggests. The researchers also saw increased activity in the medial prefrontal cortex, which sits in the center of the brain's frontal lobe. This area has been linked with self-expression and activities that convey individuality, such as telling a story about yourself.[90]

As Dr. Limb explained, "'What we think is happening is when you're telling your own musical story, you're shutting down impulses that might impede the flow of novel ideas.'"[91]

---

90   "This Is Your Brain on Jazz," Johns Hopkins Medicine News and Publications.
91   Ibid.

In other words, when humans create—music, dance, paint, carve, write, etc.—the brain selects which signals to heighten and which ones to ignore, to the point where it blocks judgment and planning in favor of language and storytelling. But the dorsolateral prefrontal cortex is also involved in working memory. Shutting it down would mean impaired recall. Perhaps this is why dancers don't remember what they did after an improvisational performance, or the ideas that surface while trance dancing. Other scientists claim that blocking regional brain signals is nothing more than an energy-conservation mechanism that kicks in when the brain is over- or under-whelmed by stimuli. Certainly, the biological origins of altered consciousness are not easy to discern. Yet understanding the nuts and bolts of what's happening can make surrendering to trance easier, so bear with me as we investigate what's going on.

In the late 1700s, scientists discovered that a mysterious invisible force animated Earth's creatures. Italian doctor Luigi Galvani proved in 1791 that nerve cells used electricity to communicate with muscle tissue, which forever joined biology with physics. Over the next hundred years, particle physicists uncovered the basic elements of atomic matter—negatively charged electrons orbiting nuclei of positively charged protons and neutrons, the essence of our 5 percent of the universe. They also discovered that electrons emitted energy if they were dislodged from their orbits. Even more important, the unbalanced charge of the remaining particles left the atoms destabilized until other electrons took their places. This initiated a domino "flow" effect as adjacent atoms stole each other's electrons. During evolution, both animals and plants took advantage of this phenomenon, but while one used it to capture and transform the sun's energy into glucose (photosynthesis), the other developed specialized cells called nerves or neurons to help them react to their surroundings.

Nerve cells have three parts: a central body (or soma) that contains the nucleus; intricately branched filaments called dendrites that turn incoming chemical signals (neurotransmitters) into electrical charges ("action potentials"); and an axon, a long fiber that transmits this voltage along its outer membrane (by altering its sodium and potassium ion concentrations[92]). Axons also end in branching filaments, which secrete neurotransmitters when incoming electrical charges stimulate them.

---

92   Sodium ions flow in and potassium ions flow out.

To help prevent closely packed fibers from short-circuiting each other, specialized "glial" cells wrap around individual axons to form protective casings. The more an axon is used, the thicker this sheath becomes and the faster it conducts a charge, hence "practice makes perfect." The absence or presence of this sheath—called myelination—is important for trance induction. Typically, peripheral nerves (sensory and motor neurons) are myelinated and appear white, while un-myelinated gray axons are found in the brain and spinal cord. Initial learning occurs when new pathways are blazed between nerves unaccustomed to communicating with each other. To ensure the right neurons fire, axons flood synapses with neurotransmitters. But as the pathways strengthen, sensitized dendrites no longer need to be over stimulated and the neurotransmitter "rush" decreases, which explains why trance neophytes react differently to induction than experienced practitioners.

The spaces between the axon terminals of one neuron and the dendrites of another are called synapses or synaptic clefts. As implied above, electric signals do not jump from one cell to another but are passed chemically. Axons secrete neurotransmitters into the synapses, which induce nearby dendrites to generate impulses. Different types of nerve cells release different neurotransmitters. The most common is glutamate. Others include acetylcholine, norepinephrine (a form of adrenaline), serotonin, dopamine, and the body's natural opiates, endorphins. For example, only a few clusters of neurons

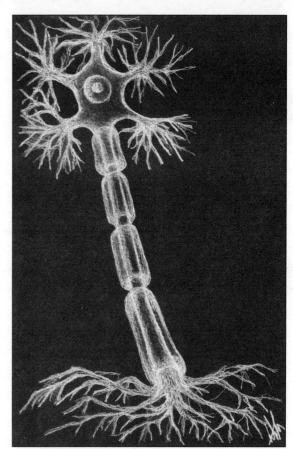

Figure 24: Neuron (dendrites around soma at top, with axon, wrapped in glial cells, leading to neurotransmitter filaments)

in the brainstem manufacture serotonin, but their axon terminals are spread throughout the cortex and cerebellum.

Two neurotransmitters in particular are involved with trance: serotonin and dopamine.[93] Serotonin is associated with many things, but its lack is often cited as a possible cause for depression. Sustained intense physical activity such as dance or running encourages serotonin secretion. Yet it is known as an inhibitory, rather than excitatory, transmitter, meaning that it keeps stimulants in check by turning off their secretion. Serotonin also helps regulate digestion, carbohydrate cravings, sleep, pain response, and the immune system.

Drugs like opiates and cocaine affect the brain by occupying or interfering with the dendrite receptors normally reserved for neurotransmitters. With nowhere to go, displaced neurotransmitters flood synapses and over-stimulate surrounding dendrites until the imposters are metabolized or carried away. This results in the sensation recognized as a "high." Normally, neurotransmitters are quickly whisked away or reabsorbed by axons, but drugs, prolonged physical activity, and also the contrary—a lack of stimulation—can disrupt the cycle.[94] Interrupted cycles may also contribute to mental illnesses such as depression, specifically through serotonin, dopamine, and/or norepinephrine deficiencies. This is why current treatments hinge on increasing their presence. The hypothesis is that, similar to recreational drugs, if "reuptake inhibitors" prevent neurotransmitter re-absorption, they will accumulate in the synapses. Yet problems exist. Current antidepressants actually take weeks, not minutes or hours, to cause an effect. Researchers are now investigating the hippocampus and neurotrophins, neural growth stimulators, for possible cures.[95]

Brainwaves

Let's move on and talk about another physical property of neurons, their tendency to fire in unison to conserve energy. This process, called entrainment, permits electrical

---

93   Michelle Shiota and James W. Kalat, *Emotion*, 342.

94   James W. Kalat, *Biological Psychology*, 71–77.

95   Ibid., 463–66.

signals to be transmitted in networks.[96] This also applies to externally generated signals such as loud persistent drumming, which is why listening to music stabilizes concentration for those with difficulty focusing (such as children with ADD who listen to music to help them study).[97] But for our purposes, it is the first of two reasons why electricity is not only the spark of life, but also the essence of trance. It travels in waves.

In 1924, while researching telepathy, a German psychiatrist named Hans Berger invented a groundbreaking machine, the electroencephalograph or EEG, to record the faint electromagnetic signals generated by the brain's 50–100 billion neurons.[98] He and the rest of the scientific community were surprised to discover that these signals were synchronized into distinct frequencies. Apparently, cerebral neurons adjusted their firing patterns to match their neighbors. They dubbed the pulses "neural oscillations," or "brainwaves," because of their cyclic, "wave-like" nature. Today we know these oscillations can be generated by individual cells, local groups interacting with each other, or entirely different regions communicating together, but in the beginning, early machines only detected the stronger signals of entire regions. Thanks to Dr. Berger's invention and a century of research, we now know that the brain emits five distinct frequencies—each associated with different activities. We also know that different levels of consciousness are associated with different frequency combinations and that each brain has a unique signature pattern, much like a fingerprint. Even better, doctors can now determine brain health by its spontaneous or resting-state activity. As you may expect, trance has its own telltale signature. So do auras.

What do auras have to do with the brain's electrical signals? Auras are the electromagnetic fields that surround matter, but particularly living organisms that use electricity. Occasionally, sensitive individuals can see these fields, feel them, or, even more rarely, read them. According to the Bible and the Islamic *hadith*,[99] strong visible auras have long been considered a sign of holiness. Muhammad is said to have emitted light

---

96   Jim Robbins, *A Symphony in the Brain*, 29.

97   Joseph LeDoux, *The Emotional Brain*, 210.

98   Each EEG electrode reads the activity of about 100,000 neurons.

99   As is discussed in more depth in chapter 5, the hadith are collections of the Prophet Muhammad's words, actions, and habits, compiled during the late ninth century by various religious scholars.

from age five, as did his father. Moses and Jesus were described as having "halos," much like the Dalai Lama today and experienced Buddhist monks, who are said to "shine." For millennia, strong auras have been associated with divine communication. Shiny Buddhist monks also imply something else—that even though some humans naturally produce larger auras (Jesus, for example), generating robust synchronized firing patterns is a skill that can be learned. Tibetan holy men manipulate the amplitude and frequencies of their cerebral oscillations through practice, not genetics. This has many implications and is the basis of the bio or neural feedback industry. It is also important for trance dancing—because as you will soon see, altering brainwaves alters consciousness. Hence, part of trance induction involves learning how to control the brain's electrical currents. Remember that "like a firefly or a neutrino, an individual nerve cell is influenced by what others are doing, and in turn can affect them. This opens the way to possible large-scale synchronization."[100]

The Brain's Five Frequencies

Cerebral neural oscillations come in five flavors, measured by amplitude (strength) and frequency (undulation speed or cycles per second, measured in hertz). In the beginning, researchers detected only four frequency bands: delta (1–4 Hz), theta (4–8 Hz), alpha (8–13 Hz), and beta (13–30 Hz).[101] But as technology advanced, they discovered a fifth, gamma (30–70 Hz), previously dismissed as "white noise." Let's take a look at how these frequencies affect our brains. (Note: The traits described below occur when a band is dominant, yet all frequencies are generated to some degree.)

> **Gamma:** This is the fastest frequency—and the hardest to produce, since the mind must be quiet to access it. It ranges from 30–70 Hz, although 40 Hz is the most common. Thought to be responsible for passing information rapidly from one cerebral region to another, it appears during idea formation, language processing, and any learning where simultaneous access to widespread information is required. Gamma is particularly prevalent in the brains of meditating Tibetan monks,

---

100   Nigel Calder, *Magic Universe*, 89.
101   The boundaries between frequencies are "fuzzy," or approximate, within a few hertz.

which is why it is associated with auras, expanded consciousness, spirituality, and peak concentration. These oscillations are thought to originate in the thalamus.[102]

Beta: This frequency band is the largest component of Oliver Sacks's "rational" consciousness signature, and is where most people spend their waking lives. It occurs during logical thinking, problem solving, judgment, decision-making, and concentration. Frustrated meditators sometimes complain, "Beta will do anything to stay active!" It increases with anxiety and decreases with muscle activity (an important factor for kinetic trance induction).[103] Insufficient beta can contribute to mental or emotional disorders such as depression, ADD, and insomnia, while stimulating these frequencies can improve emotional stability, energy, and concentration. On a sliding scale, anxious people produce too much beta, while those with ADD not enough. Beta is often subdivided into Low; a fast idle (or Beta 1, between 12–15 Hz); Beta; high mental engagement (or Beta 2, between 15–22 Hz); and Hi (or Beta 3, between 22–38 Hz), which overlaps low-end gamma and occurs during complex thought, new experience integration, high anxiety, or excitement. Beta signals are prone to fragmentation (when different regions working simultaneously produce slightly different frequencies). Lower wavelengths, however, tend to synchronize with each other, which is the reason slower frequencies produce more powerful, farther-reaching signals than the higher bands.

Alpha: Often called the "Bridge to the Subconscious," this frequency range (8–13 Hz) was one of the first Hans Berger discovered in 1924. He found that when test subjects rested quietly with their eyes closed, their brains produced a 10 Hz signal. But the minute they opened

---

102   Xiaoxuan Jia and Adam Kohn, "Gamma Rhythms in the Brain."

103   Researchers have found decreases in alpha and beta activity when subjects moved. During constant muscle activation, spinal column oscillations synchronize to the beta oscillations of the motor cortex.

their eyelids, smaller, faster beta waves took over. Research has since shown that alpha is the brain's idling frequency—what it produces right before and after sleep when the eyes are shut. Daydreaming, fantasizing, or visualizing objects also produce alpha. It is linked to reduced pain, stress, and anxiety, memory recall, and subconscious emotional experiences. For example, without alpha, people can't remember their dreams. But alpha's sharp, vivid images do not convey meaningful content, except when combined with theta's symbolism and metaphor.[104] Alpha is active during trance dancing[105] and is often the goal of neural feedback training—except for sessions treating ADD/ADHD, migraines, and/or seizures, which aim for beta instead. Similar to gamma, alpha is thought to originate in the thalamic pacemaker cells.

Theta: These frequencies (4–8 Hz) unlock your subconscious door. Humans descend into theta right before and during sleep, or during the deeper stages of meditation. These oscillations generate darker, less distinct, but intensely personal images and heighten intuition or the perception of information transmitted on wavelengths beyond the human sensory range (things picked up from auras, for example, or by the reptilian or emotional limbic systems; i.e., "gut feelings"). Theta produces bursts of profound creativity and inspiration that are nicknamed "theta flares" (as in "Ah HA!" or "light bulb" moments)—although other wavelengths are needed (alpha) to raise them into consciousness. Flares are often accompanied by strong psychic feelings and often received as divine gifts of profound truth. They surface suddenly, like lightning bolts "out of the blue," and can be preceded by washes of bluish purple if the eyes are closed.

Particularly important for our purposes, a predominance of waking theta (generated while awake) indicates "altered consciousness." And as hypnotists have discovered, the mind is particularly receptive

---

104   Wise, *The High Performance Mind*, 4.

105   It produces a frequency of 8–10 Hz. Aldridge and Fachner, *Music and Altered States*, 33.

(even hyper suggestible) here—to internal subconscious messages, suggestions from third parties, and communication from the cosmos. This is because theta circumvents the main impediments to new ideas—the conscious reasoning, learned behavior, and critical analysis functions of the prefrontal cortex, which are conducted in beta.

Researchers have also found that theta is involved in memory formation, since it registers during learning and memory retrieval. Furthermore, these frequencies stimulate emotional recall, particularly anything so overwhelming it was suppressed—traumas, childhood fears, nightmares, or incompletely processed events that in extreme cases underlie PTSD.[106]

In spite of theta's link with traumatic emotion, however, spending time here is therapeutic and often produces a calm that lasts for days—precisely because whatever surfaces is forced to undergo objective reexamination. This reduces an incident's latent emotional power, and therefore its ability to provoke cortisol secretion (a stress hormone), disturb neurotransmitter uptake, and interfere with sleep. Objective re-examination also transfers memories out of the emotional storage bin of the amygdalae (the two small masses of gray matter that are part of the limbic system) and into the hippocampus's long-term "historic narrative" regions.

Delta: At 1–4 Hz, this is the slowest of the brain's frequency bands. It provokes the profound dreamless sleep animals need to repair cells and "reset" their internal clocks. Without daily sessions here, higher reasoning, problem solving, and mood suffer, with depression following close behind. Time here is also necessary to stabilize growth and stress hormones, the immune system, appetite, breathing, blood pressure, and cardiovascular health.[107]

---

106 PTSD is the severe psychological damage that affects people who have experienced intense fear, helplessness, or horror in connection with a life-threatening event.

107 "The Benefits of Slumber: Why You Need a Good Night's Sleep," *NIH: News in Health*.

Delta is the brain's "loudest" frequency; its high amplitudes penetrate where others are blocked, similar to radio waves on the electromagnetic scale or the deep sound concussion waves of bass drums. Delta also travels the furthest. Some consider it the source of empathy, since, similar to theta, it is associated with assimilating subliminal information. High levels of waking delta correlate with receptivity to other people's needs, feelings, and thoughts. It is also the dominant wavelength of premature babies.

Delta may be the brain's strongest frequency, but it does not support consciousness (precisely because it is so strong—it entrains the other neurons). Yet most advanced life forms require time at these wavelengths, in spite of the dangers (extended periods of unconscious immobility). In fact, if animals are deprived of sleep, they die (humans included). Theta, although it can be experienced consciously, is most beneficial when produced during sleep. But why? Why is sleep essential for so many life forms—mammals, birds, reptiles, and insects alike?

Sleep

Even though we spend a third of our lives in a general state of oblivion, many of us know surprisingly little about it. Case in point: human sleep is not just one state, but four, roughly divided by frequency and whether or not we are dreaming.[108] Watching an alternate universe unfold around us, however, is the realm of the fourth stage, Rapid Eye Movement (REM). Before that, the brain cycles through three other stages first. The initial phase between sleep and wakefulness—alpha and high amplitude theta—is where we spend the least amount of time, typically 7–10 minutes (unless we have trouble dozing off and then it can be hours). We are often acutely aware of this level, though, because it produces "hypnagogic hallucinations": unnerving sensations of falling, ringing bells, voices calling out, or unexplained startle reactions ("myoclonic jerk"). Stage Two, on the other hand, is where we spend the most time; our heartbeats slow, body temperatures drop, and

---

108   In 2007, the two deepest stages of the traditional five sleep categories were combined into one.

we gradually sink deeper into the void. Here, theta is interspersed with delta and unique electrical phenomena called K-Complexes and Sleep Spindles, which signal the transfer of recently acquired knowledge into long-term memory. This transfer refreshes the brain's ability to absorb more information, i.e., learn. The third stage, or Slow-Wave Sleep (SWS), is the deepest state, when delta predominates. Memories are consolidated, growth hormones secreted, neurons replenished with glucose, and neural impulses are synchronized with long-range internal—and external—signals.

Four or five times per night, the brain cycles through three of these four stages: 1–[2–3–2–REM]—unless we wake up, and then stage 1 gets involved again. Early cycles exhibit more deep sleep (stage 3) than the last two, which favor REM.[109] Experiments have shown that dreaming aids long-term memory retention,[110] and, similar to trance, occurs while the lateral prefrontal cortex is deactivated. This is the region that sifts ideas to match expectations and culturally acceptable behavior. Disabling it permits uncensored thoughts and creative mind flares to surface unimpeded. It also allows the slower external signals bombarding us from the cosmos to enter unfiltered.

Something else is deactivated while we dream—our ability to move. During REM, neurons in the brain stem (the pons) inhibit the neurotransmitters that stimulate motor neurons (serotonin is involved), causing temporary paralysis.[111] Forced immobility can be terrifying if a sleeper awakens under the effect, but the flip side is that people and animals would hurt themselves (or be eaten by wily predators) if they blindly enacted their dreams.

Most psychic or prophetic visions occur in the twilight zone after sleep, as we surface from theta to beta, but before the lateral prefrontal cortex kicks in again. Scientists refer to these surreal sensations as "hypnopompic hallucinations." They may seem similar to the hypnagogic phenomena mentioned previously, but they are formed under different circumstances. Before slumber, the prefrontal cortex is active and tries to make logical sense of theta's perceptions and symbolic or metaphorical messages. After sleep, it remains of-

---

109   Kalat, *Biological Psychology*, 276–85.

110   Jason Goldman, "What Do Animals Dream About?" This article summarizes several studies on sleep research.

111   Kalat, *Biological Physiology*, 281.

fline as we surface, which enables unusual thoughts or ideas to be assimilated without rationalization. Hence, being able to voluntarily suppress this region could have enormous advantages—which is precisely what MRI studies of jazz and other improvisational musicians show.[112] Through practice, artists learn to block the prefrontal cortex when they concentrate, a skill now understood as essential for creativity, invention, inspiration, and yes, improvisation. Put another way, evolution selected for this trait because it enabled creative problem solving.

Dr. Oliver Sacks has noted that while "some researchers believe in the objective reality of a spiritual or supernatural realm, to which the mind might be given brief access in various physiological states, such as dreaming, hypnopompic states, trance states, and certain forms of epilepsy," he felt that "the majority of psychical or paranormal experiences are, in fact, hallucinations—hallucinations arising in states of bereavement, social isolation, sensory deprivation, and above all in drowsy or trancelike states."[113] I belong to the group that believes in "the objective reality of a spiritual or supernatural realm." In other words, I believe the visions we see, the voices we hear, and the mind flares we receive when our critical thinking faculties are shut down (during trance or sleep) may be actual encounters with another—spiritual—reality, a reality just as genuine (but not as solid) as our conscious beta world. It could be that accessing these alternate universes is as simple as turning a radio dial, i.e., synchronizing our brainwaves to a slower frequency station. What is reality, anyway? Unfiltered input, or what our culture determines we should see, hear, and react to? Humans are susceptible creatures with easily trained, malleable brains. It is possible we might be seeing, hearing, and feeling only the sensations we have been taught to expect.

Healing Brainwaves

Brainwaves play a vital role in healing. Since the 1960s, therapists have employed "neural feedback" to teach patients how to function in frequencies they normally have trouble generating. Once called "biofeedback," this process utilizes electrodes or other brainwave-

---

112 Also see "Your Brain on Improv," Dr. Charles Limb's TED talk on the subject: https://www .ted.com/talks/charles_limb_your_brain_on_improv/transcript?language=en.

113 *Hallucinations*, 215–16.

measuring devices to guide patients to specific frequencies and keep them there until their brains learn to generate them on their own.[114] This possibility was first reported by E. D. Adrian of Cambridge University in 1934 and later developed into a protocol in the 1950s and 1960s.[115] Since then, researchers have actually alleviated some mental health issues by training patients to change their signature brainwave patterns.

Another therapy based on altering the brain's electrical output is Alpha/Theta Neurofeedback.[116] This uses the border between alpha and theta (around 8 Hz) to revisit repressed memories and bring about catharsis. Normally, alpha waves are higher in amplitude, or more powerful, than theta waves. But during therapy, the practitioner helps the patient lower alpha and raise theta until the two are equal, a "crossover." This juncture, experienced as an objective "witness state," enables patients to replay traumatic events at arm's length, as if on television. This gently reintegrates the past without further trauma by retagging the memories for storage in regions besides those governed by the amygdala and its fear-based emotions.[117]

Therapists are also experimenting with transcranial Direct Current Stimulation (tDCS). Instead of teaching patients to manipulate their brainwaves, they stimulate specific regions of the cortex with electrodes. There are two types of stimulation: anodal, which excites neurons, and cathodal, which inhibits them. Although tDCS is still experimental, studies suggest it may be useful to treat brain injuries, depression, anxiety, Parkinson's disease, and chronic pain. Some suggest that healthy adults can benefit from it, too, enhancing language and math skills, attention span, problem solving, memory, and coordination, but this has yet to be proved conclusively.

In the process of developing these therapies, science has also uncovered a great deal about the biological mechanisms behind trance induction. Simply listening to music, for example, generates theta, but adding the right percussive rhythms intensifies it. Two favorite African trance techniques used together are loud percussion at 4–7 beats per

---

114 Robbins, *A Symphony in the Brain*, 7.

115 Ibid., 42, 56, 89.

116 Ibid., 159–163.

117 Ibid., 163.

second[118] with binaural beat stimulation, where slightly different rhythms are played in each ear. Rattles, frame drums, clappers, or finger cymbals work best for this. Islamic exorcists and Sufi dervishes lull the mind into descent with prolonged Quranic chanting, hyperventilation (through the loud repetition of short phrases), or overexciting the vestibulocochlear nerve by whirling.

Scientists have also discovered that excessive theta can wreak havoc. Since generating theta is what this book is all about, you should know what too much of a good thing can do. For example, strong signature theta (higher than normal "idling" or resting theta levels) is associated with drug addiction, alcoholism, head injury, stroke, cerebral palsy, Parkinson's disease, depression, seizure disorders, attention deficit disorder, hyperactivity, and a wide variety of learning disabilities.[119] Migraines and seizures, in particular, are caused by large, synchronized theta waves (predominantly) that spread across the brain and interfere with normal activity.[120] And even though the above disorders mainly arise from genetics, sickness, or injury, trance dancing CAN bring on symptoms in those prone to them already. **So if you have had a stroke, cerebral palsy, Parkinson's, a head injury, migraines, or seizures, this form of kinetic trance induction is NOT for you.** At any rate, to prevent signature theta disorders from interfering with normal activity, neural feedback practitioners teach patients to heighten beta and inhibit theta, although suppressing a frequency is easier than amplifying it.[121]

To understand how theta is involved with seizures, let's look at the mechanisms behind an epileptic attack. These occur for a variety of reasons, but they usually begin as a sudden, abnormal electrical discharge that reverberates through neighboring brain tissue like ripples from a stone hitting water. In generalized attacks, the wave engulfs both sides of the brain. During partial seizures, it only affects specific regions. The initial shock usually stems from a genetic malformation or injury and spreads in seconds, while migraines, which follow a similar pattern, take longer to disseminate. People

---

118   This is the theta frequency band, which may or may not be accompanied by flashing lights or flickering flames. In experiments, this generated matching EEG waves and hallucinations.

119   Robbins, *A Symphony in the Brain*, 74.

120   Oliver Sacks, *Hallucinations*, 130.

121   Robbins, *A Symphony in the Brain*, 42.

rarely have complex hallucinations during migraines, whereas epileptics may see intricate visions.[122] What sets both off is the subject of intense research. One potential culprit may involve serotonin levels in the striatum region of the brain.[123]

This brings me to ecstatic seizures, or theophanies—rare electrical events accompanied by ecstasy or transcendent joy that are experienced as divine epiphanies or revelations. These episodes, generated in the cortex's right temporal lobe (which is known to be linked to divine communication), are important when discussing the Invisibles. They only occur to a chosen few … like the Prophet Muhammad, Joan of Arc, and perhaps countless less-documented prophets throughout the ages. Obviously, without physical evidence we can only compare historic symptoms to modern case studies, but the similarities are striking … notably the presence of ringing bells. The Prophet Muhammad's episodes are documented in the hadith; Joan of Arc's can be found in her trial records. It would seem that the same parts of their brains were being stimulated.[124]

"Does God answer me if I believe?" One of the holy grails of consciousness research today is the biological origin of spirituality, faith-based healing, and the placebo response.[125] Not surprisingly, research has shown that the more people believe in a divine entity, the more likely they will be cured.[126] Even middle school students doing biology experiments learn that part of what human control groups measure is the result of "doing nothing" to people who believe you are doing something to them. History has shown that when some humans truly believe they are undergoing a treatment that will cure them, they miraculously cure themselves. And the details matter; i.e., how and where medication is administered, whether the patient likes the clinician or not, the patient's culture, etc. But more often than not, results hinge on the depth of a subject's religious propensity. If the patient believes—in something—the placebo effect will be stronger than if the subject is a non-believer or an atheist. The question then becomes, is

---

122 Sacks, *Hallucinations*, 130.

123 "Computer Says 'Try This,'" *The Economist*, 85.

124 Sacks, *Hallucinations*, 155, 158.

125 From the Latin "I shall please," the placebo response is an improvement in health or behavior not attributable to an administered medication or invasive treatment. Nikola Kohls et al., "Spirituality: An Overlooked Predictor of Placebo Effects?", 1838–48.

126 Giordano, "Spirituality, Suffering, and the Self," 179-91.

the cure based on biology or another sort of intervention? Science doesn't know … yet. But researchers at NIH and elsewhere are getting closer. Within the past two decades, they have actually measured the biochemical consequences of positive thinking in cases of pain, depression, anxiety, fatigue, and some Parkinson's symptoms.[127] What was once considered a sham is now a hot topic of cutting-edge medicine.

The fact that belief has a significant and measurable biological effect is no longer doubted, particularly for the above ailments. The question remains, though, how it works. Recent genetic studies may hold a clue. They found links between gene mutations of neurotransmitter metabolic enzymes and the strength of placebo responses. Dopamine and serotonin receptors in particular were involved; the mutations caused these neurotransmitters to collect in the synapses, much like the effects of recreational drugs, antidepressants such as Prozac … and trance dancing.[128]

One last healing phenomenon before we move on. Loss of consciousness, as discussed previously, is not necessarily a bad thing. As you saw in my description of a zar hadra, the desired outcome of a zar is repeated fainting. These "inhibitory collapses" are considered to work similarly to electric shock treatments. Like rebooting a computer, turning off the power forces the brain to start afresh. In the beginning, trance dancers pass out because their brains are overwhelmed by stimuli (particularly cranial nerve VIII, the vestibulocochlear nerve, and the auditory thalamus). With experience, however (for example, at weekly *hadarat*), the brain learns to shut down on cue. This is why anthropologists consider the zar nothing more than a therapeutic context for inhibitory collapse. This makes sense. Electric shock therapy, or Electroconvulsive Therapy (ECT), is still used to treat acute cases of depression (the primary ailment of zar patients) that are unresponsive to drugs or psychotherapy.[129] And since many of Africa's women have no access to hospitals, much less psychiatrists, the zar is their only therapy. But two hundred and fifty years ago, when electricity was a figment of scientific imagination, the

127   James Giordano and Joan Engebretson, "Neural and Cognitive Basis of Spiritual Experience: Biopsychosocial and Ethical Implications for Clinical Medicine," footnotes 43–61, 216–25.

128   "Are You Easily Pleased?" *The Economist*, 71–72. This is an overview of studies by Kathryn T. Hall, Joseph Loscalzo, and Ted J. Kaptchuk published in "Genetics and the Placebo Effect: The Placebome," *Trends in Molecular Medicine* 21(5), May 2015, 285–94.

129   Shiota and Kalat, *Emotion*, 342.

zar was already well established as a cure for mental illness and jinn gone awry. It makes you wonder what other cures our ancestors discovered that have disappeared into the mists of time…

Short-Circuiting the Brain

This brings us to the second reason electricity is the essence of trance: it overwhelms its conduits and short-circuits the brain.

It's one thing to understand the flow of energy throughout the body, but quite another to fathom the intricacies of the tissues that use it—much like how familiarity with gasoline won't tell you much about the engine burning it for fuel. Which brings us to the most complicated organ of all… the brain. Without it we would be a sponge, a starfish, or a plant. What follows is an abridged anatomy lesson of the brain's bits and pieces affected by trance, particularly cranial nerve number VIII (the vestibulocochlear nerve), the thalamus, the prefrontal cortex, and the amygdalae. If I have exceeded your tolerance for biology, go ahead and skip to Part Two and the Invisibles! However, if you do, please take a look at the homework at the end of this chapter nonetheless. The exercises will help acquaint you with waking theta.

––––––––––

For all its marvels, the brain only weighs about 3 pounds, 90 percent of which is salt water. It has three or four distinct layers, depending on where you categorize the thalamus and hypothalamus. Closest to the skull is the cerebrum, or cortex, which houses what makes us human (i.e., consciousness). Directly underneath the cortex is the mammalian brain, or limbic system, where pain, pleasure, and the emotions are processed. The diencephalon is below that (the thalamus and hypothalamus), and underneath everything is the brain stem, nicknamed the "reptilian brain" because it evolved first. It regulates the basics of life (breathing, blood pressure, movement, and body temperature) and transmits signals from the spine and the twelve cranial nerves to the cortex.

When the senses send external information to the brain, the signals enter through the brain stem where they are quickly analyzed for danger. Next they travel through the thalamus, the brain's main relay station (a dual structure, one on each side), which shunts the information to four different regions for analysis, reaction, and storage. Feedback loops complete the cycle, to alert organs and muscles if a response is needed. Curiously, there are 10 times as many feedback connections out of the cortex as there are pathways leading into it. Together, the brain and spinal column make up the central nervous system (CNS). All other nerves form the peripheral nervous system (PNS).

Besides having four layers, the brain is divided into two hemispheres, the right and left, with four lobes each: frontal, occipital, parietal, and temporal. The nervous system is also divided in two: the autonomic nervous system (ANS), which operates subconsciously and controls involuntary movement, and the somatic nervous system, which governs voluntary control. The ANS again has two parts: the parasympathetic, which is dominant during relaxation, and the sympathetic, which activates in times of stress and governs the "fight or flight" response and cortisol release.

The reptilian brain or brain stem is, as I mentioned, the most primitive part of the human brain, having evolved first with reptiles, our ancient ancestors. Its three parts, the midbrain, medulla, and pons, ensure survival through reflexes, fine touch, monitoring the environment's fainter vibrations, and maintaining bodily rhythms and automated tasks (heart rate, blood pressure, breathing, digestion, urination, etc.). The pons, from the Latin word for "bridge," also regulates sleep and plays a role in hearing, taste, eye movements, facial expressions, equilibrium, and the startle reflex. The medulla, the enlarged portion of the upper spinal cord, relays the cranial nerves and is where the spinal axons cross over before entering the opposite sides of the brain.

The mammalian brain, or limbic system, is a group of structures on top of the brainstem (under the cortex) that processes the prime emotions: fear, anger, sorrow, and joy. One twin structure particularly affected by trance is the amygdalae (pl) (the word "amygdala" [s] is from the Greek word for "almond," after its shape; pronounced "uh-MIG-duh-luh"). Each temporal lobe has one. They govern fear and the "fight or flight" response, among other things, by relaying information back to the pons and other startle reflex areas. They also split incoming signals and send some to the prefrontal cortex for in-depth analysis and the hippocampus to generate emotional memories.[130] Abnormal amygdala function has been linked to anxiety, autism, depression, post-traumatic stress disorder,

---

130   Shiota and Kalat, *Emotion*, 117–18.

and phobias. The other limbic structure stimulated during kinetic trance is the hippocampus. It sends and retrieves memories to and from the cortex for long-term storage and is particularly sensitive to rhythmic movement and theta vibrations.

The diencephalon, also beneath the cortex, contains the pineal gland, thalamus, and hypothalamus. The thalamus is the brain's major relay station and its malfunction causes many trance symptoms. Similar to the amygdalae, there are two, one per hemisphere. They connect the spinal cord and cranial nerves to the amygdalae and the sensory regions of the cortex. Each contains clusters of specifically dedicated sensory neurons, thalamic nuclei that partially process incoming information before relaying it. The thalamus also regulates other things such as pain perception and the body's reaction to it, brainwave frequencies, and which sensory information reaches consciousness awareness.

The cerebellum is the highly folded area at the very back and bottom of the skull that, among other tasks, integrates spatial orientation information from the vestibular system and coordinates limb activities. It, too, is divided into two parts and is stimulated by music, dancing, or movement, and particularly complex or unknown sounds.

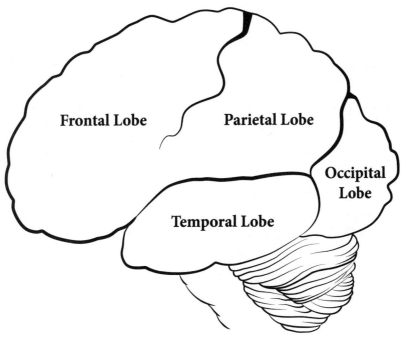

Figure 25: Brain lobes

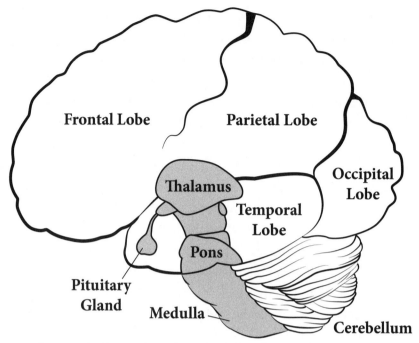

Figure 26: Brain stem (medulla and pons), thalamus, and pituitary gland

The cortex or cerebrum, the seat of human consciousness, is where reason, language, and creative thought happen. Here, information is analyzed and stored, impulses controlled, and actions modified to suit social norms. While the outer cortex is gray, from the billions of nerves that compose it, the inner portion is white, from the myelinated axons that extend into the underlying layers below and the spinal cord. As mentioned, the cortex is divided into two hemispheres, right and left, and four lobes, each with different functions. The left hemisphere is responsible for language, logic, numbers, and lists, while the right is involved with creativity, rhythm, spatial awareness, and imagination. Besides planning, the frontal lobes control speech and movement of the opposite side of the body. The parietal lobes analyze the sensory input of touch, pressure, temperature, and pain localization. The temporal lobes process hearing, memory (particularly the hippocampus), and the sense of self, as they are directly linked to the limbic system at their base. And the rear occipital lobes manage visual input.

The Senses, Cranial Nerves,
and the Vestibular Complex: Hearing and Balance

Now we come to the heart (or ear) of Middle Eastern kinetic trance induction, cranial nerve VIII or the vestibulocochlear nerve, which is the easiest of the twelve pairs of cranial nerves to overload. Normally, these "super-highways" shuttle large quantities of information around quite efficiently—that is, until they are overwhelmed by stimuli. Nerve number eight transmits auditory and balance signals to the auditory cortex from two different places in the inner ear (the cochlea for hearing, and in between the semicircular canals and vestibule for balance). After merging outside the cochlea, the combined nerve enters the brain stem, where the pons meets the medulla and eventually feeds into the auditory nuclei of the thalamus ("medial geniculate nucleus"). From there, signals are relayed to four different places, but primarily to the auditory cortex in the temporal lobes and the auditory nuclei of the amygdalae, in case an immediate startle or "fight or flight" response is needed.

Cranial Nerves

I	Smell (olfactory)
II–III–IV–VI	Vision
V–XI	Touch and muscles for the head
VII–IX–XII	Taste, facial, throat, and tongue muscles
VIII	Hearing and balance
X	Touch via the spinal column, motor and autonomic functions

The thalamus is the weak link here, the electrical bottleneck of the body's converging circuits. Signals from balance disruption, loud music, dancing, and external pacemaker rhythms overwhelm its nuclei, forcing this ancient structure to partially shut down—to "blow a fuse," so to speak. And when it can no longer respond to pain or even maintain consciousness, anesthesia and/or inhibitory collapse ensues (along with other symptoms described in chapter 3). The longer dancing continues, the more overwhelmed the thalamus becomes. The further its pacemaker cells entrain with external frequencies, the harder it becomes to maintain bodily rhythms. Obviously, there are degrees, but I think you get the point. Nevertheless, like the rest of the nervous system, the thalamus learns to adapt. Over time, the glial cells insulate exposed axons, electric spillover is reduced, and uncontrolled trances become harder to provoke. Training replaces overload. Culturally appropriate responses are learned, and milder altered states manifest on cue.

––––––––––

Yet biology only tells half the story, the solid nuts-and-bolts "why" for shifts in reality. What about the other side of the equation—the nebulous "what" that seeps through once the gossamer fabric of consciousness is torn? These rifts are two-way portals; what leads into the Invisible Realm also leads out.[131] But before we shift gears and move on to Part Two and the Invisibles, here are some exercises to introduce you to waking theta, your bridge to the ethereal world.

Homework: Exploring Theta

As you fall asleep, look for purple theta clouds. Try to remember the 3D images they lead you to. However, the best time to experience theta and alpha creativity is in the morning as you wake up. Find a morning when you can sleep in. The previous night, before falling asleep, think of a question or problem you would like answered. Write it down in your journal. As you wake up the next morning recall your question, then let your mind wander, half asleep, half awake. The answer should come to you as a vision or an idea that "pops" into your head. Even if the vision is complicated or emotionally charged, write it down before the details fade.

––––––––––

131   The neurology of religion is called Neurotheology. The neural connection to God is thought to be the frontal lobe conduit to the inferior parietal lobe, including the anterior convexity of the frontal lobe, the inferior parietal lobe, and their reciprocal interconnections. It is believed that these regions generate concepts of gods, powers, and spirits, particularly when electrical spillover between neurons occurs.

PART TWO

Spirits

5

....

Spirit Speak

What follows is the first part of a forgotten late-nineteenth-century eyewitness account of two zars in Cairo, when the cult was in its prime and women from all walks of life participated in these powerful, bloody rituals. The author, Eugenie Le Brun, born in France in 1873, was a distant relative of Charles Le Brun (1619–1690), the famous French painter and art theorist that Louis XIV once called "the greatest French artist of all time." As a young woman, Eugenie met a well-to-do Egyptian law student in Paris, Hussein Rushdi Pasha (one of Egypt's prime ministers during WW1), whom she married for love and followed to Cairo around 1893. Not long after, she started Egypt's first literary salon for women. Through it, she became a major influence on Egypt's first feminist, Hoda Shaarawi, who founded the Egyptian Feminist Union in 1923.[132]

Since Le Brun's book was originally written in French, I have translated and edited the two zar chapters to illustrate how life-altering these ceremonies could be. And although the text is biased and Eurocentric, try to look past the prejudices of the author's era and social status. In spite of her tone, she had an immensely positive influence on early Egyptian feminists.

---

132 Eugenie Le Brun (Madame Rushdi) tackled a more difficult subject in her second book, *Les Répudiées* (The Divorcees). Published in 1908, the year of her death (at age 35), she examined the perceived "backwardness" of Egyptian women, a condition she felt arose from social customs rather than Islam.

Sur Les Zars

Harems et Musulmanes d'Égypte by Eugenie Le Brun[133]

I would like to talk about the women—seventy-five percent of them African—who say they are possessed by the Devil. What fertile fields for the Red Cross and Spiritism! More likely these people belong in Salepetre [a French mental hospital]. But in Egypt, as in Paris, the two domains are related.

Judge for yourselves!

Similar to Christians, Muslims admit to the existence of supernatural beings called angels and devils. But they also believe in spirits who live underground and, especially, who float about in dark rooms and ruins. These spirits are divided into two kinds: afreet and jinn. Afreet are born at the time and place of an accidental death and their haunting induces persecution deliriums and a desire to commit suicide. Jinn, on the other hand, are a type of invisible humanity—jealous twin enemies, if you will, that seek to harm us.

Commonly, jinn are also called afreet out of carelessness, but this never leads to confusion among the locals. I shall therefore continue this custom and call these spirits afreet. The possessed call them other names as well, according to their category and country of origin (the Sudan, the Arabian Peninsula, Egypt and elsewhere). All are harmful and formidable. It is enough to be near one after an illness or violent shock, for it to take over your body and "ride" you. These entities do not emulate Mephistopheles, incarnating in human form to tempt souls away from God. They are more like facetious werewolves, who enjoy scaring and occasionally mystifying, wayward humans. But the similarity ends there. To initiates, afreet appear in human form, have a social hierarchy similar to ours (with sultans, pashas, beys, masters, and valets), and are divided into males and females. The females apparently love clothes and have whims, just like human women. Naturally, afreet marry and reproduce, which leads to interesting consequences when spirit families unite their various hosts. Absolute strangers call each other sister, daughter, or mother, according to their possessor's relationships.

---

133   Le Brun, *Harems et Musulmanes d'Égypt*, 255–74. My translation, edited for length.

Although these entities occasionally inspire prophetic trances, their main role is to cause what we call hysteria. Our morbid state of neurosis is easily explained by their presence in the human body. They hate doctors as much as prescriptions, yet nevertheless require treatment. And when they want amusement, they abuse their miserable hosts until their "horses" throw them a party, known as a zar.

But not all zars are alike! Some cost the price of a wedding, while other simpler affairs cost far less. Private zars are paid for by individuals and held in their homes, while public rituals are offered weekly by sheikhas in dedicated houses or near the tombs of saints. Sheikhas, sometimes called kodias, also host annual "moulids," where initiates gather to exchange gifts and commemorate the approach of Ramadan.

The most famous sheikha in Cairo is an old African woman, the freed slave of a prince, who speaks nothing but Turkish. Extremely spoiled (her master gave her several town houses and a country estate), she is, nevertheless, intelligent and particularly gifted in contacting the spirit world. Her zar is by far the most select. I was able to attend one, but before I tell you about it, let me describe the private zar I went to first, so you can compare the two.

My heart still pounds when I remember that first zar. It was in an old house, set back from the street, on a narrow intersection. Judging from the house's interior, I had no doubt its mistress was sick, obsessed with the idea she was haunted by afreet. What a room to choose for a party— the darkest of several dilapidated halls! A rickety mahogany pedestal table stood in the center on an old Persian carpet. Next to it sat the lone souvenir of the mansion's bygone splendor, an enormous silver chandelier crowned with two candles. On the other side of the table, planted in the ground, jutted a heavy iron spike.

I was curious to see the owner—who eventually appeared, occupied with last-minute instructions. Tall and large, with healthy skin and a clear complexion, she was neither overexcited nor depressed. The light white fabric draped over her head and galabeya reminded me of classic statues of the Virgin Mary. As I watched her—calm, crowned by an imaginary white halo—I couldn't help but think, "Why the disorder? Why so much neglect? She seems fine. What's her excuse?"

I stared at the threadbare cushions intended for our use. Some guests were already kneeling on them. I peered at their faces. They seemed no different from other women. The room was full, and still latecomers appeared. A group of Africans took over a corner of the room, their hands lazily caressing primitive instruments: enormous frame drums with sets of copper disks (*crotales*), smaller tambourine-like cousins without inlay or cymbals, and ceramic goblet drums with skins stretched over one end of their cylinder bodies. This was the preferred orchestra of the afreet! To me, they made a terrible noise, enough to damage sensitive eardrums! Yet apparently, this infernal din was organized into numerous rhythms and tones—impossible for the uninitiated to tell apart—but ecstasy-inducing for those who could.

As the musicians prepared their drumheads, acrid, intoxicating smoke rose into the air. The kodia was sprinkling powder over hot coals in an incense brazier. Someone lit the candles and a circle of women converged around the pedestal table, now covered with offerings: soap, sugar, pastries, honey, molasses, and a sad bouquet of roses. The high priestess chanted prayers and made cabalistic gestures over the food while the sisterhood replied in chorus. The kodia sprinkled more incense. It was time for the formal fumigation ritual to begin.

The heroine of the party went first. Her veil over her head, lowered almost to the brazier, she deeply inhaled the smoke. Then she offered her ears, the palms of her hands, her armpits, and the soles of her feet, and with a shameless gesture, lifted her dress to allow the fumes to penetrate underneath, all the way up to her belt. The same words and gestures were repeated for select guests—and the sacrificial ram, which was brought in and held steady by two assistants. Eventually, the incense basin passed to other hands and the bakhour ritual continued, without prayers, from group to group. The air grew heavy and irritating. My pulse beat faster and a headache spread from my temples. Their conversations grew—until suddenly, drums ripped through the air.

The sound was deafening! What sensations did those hammering black fingers excite in the audience's nerves? What message did those savage voices send to their brains? What mysterious power did this feverish beat possess to impel these women, squatting so lazily, to frenetically agitate their limbs?

Eyes rolled back into sallow, hardened faces. Smiling expressions sobered into masks of infinite desolation. Near me, a young woman, who had laughed at my reticence and disgust, now threw herself on the ground, beating her head on the carpet and rowing her arms in who knows what untouchable liquid. Others helped her up and she joined the frenzied group circling the pedestal table—the dance had begun!

The movements consisted mainly of upper-body oscillations, bent-over busts sagging like ripe grape clusters tossed violently in a disastrous wind. Swaying hips rhythmically swelled and hollowed thin galabeyas in continuous waves. Slow, measured footwork—a continuous forward stumble—"won space" as participants advanced little by little around the circle. They numbered a dozen, with changed faces and sad, tragic airs about them, drunk on noise and perfume. Some in front wore garish red or green rags. Others covered their faces with transparent veils, the edges flitting about their silhouettes like a flush of bad dreams.

Pushed by servants, forehead and neck decked with gold streamers, horns festooned with ribbons, the ram made another entrance. Its owner grasped its greasy fleece with two hands and leaning over its rump, staggered lewdly—like a delirious bacchante—three times around the room. Then the infernal circle broke up, as some of the dancers followed the woman and the animal outside. A crowd gathered at the door, heads curiously craning forward, the chanting and tambourines raging. Emotions surged, a dispute broke out, then suddenly the crowd parted to let the filthy stream back in. Staggering, eyes closed, face and hands covered with blood, her white veils splattered red, the possessed woman led her blood-stained entourage back into the room. The kodia preceded her, arms outstretched, holding a plate of jewelry bathed in blood.

Blood! Blood everywhere! They had rushed at the victim, its throat cut, squeezing and ripping the wound with their fingernails. They drank and sucked the insipid, warm liquid, then returned inside to surrender themselves, more frenzied than ever, to the circle and their diabolic possession.

They danced, and danced again, more and more numerous, until suddenly, immobilized by silence, my nightmare ceased. Some fell to their knees in a swoon, exhausted; others appeared completely lost. The kodia ministered sacramental gestures to each, blowing and whispering in their ears to end their stupors. Instantly calmed, the women regained their places with the steady gait and placid demeanor of a patient who has just taken her prescribed medicine.

Enough! Let's get out of here! My lungs need fresh air and my eyes want sunshine!

I'd like to note that this story brings up a tricky subject for Westerners (myself included): animal sacrifice. When I hosted a hadra for my bandleader's family in 2006, they suggested I offer a sacrifice. When I said no, I didn't want to kill anything, they asked if I ate meat, which I do. Busted. Of course, they rightly pointed out that their tradition was in line with my carnivorous habit. But I still said no. I didn't want the animal's death on my conscience. I know, the only way not to be a hypocrite is to become a vegetarian, but I'm not there yet. And I'm not the only Westerner with this conundrum, hence the difficulty. The ceremony is what it is, however; zar spirits are attracted to blood, and the ritual is all about giving them what they want. Plus, the final contract between host and possessor must be sealed in blood. Ultimately, though, Westerners can pick and choose what to include—or avoid—in their trance dance ceremonies.

Spirit Speak

Now we come to the holy grail of trance dancing: communicating with the spirit world. There are many ways to facilitate otherworldly interactions; vision quests are one. Improvised creative endeavors are another (dancing, drawing, etc.). Prolonged exercise or meditation help, as does gazing into crystal balls or scrying bowls. But all these activities require one essential element to work—an open mind. If you don't expect (or want) contact with the Invisibles, it probably won't happen—unless you are one of the genetic few born with the "veil," or second sight. For everyone else, communication is a learned process.

The million-dollar question is, how do you communicate with something you can't see and aren't sure exists?

Let me ask a different question … do you pray? If so, how do you receive answers—visions, voices, just "knowing," or a coincidence that points you in the right direction? Humanity has communicated with the spirit world via prayer for eons, perhaps since the dawn of our species. It's not hard; the message-sender quiets the mind, usually closes the eyes, concentrates on an issue, and then thinks or speaks a message. It's a timeless practice based on a simple premise—someone or something is listening—and the stronger the conviction, the greater the likelihood of a reply … favorable or not.

To believe or not to believe, that is the question—and the choice.

Even without concrete scientific evidence, billions of people today *do* believe that non-corporeal life forms exist, or at least one—God, Allah, Yahweh, or whatever name you call the Creator of the Universe. Even Albert Einstein, the twentieth century's greatest mind, proposed that "the presence of a superior reasoning power … is revealed in the incomprehensible universe."[134] Einstein also stated that his religion "consists of a humble admiration of the illimitable superior spirit who reveals himself in the slight details we are able to perceive with our frail and feeble minds."[135] He also observed that "Everything is determined … by forces over which we have no control. It is determined for the insect as well as for the star. Human beings, vegetables, or cosmic dust, we all dance to a mysterious tune, intoned in the distance by an invisible piper."[136]

Einstein's conviction is not surprising. As we saw in chapter 1, humans are "wired" to believe in the divine. Yet the Father of Relativity did not imagine his Celestial Conductor as the petty, meddling revenge-seeker depicted by organized religions. He envisioned a distant brilliance that could conceive of not three dimensions but thousands, not one universe but an infinite number, and not one Big Bang but an eternity of explosions.

---

134   Qtd. in Peter Galison et al., eds., *Einstein for the 21st Century*, 36.

135   Qtd. in "Dr. Albert Einstein Dies in Sleep at 76," *New York Times*.

136   Qtd. in an interview with G.S. Viereck in *The Saturday Evening Post*. Also qtd. in Ronald Clark, *Einstein*, 422.

"I do not believe in the God of theology who rewards and punishes the objects of his creation and is but a reflection of human frailty," Einstein once said; "the idea of a personal God is quite alien to me, and seems even naïve."[137] And while "I see a clock ... I cannot envision the clockmaker. The human mind is unable to conceive of four dimensions, so how can it conceive of a God, before whom a thousand years and a thousand dimensions are as one."[138]

Nevertheless, belief in one supreme, albeit invisible, entity paves the way for belief in other non-corporeal life forms. If one such being exists, then, logically, so could many. Earth and its animals, insects, and plants took roughly 13.4 billion years to evolve out of a cloud of stellar dust.[139] Given that much time, the spirit world could be just as diverse.

Of course, if you're an atheist, which many scientists tend to be nowadays, this argument falls apart. True, there is no irrefutable proof that non-corporeal life forms exist. But that doesn't mean they don't; only that our senses and inventions haven't detected them yet. Nevertheless, for unbelievers, the laws of physics easily explain away miracles. In today's world, the wonder of ignorance is gone. But as Einstein maintained, "science without religion is lame, [and] religion without science is blind."[140]

So, in a spirit of open-mindedness, suspend disbelief for a minute and let's consider possible scientific explanations for non-corporeal life forms and how they might communicate with us.

Before we start, though, I have a disclaimer to make. I am only familiar with Middle Eastern and East African spirits, specifically the branch called the jinn. I know next to nothing about angels or other Invisible species. Nevertheless, as you saw in chapter 2, East Africa is considered the birthplace of *Homo sapiens*. It is also the birthplace of the zar, the subspecies of jinn that accompanied our ancestors, under different names, as they migrated throughout Africa—and more recently, across the oceans in slave galley holds.

---

137 From an autographed letter to Beatrice Frolich, Dec. 17, 1952, Albert Einstein Archives, Jerusalem (AEA), Archival Call # 59–797.

138 Qtd. in Alice Calaprice, ed., *The Expanded Quotable Einstein*, 208.

139 The Big Bang that created our universe is thought to have occurred 13.8 billion years ago.

140 Qtd. in Calaprice, *The Expanded Quotable Einstein*, 213.

Orisha, bori, loa, zar, and other similar entities share a common African history and an unusual predilection: human cohabitation—i.e., they enjoy "possessing" solid life forms. But Invisibles don't always communicate via possession. In fact, most entities, including the "Clockmaker" Himself (although God is considered to have no gender), usually employ more "hands-off" methods, such as those described in an unusual but impeccable source—the Quran.

The Quran

The Quran is Islam's equivalent to the Christian Bible or the Jewish Old Testament—with one notable exception. Muslims believe it contains Allah's exact words as dictated to the Archangel Gabriel. The Quran's human author, the Prophet Muhammad, received these Revelations from Gabriel over a period of twenty-two years, beginning in 610 CE. I explain more about the Quran in the next chapter, but for now, suffice it to say that Muslims believe its contents came verbatim from God. And God had a lot to say about some of the Invisibles—particularly human souls, angels, demons, and jinn. So did Muhammad, whose sayings were recorded in the hadith.

The hadith are collections of the Prophet's words, actions, and habits that were compiled during the late ninth century (more than two hundred years after Muhammad's death) by various religious scholars; some mention Muhammad's encounters with the jinn. Several of these compilations, mostly named after their authors, are considered the most respectable among Sunni Muslims (particularly the first two): Hadith *Sahih al-Bukhari*, Hadith *Sahih Muslim*, Hadith *Sunan Abu Daoud*, Hadith *Jami at-Tirmidhi*, and Hadith *Sunan as-Sughra* (also known as *Sunan an-Nasa'i* after the imam who compiled it).[141] They are used to help read and interpret the Quran.

I should also mention that even the Quran was not codified, i.e., standardized, until after the Prophet's death in 632 CE. In 633, many of his compatriots were killed in battle, so Muhammad's successor, Abu Baker, ordered a definitive version be compiled

---

141   The word *sahih* has several meanings, but when applied to the hadith, it denotes information (usually concerning the Prophet Muhammad) that is "correct, proper; true, veritable" and "reliable" (*Arabic English Dictionary*), verified by scholars at the time the collections were codified.

and preserved. Muhammad had relied heavily on his literate companions to record the holy Revelations, and with their untimely deaths, those remaining realized the necessity of standardizing what up until then had been stored in Muhammad's brain. The process took twenty years, completed by 650 CE, and produced the version that is read and recited today. The passages from the Quran that I quote in this book are my translations of the Arabic text.

For now, though, let's concentrate on what Allah revealed about Invisible communication. In the Quran, demonic communication is occasionally referred to as "*waswasa*,"[142] or whispering. "Whispering," of course, implies words spoken so softly only one person can hear them, or thoughts transmitted by "inner voices"—i.e., "mental telepathy." Yet we know that for humans to "hear" (or think they hear) something, the auditory regions of the brain must be stimulated, either electrically or chemically. And this is not as unusual as you may think. Oliver Sacks points out in *Hallucinations* that many recent studies confirm it is not uncommon for people to hear voices—and that most who do are not mentally ill. In fact, humans have a global history of hearing voices. Up until the eighteenth century, ethereal messages were accorded great importance—take the oracles of the Greek and Roman gods, for example, or the commandments dictated by Abraham's One God. In fact, hearing is far more important than seeing (visions) for worship, because language conveys unambiguous meaning when images do not.[143]

In our day-to-day lives, "inner voices" may not seem extraordinary, but comprehending external "whispering" is actually quite complicated. For noises to be understood as language, not only must the brain's auditory cortex be stimulated, but the language and vocabulary regions as well, simultaneously. And yet it happens. Even more amazing, apparently during possession or medium visitations, some entities are able to replace their host's unique electrical signature (or "brain map," which is like a fingerprint) with their own. Felicitas Goodman mentioned that some possession-study

---

142   Quran 7:20: "Then Satan whispered to them [Adam and Eve]"; Quran 20:120: "Then Satan whispered to him"; Quran 50:16: "And We created man and know what his soul whispers to him"; Quran 114:4–5: "From the evil whisperings of the one who withdraws [an epithet of Satan] who whispers in the chests of the people."

143   Sacks, *Hallucinations*, 59–60.

participants even registered the same brain maps when specific entities manifested (or, in cases of Multiple Personality Disorder, when certain personalities appeared).[144]

But how can entities we can't even see influence brainwaves?

I don't know, but I have some theories...and the Quran offers several clues. First of all, Islam's holy book clearly states that these entities are made from different stuff than we are:

"We created humans from clay, from molded black mud.
The Jinn We created before, from the fire of a scorching wind." (15:26–27)

According to this, the jinn are a pre-Adamite race composed of air (gas) and fire (plasma)—as opposed to humanity's earth (solid) mixed with water (liquid), i.e., mud. The jinn share the planet with us "solids" (and suffer the consequences of our pollution) but live apart in a world that also produces things of beauty, under laws of apartheid. Also note the pronoun "we" in the above quote. This "Royal We" could be seen as implying more than one Creator (or a Creator race, even!), yet that would be in direct contradiction with Islam's first premise: there is no god but God. The Quran's point of view changes, however, from *surah* to *surah*.[145] In the section below, God is referred to in the third person:

"He [Allah] created humans from clay like pottery
And the Jinn from a smokeless flame of fire...
Lord of the two Easts and the two Wests...
He released the two seas that meet;
Between them a partition/isthmus they do not seek to attain [transgress] ...
From both come pearls and coral." (55:14–15, 17, 19–20, 22)

It is possible that "a smokeless flame of fire," like the "fire of a scorching wind" in the previous verse, refers to plasma—the fourth ionized gaseous state of matter. It exists all

---

144   *How About Demons?*, 39.

145   The Quran is divided into chapters (*surat*, plural of *surah*) and verses (*ayat*, plural of *ayah*). For a list of surat, see appendix 1.

around us but we can't see it, just like unpolluted air. Plasma is present in fire, is sensitive to charged particles, and conducts electricity (remember the lightning bolt example from chapter 1?). Therefore, it could influence brain waves. Also, a well-known jinn fact is that these entities appear at dusk and prefer low light or dark environments.[146] If jinn are indeed plasma-based, without traditional "skin" to contain their size, direct sunlight would heat and expand their molecules into unwieldy dimensions. On the other hand, Invisibles may always be present but we only perceive them at twilight because the motion detector neurons in our eyes ("rods") work best under low light conditions. Or perhaps darkness triggers slower brainwaves and we only detect these entities at lower frequencies.

One possibility is that jinn appearances are linked to rifts in the Earth's magnetic field, which allow them passage into our atmosphere from outer space or another dimension. The Quran offers this clue: "Indeed, he [Iblis] and his tribe [the jinn] see you from where you see them not" (7:27). If the jinn do live in another plane of existence, their visibility would depend on how their world intersects with ours. According to Muhammad, they flow through humans like blood[147] (or electricity through nerves, since during Muhammad's lifetime [seventh century CE], the function of nerves had yet to be discovered).

Another possibility, albeit terribly farfetched, is that some Invisibles might be composed of dark matter. This would explain their invisibility and the fact that jinn do not have mirror reflections, since by definition, dark matter does not interact with photons or other electromagnetic energy. The Quran clearly states that otherworldly inhabitants vary in composition; jinn are made from fire (or plasma), and humans, although solid, are animated by "God's breath," an entirely different substance: "When I have shaped

---

146   According to both Hadith *Sahih al-Bukhari* (#3280) and Hadith *Sahih Muslim* (#2012), Muhammad warned the faithful to "gather your children when darkness approaches, for devils [*shayateen*, i.e., the jinn] spread out then ... " However, the belief that spirits emerge at dusk can be traced as far back as pharaonic times.

147   This is mentioned in Hadith *Sahih al-Bukhari* (#2035, 2038, 2039), originally from Muhammad's Jewish wife Safiyah: "The Devil flows through the son of Adam like blood."

him, and breathed into him from My spirit" (Quran 15:29). Plus, a well-documented Hadith states that angels are made from light (photons).[148]

Of course, it is also possible that Invisibles only exist in our mind's eye. A lack of reflection implies a lack of matter for photons to bounce off of. That's not to say Invisibles aren't present, though...if they can stimulate the hearing portions of our brains (auditory cortex), why not the visual portions (visual cortex) as well? Nevertheless, witnesses of jinn manifestations are often convinced these entities were far more than mere electrical shadows. They recalled heightened emotions, movement in their peripheral vision, the sense of a nearby presence, and the intuition that surrounding auras or magnetic fields were disrupted—testimony that points to something...if not physical, then at least external.

Heightened emotions in these circumstances could stem from a "fight or flight" response, an immediate reaction to a possibly dangerous situation. As we saw in the previous chapter, this alternate neural pathway evolved to induce split-second reactions to sensory input by bypassing the slower cortical analysis loop that feeds consciousness. Signals still travel via the brain stem and the thalamus, but feed into the amygdalae before arriving in the cortex. Since the brain stem contributes to this pathway, the changes in environmental vibrations it measures tend to surface through the amygdalae as emotional, nebulous, and hard-to-pinpoint intuitions. My friend Orion Foxwood, a gifted faerie seer and conjurer, refers to the process of honing these perceptions as "bringing the subtle senses out of dormancy."[149] It would seem this circuit's faster reaction time and lack of cortical filtering makes it better suited to detecting Invisibles.

I just threw a lot of conjecture at you! But until science proves, first of all, whether or not Invisibles exist and, secondly, if they do what they are made from, we are all free to wonder—and think outside the box. I'm sure if you put your mind to it, you could come up with theories, too—as have the ancient Egyptians, Hebrews, Greeks, Arabs, Renaissance philosophers, and quantum physicists. As Einstein said, "Imagination is

---

148   From Hadith *Sahih Muslim* (#2996), quoting Muhammad's youngest wife: "Aisha reported that Allah's Messenger said 'He created the angels from light and the Jinn were created from smokeless fire and Adam was created as was described [in the Quran] for you [i.e., fashioned out of clay].'"

149   Personal interviews with Orion Foxwood, from 2011 to 2014.

more important than knowledge. For knowledge is limited, whereas imagination embraces the entire world, stimulating progress, giving birth to evolution."[150]

Enough speculation about brainwaves. Let's talk about something even more controversial, the ultimate form of spirit communication—possession!

Possession

Possession is founded on an ancient concept—that nebulous entities inhabit the bodies of animals, humans, and jinn alike. These divine sparks then return to the Invisible realm, sometimes only after the physical death of their hosts, enriched by their experiences on Earth. Based on this concept, Felicitas Goodman suggested an excellent everyday analogy for possession: a car, its owner, and a friend who wants to drive the car. During possession, the car owner relinquishes the driver's seat (his body) so his friend (an Invisible) can temporarily take control. The question is, what happens to the car owner? He could sit in the passenger's seat and watch, for example (a metaphor for what happens in lucid trance), or hand over the keys and get out of the car (i.e., lose consciousness). According to Dr. Goodman, the choice apparently depends on culture.[151] Those with ties to Africa cultivate different spirit relationships than those with Eurasian roots. Also, African spirits (which include the jinn) are more positive than negative; they heal and divine, give voice to the powerless, and help the socially ostracized fit in. Their human hosts (trance dancers) often demonstrate a predisposition to possession. Chronic crises, illnesses, or sudden nervous collapses without ritual intervention are considered signs a spirit wishes to embody and that their chosen host should be initiated. Brazilian Umbandists, for example, believe their possessors help restore health and happiness, not cause sickness and misery. The spirits wait until they are invited before entering a host and leave when they are told (at least most of them). Sometimes, practitioners may even choose their possessors.

This experience is similar to that of modern ravers. In his in-depth study of global rave culture, Robin Sylvan writes that it's "not simply that spirits are present in the dance-floor experience at raves, but that ravers can develop a conscious and mutually

---

150   Qtd. in Calaprice, *The Expanded Quotable Einstein,* 10.
151   *How About Demons?,* 1.

beneficial relationship with them." A raver he interviewed described the experience as follows: "While we're dancing … we also have a lot of help on the other side dancing with us…. The light beings, the ones you really want to be dealing with, are polite. And they'll wait for an invitation. And the guys you don't want to deal with are impolite and you have to keep them out—you know, the darker ones. Spirits are just like people…. And there's people you want to invite in your home and there's people you don't…. And that's part of what the ceremonial container is about."[152]

But there are exceptions to every rule. Umbandists do, on occasion, experience entities from the dark side, and some souls of African descent allow themselves to be misused for evil—Vodun or harsher forms of Candomblé are good examples. Possession by these spirits can result in death.[153] This is similar to Eurasian possession, which nearly always produces sinister outcomes. Noxious European entities invade victims after physical or psychological trauma when their defenses are weakened, then manifest through illnesses only curable by banishment or exorcism. Their toxicity varies, however. For instance, while Japanese ghosts may only cause trouble when they are unhappy or feel neglected, demonic entities enjoy abusing their victims … with catastrophic consequences. The chronic depression and frightening visions they cause, interspersed with violent trances of intractable raging, ruin people's lives, if not kill them outright. For example, the Catholic Church diagnoses demonic possession, and deems exorcism necessary, when a demon speaks through its victim's mouth and manifests a violent aversion to anything sacred.[154]

Another form of spirit communication I would like to bring up before we change subjects is glossolalia or "speaking in tongues," i.e., holy possession. The intimate relationship so many Evangelicals and other people of faith have with God is a continuing conundrum for researchers. One theory is that worshippers learn to communicate through specialized exercises and prayers. These techniques are simpler for those with concentration skills, but prove that communion with the divine can be achieved through practice. According to Oliver Sacks, congregants learn to imagine divine experiences with heightened sensory

---

152 *Trance Formation*, 88–89.

153 Goodman, *How About Demons?*, 89.

154 Ibid., 96.

detail, until one day, their minds leap from wishful thinking to hallucination and they actually hear and see God instead of simply imagining Him.[155] That's the scientific explanation, at any rate. If you ask the worshippers, they will say the Spirit of God possessed them.

One defining characteristic of the Evangelical Pentecostal movement is that followers "speak in tongues." A subset of Protestantism, Pentecostalism resulted in the formation of numerous new denominations and has become a growing phenomenon both in America and internationally. One of two founders, Charles Fox Parham (1873–1929), began his divine calling as a Protestant lay preacher but then founded his own church, the Bethel Bible College of Topeka, Kansas, in 1900 at age twenty-seven. He and his students determined that, according to the story of the Pentecost, speaking in tongues was a necessary part of being baptized by the Holy Spirit.[156] The Bible describes it as follows:

> And when the day of Pentecost was fully come, they were all with one accord in one place.
>
> And suddenly there came a sound from heaven as of a rushing mighty wind, and it filled all the house where they were sitting.
>
> And there appeared unto them cloven tongues like as of fire,[157] and it sat upon each of them.
>
> And they were all filled with the Holy Ghost, and began to speak with other tongues, as the Spirit gave them utterance.[158]

Felicitas Goodman spent considerable time researching glossolalia and analyzing its speech patterns. She found that church initiates were encouraged to imitate experienced members during introductory prayer sessions. They were highly motivated because they believed they wouldn't go to heaven unless they were "baptized." She also noted that Pentecostal rituals included conventional trance induction aids, such as rhythmic singing, clapping, and extremely loud music, and that glossolalia occurred during trance. The Holy Spirit did not have a distinct personality, but was easily

---

155 *Hallucinations*, 248.

156 Goodman, *How About Demons?*, 52.

157 Plasma entities, perhaps?

158 Acts 2:1–4 (King James Version).

offended since It stopped visiting some worshippers after only a few visits (typical of neural habituation).[159]

To Pentecostalists, glossolalia was a mysterious language. To Dr. Goodman, it was not. She felt that the repetition of simple syllables such as "Lalalalala" did not convey either meaning or messages and that the sounds were simple nonsensical vocalizations. Computer analysis of these "utterances" confirmed her hypothesis. They followed a typical "glossolalia curve": a strong muscular contraction of the vocal chords that gradually relaxed. On the other hand, she also discovered that during possession, demonic speech produced identical curves.[160] Apparently, Christian demons use the same glossolalia techniques as God. It would be interesting to see if orisha and zar do, too.

In summary, it appears that, similar to seizures, Invisible speech is caused by electric tsunamis that wash over the cortical regions responsible for vocalization. And while these waves can be induced through training and are subject to neural habituation, they could conceivably be caused by an external source, particularly if they engulf the right temporal lobe area associated with divine contact. Personally, I think what a worshipper utters during these events is not important, but the private message he or she takes away from the experience is. Speaking in tongues is an external sign that the congregant is communicating with the divine. To those affected, words are unnecessary. Experiencing His presence is reward enough. Suddenly, the Creator becomes very real and life after death a true possibility. In the time it took to sing hallelujah, a worshipper has answers to some of life's most difficult existential questions!

Training the Subtle Senses

Given that Pentecostals and Buddhists alike train for divine contact, the rest of this chapter is devoted to exercises to help develop your "subtle senses" and otherworldly communication skills. Enhancing concentration, memory, sensory detail perception, mental imagery, and intuition strengthen the conduits Invisibles use to communicate, which are often dulled by modern life. But before we get to the juicy details, there is something important we need to discuss first … a trance dancer's attitude toward the experience.

---

159   *How About Demons?*, 58.
160   Ibid., 122.

As noted previously, a positive attitude is essential for contacting the spirit world. Pessimism and defeatism, the scourges of depression, will prevent you from even picking up the Invisible phone, much less dialing the right number or knowing which language to speak if someone answers. Is the glass half full or half empty? If nothing happens the first time you call, will you keep trying or give up? Is your mind open to positive coincidences, even after difficult experiences? Can you see the silver lining around storm clouds? (They make for amazing sunsets and rainbows.) You must *believe* you can connect with non-corporeal life forms. They know you can. They're just waiting for you to realize it.

Don't forget, prayer is a form of Invisible communication! If you pray, you already know how to contact their world. And lastly, hearing voices does *not* mean you are disturbed, schizophrenic, or mentally ill—although if any "whisperers" encourage you to harm yourself or others, you should seek professional help. Know that **the vast majority of demonic attacks attributed to the jinn or evil spirits are mainly due to physical deformities, episodes of epilepsy, or chemical imbalances in the brain—medical conditions that can be treated. They are *not* Invisible manifestations.** Extreme Invisible communication is *very* rare and can only be attributed as such when medical doctors rule out all other possibilities. Even today, people are still being murdered during botched exorcism attempts in the Middle East and elsewhere, out of misplaced fear that they have been possessed by evil entities. There is no need for this.

Once your mind is open to the power of positive thinking, you are ready for the nitty-gritty of ethereal contact.

Developing Theta

As we have seen, theta and delta are the frequencies that Invisibles use to communicate with humans; the spirit-world radio, if you will. To hear their broadcasts, you must learn how to tune in to their channels—to recognize theta when it occurs and reward your brain accordingly (since heightened delta causes unconsciousness). If your subconscious throws up a theta flair with a great but unusual idea—*act on it*! If you don't, the flares will stop. The more credence you give these suggestions, the more suggestions you will receive. The same thing applies to intuition. If you feel a gut reaction, don't second-guess it. *Act on it* (obviously, within reason—jumping off a bridge, either literally or metaphorically, is *not* what I'm talking about here). In the beginning, you may not be right all the time. But with practice, your hunches will improve. Listen to your inner voice and follow the coincidences thrown in your path. Believe that chance events have meaning. This is the first step to understanding cosmic communication: open yourself up to its *modus operandi*, how it works.

By encouraging intuition, creativity, and other theta attributes, you sensitize your consciousness to the Invisible world. Nevertheless, keep what you find there at arm's length in the beginning. Maintain mental barriers; it's safer. Furthermore, possession trance can be *very* tricky and should be learned firsthand, in person, from experienced sources. This book cannot provide that level of instruction. Similarly, as you try the lucid trance induction techniques in Part Three, if something doesn't feel right, *stop*. Rely on your intuition! As the raver previously quoted aptly said, "Spirits are just like people…. And there's people you want to invite in your home and there's people you don't."[161] The more mental control you develop, the more prepared you will be, particularly when your subconscious throws something unexpected your way.

Lastly, sometimes the most difficult demons to face are internal. Suppressed memories can be far scarier than spirits. But the good thing about dredging up the past is that you only have to do it once. After childhood shipwrecks are hauled away, the submerged dangers are gone for good and your waterways are cleared for sailing.

Concentration

Once you recognize and encourage theta in your life, the next step is to hone your concentration skills. Total mental immersion is an important trance induction skill. For our purposes, music is the focal point: becoming so absorbed in listening that the autonomic nervous system takes over the physical task of dancing. One way to learn to ignore distractions is to read and write in noisy, bustling environments. Measure success by whether you retain what you read or whether your writing makes sense. At first, it may take several passes to understand a sentence, paragraph, page, or chapter. Practice until it takes only one pass. Another excellent method is scrying—seeing images in a crystal ball or other translucent media. It takes concentration to stare at an object for

---

161   Qtd. in Robin Sylvan, *Trance Formation*, 89.

long periods. And by teaching the subconscious to project its perceptions, you sharpen your "inner eye." And once images flow when you're sitting still, you can train them to appear while dancing.

Another concentration aid is syncopation. In music, marking anything except the downbeat requires constant vigilance, since the body's natural tendency is to synchronize with the strongest beat. Not reverting to automatic pilot takes continuous effort! I know, so far, flow is what I have asked you to seek. But for this exercise, to teach you how to focus on the music and not let your mind wander into theta-inspired reveries, try to dance against the beat—on the up beat, or the back beat or the half beat. Play with it, have fun. Release is what the whole process is about, anyway.

Memory or Event Recall

This training improves Invisible exchanges by helping you remember what transpired while you were in a trance. This is harder than you would expect. Ideas burst out of nowhere into consciousness, and then, like dreams, quickly dissipate if they aren't immediately transferred into long-term memory. Similar to a computer, the brain holds sensory input or thoughts in a temporary storage bin (like Random Access Memory) until they are transformed into permanent memories during sleep. If ideas are not reinforced within 15–30 seconds, you will forget them. And this bin has limited capacity! It can only hold seven things at a time (give or take two)—seven numbers, for example—before new information starts overwriting what's already there. And as you get older, this number goes down ...

However, researchers have found that attaching emotional significance to short-term memories helps preserve them. Stepping on a snake somewhere will certainly help you recall the place where it happened, the time of day, the weather, what clothes you were wearing, and a hundred other details. Verbal repetition ("rehearsal") also works, as does writing things down, obviously. But if you need to remember a second, third, or fourth great idea while you write down the first, and the process takes longer than 30 seconds, the following "bundling" trick may help you retain information.

Numbers and letters are useful memory jogs. One strategy is to number your ideas and then link them to words or images. A symbol or letter is easier to retain than a complex thought. Knowing the total number of ideas also alerts you to something forgotten.

My favorite method is to synthesize a thought into a single word and then make another word or phrase out of the first letters of each point I want to remember. For example, when I wanted to remember ideas related to Sleep, Time, Epilepsy, Birds & Animals, and Words versus Pictures, the phrase I emerged from trance with was "BEST PAW"... One look at my pet and the whole string flashed back, ready to be written.

Detailed Sensory Perception

Admit it, we tend to take familiar surroundings for granted. Most of us ignore everyday details because our minds are preoccupied with other things. We live in the future, the past, or somebody else's present, but rarely our own. Yet the Invisibles tend to manifest in the here and now, so let me suggest some activities to heighten your ability to live in the moment. To begin, take ten minutes at the end of the day to relive what happened during the day. Try to remember everything you did—not just the big picture, but the details. What temperature was it when you first stepped outside? Feel the weather on your skin. Don't just remember what you had for breakfast, lunch, or dinner, but actually taste it, bite for bite. Who did you meet or talk to on the phone? Remembering names is a start, but go further and remember facial or vocal details. What were they wearing? Did their socks match? Were their shoes dirty? Did they bite their nails? What did they smell like? Everyone has an odor. Make a general list of every minor detail you can think of and then check each encounter off, one by one. At first this will take time, but with practice each item will only take a few seconds to flash back in extraordinary minutiae. Then take an emotional inventory. Did you feel any strong emotions during the day? Any brief waves of joy or sadness? Try to remember what triggered them. Were the reasons obvious... or nebulous?

Apply the above recall techniques to a past trip or memory. Use photographs at first, but go beyond the images by remembering smells, tastes, textures, emotions, people, etc. Don't forget the weather and any creatures you encountered or heard (birds, animals, bugs, etc.). Then pick two spots—one outside, one inside—where you can sit comfortably and observe your environment. No detail is extraneous. Make a list of colors, smells, sounds, textures, taste, the time of day, weather, season, temperature, humidity, the ground or floor beneath your feet, the sky or ceiling above your head, and the quality of light. How do you feel? Are you happy, sad, sick, well, nervous, stressed, relaxed, etc.?

Go back to the same places on a different day, time, and season. Take a new inventory, make a new list, and then reread the old one. Actually relive the first experience. What has changed in your environment, in your life? Were pending events resolved? Has the passage of time made you feel different? Compare this with the first experience. Which period involved more stress? Did this affect your senses?

When we are young, time drags on. Yet the older we get, the faster it flies. A cliché, I know, but a universal human truth. Time is a dimension of our universe we take for granted until an event reminds us our days are numbered. Our ancestors were far more in tune with the passage of time than we are. We live inside most of the time, in climate controlled, artificially lit environments. Our bodies are separated from the sun and the Earth's rotational cues that set our diurnal rhythms and internal clocks. For example, can you guess the time of day by sunlight alone, or at night, by your diurnal rhythms? Can you wake up on time without an alarm? Our ancestors could. Do you follow the full moon cycle with more than a calendar? Do you actually go outside and track it across the sky? Do you feel different emotions during full and new moons? If so, what are they? Are you more susceptible to the cycle at certain times of the year?

The most immediate effect of time is how it regulates sleep cycles. As we saw in chapter 4, without sleep, we die. Not right away, but eventually. Deprive the brain of theta and delta and it withers. As a sensory exercise, then, consciously try to reset your sleep patterns (harness jet lag). Go 24 hours without sleep. Did your sensory input change? Write down how your body coped. Everyone reacts differently, but for most, "waking theta" visions increase—which is why shamans incorporate sleep deprivation into their vision quest rituals.

How good are you at reading emotions? Observe the people close to you. If they are not feeling well, do you know without them telling you? How do they physically manifest pain, joy, fear, sadness, etc.? Do they hold themselves differently? What about their facial expressions? Compare their reactions to casual acquaintances and complete strangers. Which emotions are you most sensitive to? Close your eyes and listen to people talk. Do you hear emotion in their voices? Does it match what you see or what you know to be true? Harder still, try to sense emotions through people's auras. What emotions do they project? What does your intuition tell you they are feeling?

Learning how to recognize and interpret intuitions will help you translate other-worldly communication. As I mentioned, the fight or flight circuit often picks up information the cortex filters out. Learn to recognize when your subtle senses are trying to tell you something. Was a faint dark cloud floating at the edge of your peripheral vision, a slight breeze ruffling your hair, a faint odor dissipating as suddenly as it entered your nostrils, or an illusory presence watching behind your back? Instead of second-guessing these sensations and searching for logical explanations, just feel them. Close your eyes, calm your body, empty your mind, and listen for an inner voice. What is it saying or telling you to do? Weigh the dangers, but take the path less traveled; heed an illogical impression if the consequences are no worse than disrupting well-worn habits. Later, when you are more in tune with how your spur-of-the-moment impulses play out, you can take risks. But first, gain experience interpreting "hunches." Like the spirits that may be inspiring them, not all are worth listening to.

Mental Imagery: Crystal Gazing and Scrying

Technically, crystal gazing is a form of static trance induction through sensory deprivation. Similar to Paleolithic shamans (and the Prophet Muhammad) who induced visions by spending time in dark caves, crystals induce visions by forcing the eyes to stare into emptiness. Nothing actually forms in the crystal; it is merely a resting place for the eyes until the visual cortex gets bored and starts producing images on its own. What you see will depend on your subconscious or the Invisibles. Ancient cultures also used bowls of water or reflecting pools for the same purpose, an activity they called scrying.

For the following exercises, you do not need an expensive crystal. A clear glass ball or translucent bowl filled with water will do. The idea is to stare into something with a different refractive index than air, i.e., something clear and colorless that reflects light differently. For comfort, the gazing surface should be at least four to five inches in diameter. The right environment is key. Too many visual distractions or reflections will prevent images from forming. Rest the ball or bowl on an empty table covered with solid dark material (I prefer black velvet). Pull up a comfortable chair so your eyes are reading distance away when seated. Lower the ambient lighting until the ball is illuminated without reflections. Lighting is important. Natural is better than electric; neon or fluorescent is not good at all. The most popular choices are candles, moonlight, sunset, and dawn, but dim electric will do—certainly nothing bright or glaring.

To start, close your eyes for about five minutes. Calm and center yourself with a passive mindset. Concentrate on a question you would like answered (having a purpose challenges your subconscious). **Affirm that only the truth can reach you.** Then open your eyes, empty your mind, and gaze into the crystal. Try not to blink too often or strain your eyes. Bring the center into focus, then look through and beyond it—a few feet at first, and then yards. *Expect* to see pictures—as I mentioned, optimism is everything. Before visions appear, the crystal will cloud over with milky gray mist, either inside the ball or in between it and your eyes. Sometimes concentric multicolored rings emanate from inside like ripples out of a multicolored bulls-eye. Before long, reflections and the outside world will melt away, leaving you staring into an endless void. This is when visions form. At first, they will be disjointed and confusing, but will improve with patience and practice, until eventually they gush like a mountain stream during spring thaw.

Begin with five-minute sessions, and then slowly increase your gazing time. As with other forms of trance, initial attempts tend not to work, so keep trying. When you are done, close your eyes a few minutes, review what you saw, and then write everything down in your journal. Wait too long and the images will be gone. Expect several types: dreamlike visions inspired by imagination or current events, and memories that will become more obscure or forgotten the deeper into trance you go. At some point, though, you will begin to see events, objects, places, or people connected to the Other World, either related to your session goal or as a message an Invisible is trying to communicate. When you witness events you would otherwise have no knowledge of, you know your psychic connection is genuine.

Don't try to force images to appear. They will come in their own time—or they may be unnecessary because you already "know" the answer. Just remember, connections are rare without faith. Like a magnet, belief attracts what the mind expects. Train your skills by recreating images: an object, a photograph, or even a fairy-tale character. Then try a place—first somewhere you've been, then somewhere you haven't. Finally, invite spirit friends to visit, if you have any.

Homework: Dancing with Fire in the Shaman's Cave

First, I want to take you on a Vision Quest. Either record the following guided meditation and play it back to yourself, or use my recording of it.[162] Lie in a comfortable, quiet, low-lit spot and listen with your eyes closed:

A GUIDED MEDITATION: THE SHAMAN'S CAVE

Let's travel back in time to when belief in spirits had no condescending voice to oppose it and skepticism was suspended…We are in the Dordogne, in southwestern France, a region dotted with sacred spaces: gothic cathedrals, Roman temples, an occasional megalith, and numerous prehistoric caves decorated with ochre and charcoal animals. One of the area's rivers, the Vezere, eroded its limestone bed into a gorge pitted with tunnels and caverns. During the last Ice Age, over fifteen thousand years ago, shamans used a number of them to talk to spirits. There's one cave in particular I think you might like.

Around a bend, upriver from the well-known tourist attractions, a ledge juts out near a cliff top on your left. You reach it by a narrow switchback path. It's not a hard climb and the view is well worth the effort. You can see for miles up there; puffy clouds marching across the horizon like ants, rolling forest-green hills, red tile roofs, yellow mustard and purple lavender fields interrupted by a lone gray cathedral spire.

The ledge extends from a grotto large enough to shelter a campfire. Smooth boulders, ideal for sitting, form a semi-circle at the rear. Several larger sarsens at the entrance stand guard against howling winter winds. Deep within, a gaping two-story crack splits the cliff face into a tunnel. This is what we've come to investigate. Don't worry, it's easy to navigate and tall enough to walk in upright. The walls are smooth from eons of storm runoff and if you listen carefully, you can hear water dripping. The odor of moist earth and damp rock grow as you descend into the hillside. At the bottom, countless crystal-clear turquoise pools empty into a tortuous underground stream.

---

162   Sands of Time Music is releasing three companion music albums to supplement this book: *Zar 2: Tumboura, Zar 3: Harim Masri,* and *Weaving Infinity,* which includes two complete trance dance sets of Egyptian music, complete with warm-ups, cool-downs, and vision quests.

But we're not going that far today. The tunnel has other interesting features besides the pools. It's not dark. Oil lamps light the way and torches mark the entrances to smaller cavities. It's these little caverns we've come to visit. There are hundreds of them, each unique, each with multicolored symbols marking their thresholds. Look carefully at the symbols, but keep walking until one draws you to it. Memorize the image, then go in.

What do you see?
Look around.
Do you hear anything, smell anything?
What do you feel? Are you hot or cold?
Explore.
Touch things; rearrange them if you want.
Focus on colors and your emotions.
Do you recognize this place?
Is anyone there?
Please, stay as long as you want.

When you're done, retrace your steps back up the tunnel to the grotto. Stand on the ledge and recall your experience in the cave.

What comes to mind first?
A specific image or sound? A smell, a sensation?
Gaze into the distance—at the countryside, the open sky, and the river below.
Is anything different or new?
Has the weather changed, or the time of day?

As you climb back down the cliff, decide which memory is the most vivid. This is your "key" to return.

Come explore any time. You are always welcome.

Now return to the homework from chapter 1, Dancing with Fire. Only this time, increase the fast rhythmic music to 15–20 minutes and dance on a rug. As the music begins, relax your gaze and allow yourself to see images in the carpet and the room around you. Mirrors, windowpanes, or light-scattering objects are particularly helpful vision inducers. Close your eyes. Visualize the Shaman's Cave ledge and enter the tunnel. Still dancing, walk down the tunnel until an entrance symbol attracts your attention, step over the threshold, and explore the space. Remember any vivid sensations. Include slower music at the end of your trance set so you can lie down before retracing your steps back out of the tunnel. Did anything stand out or seem important? Afterwards, write it all down in your journal and reread your notes twenty-four hours later.

6

....

The Jinn

The Sufi tradition, similar to Muslim tradition in general, is based on oral transmission—i.e., storytelling. Around campfires, into the night under the desert stars, tales are told, deeds are immortalized, and Allah's glorious mysteries are contemplated.

Sufi Wisdom—The Three Questions[163]

There once lived a dervish stingy with words. If a nod or sign would do, he would spare his tongue. He was a quiet, inoffensive, but shrewd man called Holy Dervish.

In the same place lived a rich, good-natured gentleman given to mischief now and then. One day he proposed to visit the holy dervish with friends. "I wish," he said, "to ask him three questions he will never be able to answer." They found the holy man sitting near his hut in a newly plowed field. The Muslim gentlemen walked up and with great mock humility said, "Holy Father, I am troubled by three questions; will you kindly answer them for me?" The dervish gave an affirmative nod.

The gentleman began, "The first question, Holy Father, is about God. People say there is a God; but I cannot see Him, and no one can show Him to me. Therefore, I cannot believe God exists. Will you answer this question?" The dervish nodded again.

---

163   From Frank Dobbins, *Error's Chains*, 750–52. Edited for length and clarity.

"My second question," the gentleman continued, "is about Satan. The Quran says that Satan was created from fire. But if Satan was created from fire, how can hellfire hurt him? Will you explain that too?" A nod.

"The third question refers to myself. The Quran says that man's every action is decreed; now, if it is decreed that I must commit a certain action, how can God judge me for that action, Himself having decreed it? Please, Holy Father, answer me."

Another nod, and while the party stood gazing at him, the dervish quietly seized a clod from the newly plowed field and hurled it with all his might at the gentleman's face. The gentleman was furious, and dragged the dervish before a judge.

Arriving in court, the gentleman stated his complaint, saying that the pain in his head was so severe he could hardly bear it. The judge looked at the dervish, and asked if this was so? A nod was the reply; but the judge said, "Please explain yourself, for nods will not do in my court."

The dervish replied, "This gentleman came to me with his companions, and asked three questions which I carefully answered."

"He did no such thing," the gentleman exclaimed. "A clod of earth he threw in my face—which was extremely painful!"

The judge looked at the dervish, and said, "Explain yourself."

"I will. Please, your Honor, this gentleman said that people maintained there was a God, but he could not see Him, nor could anyone show him God, therefore he could not believe God exists. Now he says he has pain in his face from the clod I threw at him, but I cannot see his pain. Will your Honor kindly ask him to show us his pain, for how can I believe he has any if I cannot see it? Again, this gentleman asked, if Satan was created from fire, how could hellfire hurt him? The gentleman will admit, though, that Father Adam was created from earth, and that he himself is also of earth. But if he be of earth, how can a clod of earth hurt him?" As to the third question, the dervish drew himself up and said with great dignity, "Sir, if it be written in my fate to throw a clod at this gentleman's face, how can and dare he bring me before a judge?"

The judge allowed that the dervish had answered the three questions with his clod, but admonished him to answer future questions in a more congenial way, as he might not get off so easily the next time.

"You can't see air, yet you feel wind. You can't see smells, yet your nose detects odors. Invite all your senses on board. Sight is only one fractal of one large overall sense that detects vibration and rhythm. From these waves does matter flow. Rhythm is nothing more than organized vibration."[164]

It has been said that calling the jinn is like calling a pack of immense, ferocious wild dogs. They come when they want, if they want. Legend has it that they love music, dance, syncopated percussion, and incense. They can be extremely loyal or self-serving, depending on the individual. And occasionally, they will even help humans—if asked nicely, if they are attracted to someone, or if they want something. To communicate with the jinn, you must initiate the conversation. The well-mannered sort (the ones you want to meet) only manifest when invited. The "trickster" types, they're a different story—to the point where the Quran warned against contacting them. Knowing something about these entities beforehand is definitely advisable.

But before we dive into their universe, let's explore the words humans use to describe these fiery beings, along with the other Invisibles mentioned in the Quran.

What's in a Name? A Jinn Glossary

As we saw in chapter 2, the prehistoric Middle East was a crossroads for *Homo sapiens* emigrating out of Africa. It is plausible, then, that the region's vocabulary is flavored with 70,000 years of human history—from Paleolithic shamans, Mesolithic Natufians and Anatolians, all the way to the Greeks and Romans. Each culture invented things (or ideas) and named them—or adopted the ways and nomenclature of their predecessors. By the time the Quran was transmitted in the 600s CE, the Arabian Peninsula, particularly the pilgrimage destination of Mecca, was steeped in eons of cross-cultural exchange. Let's quickly go over the major Arabic names for non-corporeal life forms. You'll be surprised what's in a name!

---

164 Orion Foxwood, personal interview.

Jinn (sometimes spelled *djinn*) and *Jaan*: These two words are used synonymously in the Quran as "collective plurals," meaning they refer
to a group. *Jinni,* masculine, and *jinniya,* feminine, are the singular
forms, all from the Arabic root *j-n-n,* "to cover, as in to shadow, hide
or be hidden." Other derivatives are *megnun (majnun)*—"mad" or
"crazy" (one whose "intellect is hidden" or "with jinn," i.e., possessed);
junun—"madness, insanity, dementia, possession, obsession," or the
other end of the spectrum, "ecstasy, rapture"; *janun*—"embryo, fetus"
(hidden inside the womb); *janaan*—heart or soul; *jannah*—"heaven,
paradise, or an enclosed garden," i.e., "hidden, beautiful spaces" (to
differentiate between a garden and heaven, Arabic speakers use *ja-
neineh* for the physical version; a garden covers the earth with green,
trees, and other plants, and so hides the ground beneath it); *jana*—
"fruit"; *janan* as a verb means "to drive someone crazy or mad," as in
one possessed by a jinni; a different form, *junna, yujannu,* means "to
be covered, concealed or hidden" (in active voice, it becomes "to cover
or hide," as in the Quran 6:76, or, when related to a garden, *jana* is "to
gather [fruit], collect, pick, or, on an entirely different note, to commit
an offense or crime"!).

Many scholars believe the word "jinn" is not Arabic at all, but borrowed from Latin. As I mentioned in chapter 2, genii (plural) were
Roman spirit guides, tutelary deities who watched over humans from
birth, similar to ancient Greek daemons or modern Egyptian qarin.
The word comes from Latin, *gignere,* "to bring into being, beget, create, or produce." Later, the meaning of *genius* (singular) was expanded
to include "extraordinary natural talent" because exceptional achievements were thought to originate from individuals with a particularly
powerful genius. At the time, belief in (or at least the concept of)
guardian spirits was generalized throughout the Roman Empire and
beyond, including the territories populated by the nomadic Semitic
tribes of the Arabian Peninsula.

Shaytan / shayateen (pl): This is the Arabic transliteration of the Hebrew word "satan." The Quran uses the word two ways: as a proper name, Satan (2:36), Al-Shaytan, the Devil, The Rebellious One, and as a generic term for evil souls (whether among jinn or human), similar to the Christian adaptation of the Greek term "daemon." While Medieval manuscripts suggest the word "jinn" could have been a title derived from the jinn's original role as guardians of heaven—until they slaughtered each other and were thrown out of Paradise—Quranic jinn shaytan differ from Christian demons in that they are not fallen angels. Angels in the Quran are separate beings made from light, as discussed previously; jinn are made from fire/plasma and have free will. Angels do not.[165] Rebellious jinn choose their paths, just as humans choose theirs; angels might occasionally question theirs, but have no right to do so.

As for Satan's origins, surprisingly, the Jews did not initially conceive of him as the ultimate evil demon. His proper name, Satan, was used only five times in the Old Testament. But "satan" as a simple noun for "enemy" was employed freely. And in two passages concerning the same event, the older one (written first) was attributed to Yahweh (God), while the more recent one was attributed to Satan.[166] In the older Hebrew literature, especially the Pentateuch, Satan is not mentioned at all. Acts of punishment, revenge, and temptation are performed by Yahweh himself, or by his angels at his command.[167]

The later prophets Zachariah and Job describe Satan as a malicious servant of God who enjoyed his position as tempter, avenger, and torturer of humans. He was an adversary of man, though, not God, a description that resonates well with the proud, spiteful character of Iblis. The Quran implies that God created humans to teach Iblis

---

165   Quran 16:49 and 66:6.

166   Compare 2 Samuel 24 to 1 Chronicles 21.

167   Paul Carus, *The History of the Devil and the Idea of Evil*, 70–71.

humility. After being invited to pray with the angels in heaven, Iblis eventually succumbed to pride and arrogance, prompting God to test him. In the Quran, the story goes like this:

> And then [God] said to the angels, "Your lord will create a human from clay, from molded black mud.
> And when I have shaped him and breathed into him from my spirit (ruh) then fall down to him bowing."
> So the angels bowed all together
> Except Iblis refused to be among the bowers.
> [God] said, "Iblis why are you not among the bowers?"
> [Iblis] said, "I am not one to bow to a human you made from clay, from molded black mud."
> [God] said, "Then get out from it/here for you are expelled.
> And upon you the curse until Judgement Day."
> [Iblis] said, "Lord, then grant me respite until Resurrection Day."
> [God] said, "You are among those given respite
> Until the day of the appointed time."
> [Iblis] said, "Lord, with what tempted/misled me I will make seem good for those on Earth and I will tempt/mislead all of them. Except for your faithful servants among them."
> [God] said, "This is a straight path.
> As for my servants you shall not have authority over them except those who follow you from among the tempted/misled."[168]

So God both agreed to set aside Iblis's punishment until Resurrection Day and accepted the challenge by his former favorite to test the worthiness of humans, his new creation. In Iblis's defense, part of

---

168   Quran 15:28–42.

the first Pillar of Islam[169] is that "There is no god but God" (" … and Muhammad is the Messenger of God"); in other words, idol worship is forbidden. Yet since the dawn of civilization, household idols were made from hollow molded clay. Iblis refused to bow down to a creature made from the same stuff … so the question becomes then, what did God punish Iblis for: disobedience, pride, independent thought, or deductive reasoning?[170]

And when push came to shove, Iblis was careful not to cross the line with God. The Quran recounts how, on the eve of the Battle of Badr, a decisive victory and turning point for Muhammad, Iblis promised Muhammad's enemies (the Quraysh, Muhammad's tribe) that they would prevail, but he then deserted them on the battlefield:

> And the devil made their acts pleasing to them and said, "No one will overcome you today from among the people while I am near [a neighbor to] you. But when the two armies [forces] came into sight, he turned on his heels and said, "I am free from you because I see what you do not. I fear Allah and Allah is strong/severe in punishment [penalty]."[171]

Iblis: This is the Quranic name for the Devil. It is derived from *ablasa*, "to be desperate," or the noun *al-iblaas*, "desperation." It denotes someone who is broken by grief or struck dumb with despair, i.e., desperate for God's mercy. This is the superlative form, as in "the most desperate." Before banishment from heaven, he was called Azazeel.

---

169 The Five Pillars of Islam (*Arkaan*) are the mandatory acts required of all Muslims: *Shahadah*: declaring that there is no god except God and that Muhammad is His Messenger; *Salat*: ritual prayer five times a day; *Zakat*: giving alms (2.5%); *Sawm*: fasting during the holy month of Ramadan; *Hajj*: at least one pilgrimage to Mecca.

170 Henkesh, liner notes for *Dancing with Genies*, 28–29.

171 Quran 8:48.

Afreet / afareet (pl): The Quran mentions two specific types of jinn, afreet and *marid*. In current popular belief, afreet is also used to designate ancestor spirits, i.e., the souls of the dead, particularly those who died by violence and haunt the place of their demise. The root *afara* means "to cover with dust," or as a noun, "dust" or "dust-colored," i.e., tan. This could stem from the belief that jinn travel inside dust-devils or whirlwinds (*zoba'ah*) through the desert. Or, in reference to the dead, it could allude to the dust that wailing women throw on their heads to mourn the dearly departed. In the Quran, afreet refers to jinn of extraordinary strength or power; speaking to King Solomon, "an afreet of the jinn said, 'I will bring it to you [the Queen of Sheba's throne] before you rise from your place.'"[172] In everyday Arabic, the word has also come to mean mischievous, sly, cunning, crafty, or naughty (as in children)—in a nod to the trickster, prank-loving character of many jinn.

Marid / marada (pl): This jinn category is mentioned only once in the Quran.[173] It signifies a powerful entity, far stronger than average jinn but not as powerful as afareet. The word comes from the root *marada*, "to be defiant; a rebel, insurgent, demon, evil spirit, or giant." As an adjective, *mutamarid* signifies "a powerful tyrant or bully who cares nothing about breaking the law." These spirits assist Iblis and execute his orders.

Qarin / qurana (pl): These spirits, who live underground, are the modern Arabic equivalent of ancient Greek daemons, Invisible doubles that watch over humans from birth. In current Arabic, the root *q-r-n* means "to unite or join." Particularly popular in Egypt since pharaonic times, this belief was reinforced in the Quran and the hadith:

---

172   Quran 27:39.

173   Quran 37:6–9: "We have adorned the world's sky [lowest level of heaven] with stars, to guard against all 'shaytan marid,' so they may not listen to the exalted assembly, but be pelted from all sides [to repel them]."

"Each of you has a partner [qarin] from the jinn."[174] Aisha, Muhammad's youngest wife, also heard Muhammad refer to "a devil with everyone."[175] The Quran states that for anyone who forgets Allah is the most merciful, "We assign him a shaytan as a companion [qarin]."[176] "We assigned them companions [qurana]"[177] and "One will say 'I had a [qarin] who would ask Are you among those who bear witness?'"[178]

Malik / mala'ika (pl): Angel. Three sapient creations are mentioned in the Quran: jinn, humans, and angels. Jinn and humans can choose whether to be good, evil, or neutral. Angels, however, cannot. They were created simply to obey God and carry out his commands.[179] The word comes from *m-l-k,* the same root as "king" or "master." As mentioned in footnote 150, Aisha is quoted as hearing the prophet say that angels are made from light, as opposed to the fiery composition of jinn.[180] The Quran mentions different types: "the angels, messengers with wings, two or three or four,"[181] while Gabriel is said to have 600.[182] Angels "glide or swim" in heaven,[183] are able to take on human appearance,[184] but do not eat solid food.[185] A few are named. Besides Gabriel, there is Michael,[186]

---

174 Hadith *Sahih Muslim* (#2814a), narrated by Abdullah ibn Masud.

175 Hadith *Sahih Muslim* (#2815), narrated by Aisha.

176 Quran 43:36.

177 Quran 41:25.

178 Quran 37:51.

179 Quran 16:49; 66:6.

180 Hadith *Sahih Muslim* (#2996), narrated by Aisha.

181 Quran 35:1.

182 *Jibraeel* is also referred to as *Ar-Rouh*, "the Spirit"—Quran 70:4; 78:38; 97:4; 26:193 19:16–21.

183 Quran 79:3.

184 Quran 19:16–17; 51:24–37; 15:51–60.

185 Quran 51:24–28.

186 Quran 2:98.

Izraeel, the Angel of Death,[187] Malik, the guardian of Hell,[188] and Harout and Marout, the teachers of magic.[189] Israfeel, the trumpet sounder on Judgment Day,[190] is implied. Two classes of angels are singled out as well: guardian angels[191] and those who question the dead in their graves.

On a side note, fiery angels called *seraphim*, perhaps a mix of angel and jinn (light and plasma), with six wings hiding their body, face, and feet, are mentioned in the Bible.[192]

The next two terms aren't jinn per se, but are words for "soul"—the animating "breath of life" God bequeathed to jinn and humans alike:

Ruh / arwah (pl): This word for soul is derived from the root *raha,* which has many forms and meanings (such as "to go" or "to rest") but in this instance it comes from *rih/aryah,* "wind or breath"[193]—an entirely different substance from light or plasma. According to the Quran, the "living breath of God" animates the physical bodies of both jinn and humans. And while humans may not be able to see the jinn, their ethereal bodies are still able to house the same essence of consciousness as humans. As mentioned in footnote 184, the word can also mean "spirit, revelation, or the angel Gabriel, as in the Spirit of Revelation."

Nefs / nufus (pl): This popular Quranic term for soul (human or jinn) also derived from a word for breath. The root of this word, *nafasa,* means "to breathe, inhale and exhale" (along with a number of other definitions).

---

187 Quran 32:11.

188 Quran 43:74–77; Hadith *Sahih al-Bukhari* (#3265).

189 Quran 2:102.

190 Hadith *Sahih al-Bukhari* (#4813) by Abu Hurairaa.

191   Quran 50:17–18; 13:11; 82:10–12; 43:80.

192 Isaiah 6.

193 Quran 15:28–29.

It is the essence that returns to the Creator after death. "Every soul (nefs) shall taste death."[194]

While we are discussing jinn types, here are a few Middle Eastern jinn not mentioned in the Quran but popular nonetheless. The excerpts below are from a famous book about all things Egyptian, *An Account of the Manners and Customs of Modern Egyptians*, written by Edward Lane[195] and first published in 1836.[196] I mention this author often, for although he lived two hundred years ago, his observations still hold true. Egyptian rural life has changed little since pharaonic times—until the advent of television, that is.

Hatif: This popular benevolent entity is heard but not seen. Often mentioned by Arab writers, including As-Shibli, these spirits generally impart intelligent advice, direction, or warning to unsuspecting humans.

Ghool: A female shaytan or evil jinni that eats men. The male is called *kutrub*. Resembling both human and animal, these spirits appear in desolate places at night to solitary travelers. Adopting various monstrous shapes, they lure unsuspecting men off their paths, converse with them, and sometimes yield to them before killing and eating them. They also haunt burial grounds and feed on dead bodies. Several of the Prophet's companions saw these creatures in their travels: "Omar saw one on a journey to Syria, before Islam, and struck it with his sword. It is said they (and others) are the offspring of Iblis and a wife God created for him from *simoom* ('smokeless fire')[197] from an egg."

---

194 Quran 3:185, 21:35, 29:57.

195 Edward Lane (1801–1876) was a well-known British orientalist, translator, and lexicographer famous for his extensive Arabic dictionary, his translation of the Arabian Nights, and books about medieval and nineteenth-century Egypt. For more information, please see Jason Thompson's *Edward Lane: A Biography*, published in 2008.

196 The excerpts from *An Account of the Manners and Customs of Modern Egyptians* have been edited for clarity.

197 A *simoom* is a fiery hot wind, as in a desert sandstorm.

Sealah or *saalah*: Another form of shaytan, found mostly in forests. The offspring of humans and jinn, these hideous creatures feed on humans. When one captures a man, it makes him dance and plays with him like a cat with a mouse. A man of Isfahan asserted there were many in his country. Arab geographers call an island in the sea of China "the Island of the Sealah" because they are known to live there.

Ghaddar or *gharrar*: A dangerous invisible species found in the border regions of Yemen, particularly Tihameh, and Upper Egypt. It entices men to it, either tortures or terrifies them, and then leaves.

Delhan: These demonic beings found on deserted islands resemble men riding ostriches. They eat shipwrecked men, but some say one once attacked a ship at sea and captured its crew. They fought it, but its cry rendered them unconscious. Ibn-al-Wardee mentioned the *dahlan* as living on an island in the Sea of Oman. He described them as cannibal shayateen, shaped like men riding on birds resembling ostriches.

Al-ghowwasah: An inferior class of jinn, called the Divers or Plungers in the seas.

Shikk: Another demonic half-human half-jinn (divided longitudinally) creature that appears to travelers.

Nesnas: The offspring of a *shikk* and a human, this jinn/human cross resembles half a human—with half a head, half a body, one arm, one leg—and hops with much agility. It is found in the woods of Yemen as well as Hadramot, and one was even brought alive to Al-Mutawekkil. Endowed with speech, it resembled a man, except its half a face was in its chest and it had a tail like a sheep. The people of Hadramot eat it and its flesh is sweet. It is only generated in their country. A man who went there asserted he saw a captured *nesnas*, which cried out for mercy in the name of God and himself. Another race of people with heads in their breasts was discovered on an island called Jabeh (Java) in the Sea of El-Hind (India). A different kind of *nesnas* with wings like a bat was seen on Raij Island in the Sea of Es-Seen (China).

Muhammad and the Quran

Now let's talk about the book that has immortalized the jinn—and why the world's billions of Muslims believe it contains the literal Words of God.

As mentioned previously, to be a Muslim the faithful must swear "There is no god but God and Muhammad is a Messenger of God," an act considered the first Pillar of Islam. The Quran is sacred to Muslims because it contains God's revelations to Muhammad—word for word. This is also why Muslims believe in the jinn. Disbelief would imply that the contents of this holy book, and hence the words of God, are flawed.

The Quran's origins are intertwined with the life and ancestry of the human chosen to author it—Abu al-Qasim Muhammad ibn Abdullah ibn Abdul Muttalib, better known simply as Muhammad. The first Muslim wasn't just anybody. Even though he was raised an orphan, he was a member of the Bani Hashim clan of the Quraysh, the tribe responsible for tending Mecca's pilgrims at the time Muhammad was born (570 CE). These fiercely independent children of the desert proudly traced their lineage—and hence DNA—back to Abraham, the patriarch of the Jewish faith.

Mecca was a famous pilgrimage destination centuries before the Quraysh settled in the area. According to legend (and confirmed by the Quran[198]), Abraham and his first son, Ishmael,[199] built the *Ka'aba* or Cube,[200] the city's holy sanctuary, to commemorate the miraculous spring God brought forth from the desert to save Ishmael (later named the Well of Zamzam).[201] In the beginning, pilgrims included both Jews and Bedouin. But as time

---

198   Martin Lings, *Muhammad*, 1–3.

199   Muhammad's bloodline in his own words, as recorded in Hadith *Jami at-Tirmidhi* (#3605–6) as narrated by Wathilah bin al-Asqa': "Indeed Allah has chosen Isma'il from the children of Abraham, and He chose Banu Kinanah from the children of Isma'il, and He chose the Quraish from Banu Kinanah, and He chose Banu Hashim from Quraish, and He chose me from Banu Hashim."

200   Quran 2:125–127, 3:96–7, 22:26.

201   Lings, *Muhammad*, 10–11.

passed, idols were placed in and around the temple. The Jews felt these graven images defiled the sanctuary, so ceased to visit.[202] By the time of Muhammad's grandfather, Abdul Muttalib (500s CE), thousands visited the shrine every year, even though the well had long since disappeared. Guided by a series of prophetic dreams, Abdul Muttalib rediscovered the well, along with a horde of treasure, which thrust his clan into a position of power.

It is said the Quran was inscribed on stone tablets in heaven before the Archangel Gabriel transmitted it to Muhammad over a twenty-year period. Yet Gabriel's initial revelation in the Mount Hira Cave was not the Prophet's first encounter with angels. That happened long before, when he was a child of two or three. According to a hadith, two men dressed in white split open his chest, then his heart, removed a blood clot, washed the organ with snow, returned it to his body, and sewed him back up.[203] As a young man Muhammad was known for his honesty and trustworthiness, traits that eventually led to marriage at age twenty-five with one of Mecca's wealthier merchants, the doubly widowed Khadija, who was fifteen years his senior. Their union was happy and she bore him five children (in her forties!); four girls survived into adulthood. Fifteen uneventful years passed until the year before his famous angelic encounter (at age forty) when Muhammad began to have unusual prophetic dreams: "Revelation began for Allah's Messenger in the form of good visions during sleep, which came like dawn breaking. The love of seclusion came to him and he secluded himself in the Hira Cave to worship for many nights before returning to his family."[204]

Muhammad's first vision heralded a new—and final—phase of his life. It instructed him to "Recite!" and that "He who hath taught by the pen, taught man what he knew not."[205] This was a challenge for a man who could neither read nor write. At first, the visions came slowly. Two years of silence followed the initial revelation. But eventually he was instructed to proclaim Gabriel's messages and communication steadily increased

---

202   Lings, *Muhammad*, 4.

203   Hadith *Sahih Muslim* (#162c) narrated by Anas B. Malik.

204   Hadith *Sahih al-Bukhari* (#3) as narrated by Aisha. See also *al-Bukhari* (#4953) and (#6982) and *Sahih Muslim* (#160a), all from Aisha.

205   Gabriel's first message, Quran 96:1–5. Translation by Lings, *Muhammad*, 43–44.

until his death at age sixty-three. "Allah sent revelations to His Messenger continuously during the period preceding his death; and then Allah's messenger died."[206]

Two things are important here. First, the Quran's chapters, or *surat* (plural of surah), are *not* in chronological order (for example, the first Mount Hira message can be found at the beginning of Surah 96—out of 114 surat total). And second, Muhammad received these revelations during hypnopompic dreams or ecstatic fits, as the following descriptions show (different collections of hadith often contain complementary versions of the same incident or quote):

- "The Prophet was asked: 'How does Revelation come to you?' Allah's messenger said: 'Like a ringing bell and that is the hardest on me. And sometimes the angel appears as a man, and speaks to me such that I understand what he says.' Aisha added: 'I saw Allah's Messenger during Revelation on an extremely cold day. When it receded his forehead was flooded with sweat.'"[207]

- "While walking, I heard a voice from the sky. I looked up and there was the angel that came to me at Hira Cave sitting on a chair between earth and sky. I was afraid, so I returned home and said, 'Wrap me (in blankets).' And then Allah sent down [the ayat]: 'Hey you, wrapped in garments! Arise and warn [the people] ... ' up to His utterance, 'and leave the scum.'[208] After this, the revelations increased and became more frequent."[209]

- "Allah's Messenger said, 'Om Sulaim [one of Muhammad's wives], what is this?' She answered, 'It is your sweat, which I put in my perfume.' Allah's Messenger sweated in cold weather when revelation came to him."[210]

---

206   Hadith *Sahih al-Bukhari* (#4982) and Hadith *Sahih Muslim* (#3016), both narrated by Anas B. Malik.

207   Hadith *Sahih al-Bukhari* (#2), narrated by Aisha. The same event is described in *Sahih Muslim* (#2333b) and *Jami at-Tirmidhi* (#3634).

208   Quran 74:1–5.

209   Hadith *Sahih al-Bukhari* 1:4, narrated by Jabir bin Abdullah al-Ansari.

210   Hadith *Sahih Muslim* (#2332) by Um Sulaim, and a similar event by Aisha follows (#2333).

- "We were with Allah's Messenger when someone came wearing a cloak with traces of yellow. He said, 'Messenger of Allah, what should I do for Umra [hajj]?' Revelation was sent to the Prophet and he was covered with a thobe. I said, 'Omar, I wish to see the Prophet when Revelation is sent down.' Omar asked, 'Does it please you to see the Prophet when Revelation comes to him?' Then Omar pulled aside the edge of the thobe and I looked at him. He snorted and I thought it was the sound of a camel. When it had passed the Prophet asked, 'Where is the one who asked about 'Umra'?'"[211]

- "If Gabriel descended with a Revelation for Allah's Messenger, he [Muhammad] moved his tongue and lips, which was hard on him, and they knew revelation was taking place."[212]

Similar descriptions abound. Most mention Muhammad's unresponsiveness and that he sweated profusely, particularly when reemerging from a seizure. Sometimes he made noises or acted oddly—enough for his companions to shield him from the public. Yet he always remembered the magnificent verses spoken to him during these ecstatic episodes—and while he slept. The Quran instructs,

> Stand [to pray] at night, but not all night
> Half of it or a little less
> Or a little more, and recite the Quran in slow, rhythmic chanting.
> Soon We will cast upon you a heavy word.
> Indeed, rising at night is stronger and most potent and more suitable for words.[213]

Certainly, long-term sleep deprivation promotes lucid hypnopompic dreaming. Coupled with hyperventilation from chanting and the slower brainwave frequencies

---

211 Hadith *Sahih Muslim* (#1180), narrated by Ya'la.
212 Hadith *Sahih al-Bukhari* (#5), *Sahih Muslim* (#448a).
213 Quran 73:2–6.

produced by protracted rhythmic music, this form of worship is indeed "a right path" for inducing visions and connecting to the Invisible world.

So where are the jinn in all this? According to *The Dictionary of the Holy Quran*, the word "jinn" appears thirty-two times in Muhammad's holy book, the root *sh-t-n* (for "shaytan") an additional eighty-eight times, and Iblis or *b-l-s* sixteen times—for a total of 136 references (not counting angels, qarin, or souls)! Sometimes these beings are only mentioned in passing (or implied) within the larger context of God's total sentient creation, but at other times they are the subject of lengthy discussions, particularly in Surah 72, *al-Jinn* ("The Jinn"). Yet they are not mentioned regularly throughout the Quran's twenty-odd years of disclosure.

No, the jinn as a species were only introduced near the end of Muhammad's life in Mecca. Before that they were never mentioned![214] Iblis or shayateen (evil souls), yes, but not the jinn by name as an Invisible race. Take a look at the chronological surah order in appendix 1. I have marked where the jinn are cited. According to this traditional version,[215] the second time they are mentioned is in Surah *al-Jinn*, depending on the source. Either way, the jinn debut during the Year of Sorrow, Muhammad's darkest hour, when no one else would comfort or help him. They remained in his thoughts (and a subject of the Quran) for two years until he emigrated to Medina (an event known as the Hijrah) and had more important issues to confront. Nevertheless, from the time of their introduction, the Quran emphasizes that these entities are not all alike—nor evil:

> Among us are the righteous, and those who are not; We follow divergent paths...
> Among us are those who submit and those who avoid justice...[216]

So, what happened during the "Year of Sorrow"?

In 619 CE, the year Surah *al-Jinn* was revealed, Khadija, Muhammad's first (and at the time only) wife of twenty-five years, and his uncle Abu Talib, the head of his clan and

---

214   This is according to the chronological Revelation order—with the exception of the final line of the Quran, which could easily have been inserted later.

215   Nothing is certain, of course. The first time Revelation chronology was actually recorded was a century after Muhammad's death.

216   Quran 72:11, 14.

his protector, died. Within six months he lost his closest friend, his wisest supporter, the mother of his children, and physical safety. Grieving and desperate, he sought safe haven for himself and his followers in Ta'if, a town about sixty miles southeast of Mecca. But the leaders of the Thaqif tribe who governed the area wanted nothing to do with him or his new religion. As soon as Muhammad left their council, they incited the town's residents to chase him and his companions out of town. The event turned into a minor riot when the locals began throwing stones in derision. Wounded and bleeding, Muhammad and his group took refuge in a vineyard on the outskirts of town until the mob dispersed.

Despondent, unsure of what to do, but with no place else to go, Muhammad headed back to Mecca. That evening or the next, he spent the night in the mountainous valley of Nakhlah, the halfway stop between Ta'if and Mecca (subsequently called "Jinn Valley"), where he nursed his wounds under a palm tree and prayed long into the night for guidance. Apparently, a group of seven Nasebeen jinn heard him reciting the Quran and stopped to listen. They were quickly enthralled. What the ignorant people of Ta'if had brutalized him for,[217] these jinn couldn't get enough of—to the point where those hovering around the Prophet forbade their companions to speak, for fear of missing a word. The Invisible travelers then returned to their people with tidings of God's "summoner" and his message—which was intended for them as well as humans. As the Quran recounts:

> And when we directed to you a group of Jinn to listen to the Quran,
> when present they said, "Listen." When it was finished they returned
> to their people to warn them.
> They said, "Oh our people, we have heard a book that came down
> after Moses confirming what was between his hands [the stone tablets],
> guiding toward the truth and a straight path."[218]

And even though the Quran skirts around a direct meeting between Muhammad and the jinn, I believe Muhammad actually saw and communicated with the jinn at this time.

---

217   H. A. R. Gibb, *A Shorter Encyclopedia of Islam*, 396.
218   Quran 46:29–30.

The Book of Jinn

Finally, it's time to dive into the world of the jinn!

Rather than try to cram all there is to know about the jinn in one chapter, I prefer to refer you to the *Legends of the Fire Spirits*, an excellent source for the multitude of legends, tales, and anecdotes about these fascinating entities. In my opinion, there is no other English language compilation (so far) that covers the breadth and scope of Robert Lebling's work. In my book, however, I will focus on a book Lebling did not cover, entitled *Akaam al-Murjaan fi Ahkaam al-Jaan*.[219] I like to call this fourteenth-century treasure (held in Cairo's Al-Azhar library) "The Book of Jinn."

This medieval manuscript is considered by Arabic occult scholars to be an early definitive source for all things jinn, along with Ibn Taymiyah's "Essay on the Jinn."[220] Republished several times in the last century by various Arabic language editors, The Book of Jinn is even mentioned as an excellent source in *A Shorter Encyclopedia of Islam*.[221] Unfortunately, I was not able to find a copy of The Book of Jinn in English, so I had to translate it myself over the years with the help of one very patient native speaker (surprisingly, not everyone finds the jinn interesting!).

Due to the manuscript's length, I am only including highlights of subjects not covered elsewhere and have omitted the sahih chains, or provenances, attributed to its quotes and stories (they take up a quarter of the book). The 1939 printing states that an original copy of the manuscript can be found in Egypt's Dar al-Kutub (Al-Azhar) library under "Sufism and Religious Morals," #2495. Unfortunately, when I went to ask about it, the library was undergoing renovation and it had been moved.

---

219   This translates as *The Multitudes of Coral* [i.e., precious jewels] *in Judgment of the Jinn.*

220   Ibn Taymiyah was born in Harran (now Orfa, Turkey) in 1263 CE and died in prison in Damascus in 1328 CE.

221   See H. A. R. Gibb, the entry for "jinn." *A Shorter Encyclopedia of Islam* is a single, condensed volume of the earlier, definitive ten-volume set.

The author, Badr ad-Din as-Shibli, was born 1312 CE (712 Hijri)[222] in Damascus, as was his father, Qayim al-Shibliya. After studying law in Cairo, As-Shibli was hired as a judge in Tripoli in 1354 CE (755 H) when thieves murdered his predecessor. He died there in 1368 CE (769 H) at age fifty-five. He wrote three books: the *Benefits of Questioning, The Multitudes of Coral in Judgment of the Jinn*, and an instruction manual for children, *Bathroom Customs*. He apparently compiled his jinn compendium (multitudes of Quranic verses, hadith traditions, stories, anecdotes, and customs) a decade before or after the Black Death. They offer a fascinating window into Muhammad's world of seventh-century Arabia—but as to their veracity … most chapters wisely conclude with "and [only] God Almighty knows."

> **"Genesis"** [223]—In the beginning, according to the Quran, God created seven skies, seven earths, the angels, and the jinn before He created Adam. He made the jinn from fire, angels from light, and, later, humans from clay. He separated His sentient beings into four categories: angels, devils, jinn, and humans, and divided them into ten parts, nine of which were angels. The remainder He again divided into ten and made 90 percent devils. The remaining jinn and humans were divided one last time into nine parts jinn and one part human. Hence the final fractions equaled humans 1/1000, jinn 9/1000, devils 90/1000, and angels 900/1000.
>
> God made the first jinni from the "tip of a flame" and named him Soumya. He granted him a wish, but Soumya asked for three: "to see, but not be seen," to "disappear into the soil," and, after aging, "to become young before death." God granted all three. And so the jinn dwelt on Earth while the angels resided in the multilayered skies [the higher the level, the more pious the angel]. During this time, the jinn had forty [or, according to others, seventy-two] generations of kings, each given the title Suleyman [or Solomon]. The last Suleyman was also named Jaan and from him, it is thought, the

---

222 The Hijri calendar is a 12-month lunar Muslim calendar, the first year of which corresponds with 622 CE, the year of Muhammad's emigration from Mecca to Medina (the Hijrah).

223 The presentation that follows is my condensed translation and synthesis of The Book of Jinn. I bring together a number of chapters that cover the same topic.

jinn derived this name. They lived peaceably on Earth for eons, but eventually disobeyed God and began to massacre each other. God sent them prophets to guide them back to the right path, but they went unheeded,[224] or worse, were slaughtered. Finally, after a rebellious faction murdered His last prophet, Joseph, God dispatched 4000 soldiers, angels, and jinn under the command of a jinni named Azazeel to destroy the evildoers. The holy army killed most of the rebels and expelled the rest to beneath the oceans, deserted tropical islands, and the mythic Qaf Mountain chain surrounding Earth.

After defeating the rebels, the holy warriors found life on Earth pleasant and decided to stay. God rewarded Azazeel by making him ruler of the lower sky and Sultan of Earth, and allowed him to worship with the angels in heaven. But God had other plans for Earth—to replace Azazeel with a different successor, or *khalifa*. When Azazeel discovered this, he warned the angels, who asked God if His new creature would be as corrupt as the jinn they had just destroyed. God only answered that He knew what the angels did not about Adam, His new creation. Afraid they had disobeyed the Almighty by questioning His decisions, the angels circled His throne and begged for forgiveness. "I know what you do not," repeated God. "Adam will take over as successor on Earth, and his descendants shall live there. You angels will live in the skies."

And when God finished this clay *khalifa*, He ordered the angels to bow to His new creation. All of heaven's inhabitants bowed except Azazeel, whose pride and jealousy prevented him. Furious, God banished His one-time favorite from heaven, took away his preferred status, and renamed him Iblis. Rejected and despondent, the jinn leader replied, "I will misguide all of Adam's seed with what misguided me!" In other words, with pride, arrogance, disrespect, and envy.[225]

"Jinn Types"—From the hadith, it is known that God made three types of jinn: the first appear as snakes, scorpions, and burrowing creatures like worms;

---

224 An incident referred to in the Quran 6:13, per As-Shibli, *Akaam al-Murjaan fi Ahkaam al-Jaan,* 59.

225 As-Shibli, *Akaam al-Murjaan fi Ahkaam al-Jaan,* 19–24.

the second as black animals [but particularly dogs]; and the third are invisible like the wind and fly. However, other specialists say there are six types: *jinn*—pure in essence; *umaar* that live among humans; *arwah*—the spirits seen by children; *shayateen*—cunning disbelievers; *marada*—strong and powerful shayateen; and *afareet*—the most powerful of jinn. All will be subject to reward or punishment on Judgment Day, though. Similarly, God also made three types of humans: those like animals with emotions but no reason; those who resemble humans but have evil in their hearts; and those under God's shadow who are righteous. The Almighty did not intend for jinn and humans to meet, however,[226] and so He intentionally endowed humans with senses that could not detect the jinn in their natural state, as per Soumya's wish.[227]

That jinn and angels manifest in different shapes is a common theme for many holy books. The Old Testament, for example, describes Abraham's visiting angels as travelers and those who came to Lot in Sodom and Gomorrah as tempting young men. In the Quran, Gabriel appears to Muhammad alternately as a shining traveler, an entity with six hundred wings, and a being that filled the sky from horizon to horizon. And the jinn often take the shapes of snakes, scorpions, dogs, strange travelers, beautiful women, birds, camels, cows, sheep, horses, mules, or donkeys. Abdullah ibn Masud, Muhammad's faithful squire and the source for many jinn hadith,[228] was with the Prophet on numerous occasions when the fire spirits manifested. According to him, they alternately appeared as dark smoke, vultures, snakes, or tall men in white garb.

---

226 See the ayah (verse) in the Quran about a barrier between the two races: "And between them a partition..." (55:20)

227 As-Shibli, *Akaam al-Murjaan fi Ahkaam al-Jaan*, 33–41.

228 Abdullah ibn Masud also contributed, after Muhammad's death, to the final compilation of the Quran. Originally from the Banu Huzail tribe, he first met Muhammad as a young shepherd tending the flocks of a Quraish chieftain in the hills near Mecca (per Martin Lings in *Muhammad: His Life Based on the Earliest Sources*, page 48). Ibn Masud was the sixth convert to Islam and became the Prophet's "squire," tending to his needs at home and abroad. He woke him when he slept, shielded him when he washed, and carried his personal possessions. He even adopted the Prophet's mannerisms to the point where he was often mistaken for a family member. Ibn Masud died in 652 CE.

"Dwelling Places"—While traveling, Muhammad was occasionally heard speaking gibberish to unseen companions [glossolalia?]. When questioned after one incident, he replied that the jinn had come to settle a dispute. "The Muslim jinn were arguing with the disbelievers about where each should live. I replied that the Muslims should live in the villages and on the mountains and the nonbelievers should live in the valleys between the mountains and the sea." Although jinn live almost everywhere on Earth, they definitely have preferences. One jinn species, for example, dwells in human homes, floating near the ceilings to feed on unblessed food. Hence Muslims invoke God's name before entering a house or eating. Otherwise, the jinn are free to partake. Jinn also inhabit the desert, wilderness in general, rivers, ruins, garbage dumps, dark rooms, wells, baths, stables, ovens, and even outhouses. This is why people ask permission ["*Dastour!*"] or mumble one of God's ninety-nine names [usually "*Bi-ism Allah al-rahman al-raheem!*"] before entering a bathroom, lowering a bucket into a well, or lighting a fire. The jinn are also fond of markets and crossroads. [229]

Jinn have different needs when it comes to food and drink. In fact, there is much disagreement as to what and how they nourish themselves:

"Nourishment"—Pure jinn, those like the wind, eternal until Judgment Day and perhaps without gender, are thought not to eat, drink, or have children. Those with gender, on the other hand, do engage in these activities. How they go about them is also up for discussion. Some believe that instead of swallowing and chewing, the jinn breathe in the essence of nourishment—i.e., they "smell" it—or they pass through it and absorb nutrients by physical contact. Others claim chewing and swallowing are supported in the hadith and offer entities such as *saalla*, ghouls, *qutrub*, etc., as examples.

As to *what* the jinn eat, a number of hadith refer to the following incident: One night the jinn came to Muhammad and asked for food. He

---

229   As-Shibli, *Akaam al-Murjaan fi Ahkaam al-Jaan*, 42–44.

replied, "All bones with the name of God said over them that fall into your hands are much better than meat. And all [green]²³⁰ dung is fodder for your livestock." This is why the Prophet forbade his followers to wipe themselves with bones or dung after defecating; it was "the food of your brothers the jinn. When the Nasebeen jinn came to me and asked for food, I asked the Almighty that they should always find food on these things for them to eat."²³¹

Actually, if you think about it, bones and dung could be nourishing. Bones contain marrow, the essence of blood (perhaps heated by fire), and dung is plant matter softened by digestive acids. On a similar subject, it is said that Iblis eats and drinks with his left hand, therefore humans should not. And so the left is reserved for unclean activities, which makes life quite difficult for left-handed people in Muslim societies. We are considered "children of the jinn"—a class of humans, by the way, that includes Barack Obama, Bill Clinton, George Bush Sr., Ronald Reagan, and Gerald Ford, just to name recent left-handed U.S. presidents:

> **"Reproduction"**—There are several Quranic passages that imply most jinn reproduce. Even Iblis, who is "among the reprieved until Judgment Day" [i.e., among the select few who do not die], has children. The Quran clearly states God's creations are meant to reproduce in pairs: "And God made for you from your own kind, mates, and made from these mates, sons and grandsons" (16:72). The Quran also states that both jinn and "Adam's offspring" engage in sex: "…who have never been deflowered by either men or jinn" (55:74).

The deflowering of human females by jinn was apparently, if not common, then at least heard of during Muhammad's lifetime. In fact, interspecies sex is discussed at length

---

230 "Green" was added later to differentiate between the dung of grazing animals and the feces of meat eaters.

231 As-Shibli, *Akaam al-Murjaan fi Ahkaam al-Jaan*, 49. Taken from many different hadith on the subject.

in the hadith and the *sunnah* (the religious traditions that govern proper Muslim conduct). As to whether cross-species fornication is permitted … some say it is, if the purpose is to procreate. Others claim it is not, because the Quran mentions "mates of your own kind." Sex with the jinn was permissible, however, for a wife to avoid harm. Indeed, there are many stories (see this chapter's homework section) about jinn carrying off beautiful women and holding them captive as wives or concubines against their will. The shayateen also participate during human sex when men do not invoke the name of God before penetration. As with food, this omission implies an invitation to partake— which they do by wrapping around a man's urethra. Others claim that if a husband has intercourse while his wife is menstruating, shayateen, attracted by the blood, will precede him and impregnate her first.[232]

> Iblis is said to have had many offspring, but the most important were a daughter and five sons from his second wife, Lilith. The daughter's name is either Madihah or Tamadoukh, depending on the source. All agree, though, that humans wishing to use sorcery visit her castle on the water because if they satisfy her demands [usually a newborn child], she will grant their requests. She is also said to have talking (and non-talking) animals as servants.[233] As for Iblis's sons, the first is Thabir the Troublemaker. He causes mayhem by slitting open pockets [pickpocket], slapping people, and calling for *al-jahaliya* [pre-Islam when humans worshipped idols]. The second son is Al-Awar, the one-eyed Master of Prostitutes. The third, Mas'out the Liar, is Master of Deceit. Dasim the Fat, another Master Troublemaker, is fourth. He "stirs the pot" in family arguments to set kin upon kin. And the last, Zalanbour, Master of the Souq, incites disagreements between customers and merchants in the marketplace.[234]

---

232 As-Shibli, *Akaam al-Murjaan fi Ahkaam al-Jaan*, 56–57, 103–112.

233 Ibid., 157.

234 Ibid., 281.

Jinn legal status was codified and recorded from the very beginning of Islam, including relations with mankind, such as marriage and property. The Book of Jinn cites the following anecdote as an example:

> **"Jinn Justice"**—It was once brought before a judge the issue of when humans and jinn could drink from a town well. The judge asked if the jinn had appeared before them. When the townspeople replied they had not, but that they had heard their words, the judge ruled that the humans should drink from the well from sunrise to sunset and that the jinn should drink from sunset to dawn. And whoever went against this ruling was to be stoned.[235]

Aisha is also on record, in a *Sahih Muslim* hadith, as a defender of jinn rights. She insisted that killing them was forbidden unless the cause was just. Snakes found in houses, for example, must be asked three times to leave before they can be killed.[236] Indeed, because humans are able to kill jinn—sometimes unwittingly—the fire spirits are extremely wary of Adam's seed. The Book of Jinn recounts several stories to this effect:

> One night as I was praying I saw a boy standing between my hands. I tried to grab him but he jumped away and I heard him fall behind the wall. He did not come back. After that, I was told the jinn are as afraid of humans as we are of them. If jinn appear, do not be afraid, otherwise they will "ride" [possess] you. Be strong and they will leave you alone.[237]
>
> On the other hand, humans have every reason to be just as leery of the jinn, which is why strategies to defend against them are popular.

---

235   As-Shibli, *Akaam al-Murjaan fi Ahkaam al-Jaan*, 138.

236   Ibid., 101.

237   Notice the use of the verb "to ride"—*r-k-b* or *rakaba*—here, which implies possession. By the 1300s it was recognized that Invisibles possessed humans via emotional breaches, i.e., fear. Hence the advice to be strong in the face of something frightening. *Akaam al-Murjaan fi Ahkaam al-Jaan*, 139.

"Disappearing Dates: How the Surah al-Baqara Epilogue[238] Came Into Use"—The next story took place during the time of the Prophet, as told by one of his followers: We kept dates given as alms for the poor in a locked storeroom, but I found fewer every day. I informed the Prophet and he said it was the work of a shaytan. So I went into the room, locked the door, and sat down, surrounded by darkness. Later that night, a shadow covered the door and took a shape, then another and another, until finally it entered through the keyhole. I covered myself with a blanket and watched while the shadow ate from the dates. I jumped on it, grabbed it in my arms and shouted, "Oh enemy of God!" It replied, "Let me go, for I am old with children. I am a poor jinni of the Nasebeen. This was our village before your leader kicked us out. If you let me go I will not return." So I let him go. The Angel Gabriel informed the Prophet what had happened and the Prophet prayed for advice. A few days later, he asked if I had news of the jinni since the incident. I said yes, that he had returned. So I went back into the room and locked the door again. And as before, it entered through the keyhole and began to eat dates. I grabbed it as before, and said, "Oh enemy of God, you said you would not return!" It answered, "I did not return before this, and proof is that one of you did not say the epilogue of Surah *al-Baqara*. If you don't read it, we can enter at will. And so here I am this evening."

This story has many versions. Sometimes the jinni was a newly weaned boy: Someone else had a trough full of dates that he checked on regularly but found some missing. So one night he stayed to guard them and discovered a newly weaned boy. After saluting each other, the man asked, "What are you?" The lad replied, "A jinni." "Give me your hand," the man requested. So the boy gave him his hand. It resembled a dog's paw with fur and the man exclaimed in surprise, "Is this how the jinn were created?" The young creature replied, "Indeed I know jinn far hairier than I am." Then the man asked, "What brought you to do this?" The boy replied, "I heard you were generous with alms, so we wanted to share your food." The man said, "Okay, but what protects us from all of you?" "The verse

---

238   This refers to the epilogue of the second surah of the Quran, Surah *al-Baqara*, or the beginning of the third, Surah *Al-i-'Imran*: "*Allah la ilahu illa huwa al-Hay al-Qiyoum.*"

from Surah *al-Baqara*: '*Allah la ilahu illa huwa al-Hay al-Qiyoum*' [There is no god but He of Eternal Life]. Whoever repeats this for protection will make us disappear. And whoever says this at dusk will be protected from us until dawn." When he awoke, the man went to the Prophet and told him what the jinn had said. "What cunning truth!" Muhammad replied.[239]

The ayah (verse) this story refers to is called the Ayat *al-Kursi*, "the Verse of the Throne." Its ten lines are considered among the holiest of the Quran and are often recited as talismans against evil, although prayer in general is considered an effective barrier against the jinn.

One of Muhammad's followers asked the Prophet when was the best time to pray, "so that my prayers will be heard?" The Prophet replied, "After midnight until dawn is the best time, but then stop until the sun rises one spear above the horizon. That is when the sun sits "between the horns of the Devil" and pagans pray. Afterwards, you may pray again as you like, until your spear is once more equal to its shadow. Then stop, because that is the Hour of the Jinn, when hell opens its doors and the jinn come out. After sunset, pray as you like until dawn."[240] Muhammad also instructed the faithful to bring their children indoors at this time. "When the night spreads its wings, hide your children because that is when the jinn appear. Guard them inside, lock the doors, cover your jugs, and mention the name of God over both. Also, extinguish your lamps before you sleep, lest jinn or mice knock them over and burn your houses down."[241]

In spite of popular insistence that all jinn are evil, numerous stories have been passed down that demonstrate the contrary. Many jinn, particularly hatifs, have keenly developed altruistic philosophies that they share with humans willing to listen. One hatif even came to comfort a grieving man who had just lost his son, according to a story As-Shibli included in his book:

---

239   As-Shibli, *Akaam al-Murjaan fi Ahkaam al-Jaan*, 143–44.

240   As-Shibli, *Akaam al-Murjaan fi Ahkaam al-Jaan*, 305, referencing Hadith *Sunan as-Sughra* (#579) narrated by Amrah bin Abasah.

241   As-Shibli, *Akaam al-Murjaan fi Ahkaam al-Jaan*, 288.

A son died and his grieving father couldn't sleep. One night, alone in the house and mourning his son, he heard a hatif calling from a corner. "*Salama-leykum, ya khalifa.*" The man answered, "*Wa aleykum sallam,*" petrified. To his surprise, the voice began to recite verses from the end of Surah *Al-i-'Imran*, until it ended with "*Wa ma and Allah kheer lil abraar*" [God has good things for believers]. Then it said, "Ya khalifa, what is it about your son that is so special? Is he better than Muhammad's infant son, Ibrahim?"[242] Tears welled in the man's eyes, and the hatif continued, "Don't say words that anger God. You seek to push death away from your son, yet death is written for all God's creations. If there were no death, you would not all fit on Earth. Without grief, without emotion, without love, life is not worth living." The man asked who the voice was and it replied, "A neighbor from among the jinn."[243]

The jinn would not be widely known among Muslims today if not for their mention in the Quran. Apparently, Muhammad had numerous encounters with them (as chronicled in the hadith, particularly those narrated by Abdullah ibn Masud), which the Book of Jinn devotes sixteen pages to (pages 74–83). As mentioned previously, Muhammad's initial encounter with them changed his life. It gave him the confidence to break away from the only home he had known and pursue other options—the all-important Hijrah, his move to Medina. As-Shibli collected many details about this first "baptism of fire":

> **"Jinn Valley"**—After the Prophet's terrible experience in Ta'if,[244] he stopped under a palm tree on the return road to Mecca, just beyond a place called Kher Thaqeef. As he prayed in the middle of the night, a group of seven [some say nine] Nasebeen jinn [believers in God and His prophets] passed by and stopped to listen.[245] This occurred during the "Year of Sorrow," three years before the Hijrah and eleven years after

---

242 Ibrahim was the last child born to Muhammad in 630 CE. The child's mother was Muhammad's concubine (one of four), Maria al-Qibtiyya, an Egyptian Coptic Christian sent as a gift from the governor of Egypt in 628 CE. The child died sixteen to eighteen months after he was born, not long before Muhammad died.

243 As-Shibli, *Akaam al-Murjaan fi Ahkaam al-Jaan*, 130.

244 Ibid., 194.

245 Quran 46:29–32.

Muhammad's first revelation. The jinn were said to be Jewish because they mentioned Moses. Muhammad apparently left Mecca for Ta'if, the closest city to Mecca and home to the goddess Al-Lat, on the last three days of Shawal and remained absent from the city for twenty-five days, until he finally returned under the auspices of a new protector.

Sources vary as to the number and origin of these original Invisible converts. Ibn Masud and others say there were nine and listed names (sources also disagree on the names). As-Shibli listed twelve: Hasa—one resembling ocean waves; Masa—evening or one who does not keep his word; Shasir—a hyena; Masir—a barrier; Ibn al-Izb—son of the midget; Aneen—groaning; Al-Akhsam—an enemy or opponent; Menshi—high; Mashi—companion; Al-Ahqab—belt; Zoba—whirlwind or dust devil, and Omar bin Jabir—Omar, son of Jabir.

> **"Night of the Jinn in Hajoun Cemetery"**—Three months after the return from Ta'if, the jinn visited Muhammad again. One night, he went walking without his companions, who, when they noticed his absence, searched frantically for him but to no avail. At dawn, he returned from behind a hill and they asked where he had been. He replied, "A hatif from the jinn took me to recite the Quran to them." To prove it, he took his companions to Hajoun Cemetery to see their footsteps and the traces of their fires. Curious, the men asked if he had spoken with them, as well. He replied that he had. The jinn had asked him for food, to which he replied, "all bones with the name of God said over them that fall into your hands are much better than meat. And all dung is fodder for your livestock." Then he added, "So don't wipe yourself with these things because they are the food of your brothers [the jinn]."[246]

> **"Jinn Mosque"**—Masjid Jinn, also known as Masjid Haras, is a mosque in Mecca built on the site where the Prophet drew a circle for Abdullah ibn Masud, who accompanied him while he recited the Quran for the jinn. Abdullah ibn Masud narrates: While in Mecca, the Prophet once said to

---

246   Hadith *Sahih Muslim* (#450a) narrated by Dawud, and Hadith *Sahih al-Bukhari* (#3860) narrated by Abu Huraira.

the Sahabah [his companions], "Whoever wishes to see the Jinn should come with me." Besides myself, no one else came. When we reached the Mualla district of Mecca [Hajoun], the Prophet used his foot to draw a circle on the ground. He then instructed me to sit inside the circle. After proceeding a little further, he started reciting the Quran. Jinn started to gather in troops. So many came I could not see the Prophet nor hear him. The Prophet continued talking with a group of them until *fajr* [dawn].[247]

"Heights of Mecca"—Another evening the Prophet asked two of his most trustworthy companions to accompany him to meet the jinn. Only one actually came, Abdullah ibn Masud. The two walked into the hills around Mecca until they saw black clouds gathering. The Prophet halted and drew a line on the ground with his foot, between him and Ibn Masud, and ordered his friend to stay behind it. Ibn Masud sat down to wait while Muhammmad walked toward the black cloud. As the Prophet recited the Quran, Ibn Masud saw the cloud engulf him, muffling his voice and completely obscuring him from sight. After a time the fog lifted, and dispersed like wisps of smoke into the night. Yet a few wisps remained until dawn, when Muhammad returned to Ibn Masud and asked, "Are you still awake?" "Yes," Ibn Masud replied, "you asked me to stay here." The Prophet requested water to wash before praying, and Ibn Masud fetched the jar he had brought for the purpose. But on opening it, he found it contained *nabidh*, fresh dates mixed with water. The prophet said, "That's all right, it is good fruit mixed with pure water," and used it to wash for prayer. As he stood to pray, two jinn appeared and asked if they could join him. "Yes, line up behind me." And so humans and jinn worshipped together overlooking Mecca. Later, Ibn Masud asked the Prophet who they were and he replied, "They were Nasebeen jinn seeking guidance. They also asked for food." "What did you give them?" Ibn Masud inquired. "Dung" was the reply.[248]

---

247 This is As-Shibli's recounting of the circumstances behind Ibn Masud's hadith.

248 As-Shibli, *Akaam al-Murjaan fi Ahkaam al-Jaan*, 98. These incidents are repeatedly mentioned in most of the major hadith collections, with varying details. A search using the terms "bone, dung, and jinn" will pull them up.

The Book of Jinn mentions three more encounters between Muhammad and the jinn, witnessed by others besides Abdullah ibn Masud: at Farqid Oasis, outside Medina with Ibn Zubayr, and while traveling with Bilal bin Harith. Unfortunately, As-Shibli does not give further details.

Before we leave As-Shibli's world of jinn, I would like to include one last topic, Solomon's relationship with the jinn. Let me begin with Edward Lane's commentary, though. He observed that according to Biblical tradition, no one possessed as much power over the jinn as King Solomon, the son of David, which he managed through a brass and iron seal ring "engraved with 'the most great name' of God (YHWH). With the brass he stamped his written commands to the good jinn; with the iron, to the evil jinn or the shayateen." This ring, a gift of God, gave Solomon unlimited power over good jinn and bad; "as well as over the birds, winds and wild animals. His vizier, Asaf ibn Barkhiya, was also acquainted with 'the most great name,' which performed great miracles when uttered, and could even raise the dead." Through this ring, it is said, "Solomon compelled the jinn to help build the Temple of Jerusalem and various other works, converted many evil jinn to the true faith, and confined those who remained infidels to prisons."[249]

> **"Solomon and the Jinn"**—According to The Book of Jinn, "The Book of Wonders" tells the story of a Moroccan prince traveling with his army who came across something unusual in the shallow waters of an island beach—seventeen green ceramic jars [amphora] sealed with Solomon's stamp. The Prince ordered four of the jars brought to shore and opened. When the first was cracked open, a shaytan appeared and demanded, "Who made you a prophet? I will not return to corrupt those on Earth!" Then it looked around and said in surprise, "I swear I do not see Solomon or his property!" But before it could utter another word, it melted into the sand. The Prince ordered the other three jars opened, but the soldiers could not catch them, so quickly did they roll back into the sea and disappear.[250]

---

249 Lane, *Arabian Society in the Middle Ages*, 40.
250 As-Shibli, *Akaam al-Murjaan fi Ahkaam al-Jaan*, 142.

Another Solomon story, also mentioned in the Quran, concerns Bilqis, the Queen of Sheba. The hoopoe, a large, common bird in Egypt, flew to Solomon and said:

"I come from Saba with tidings.
I found a woman ruling them *who* has been given all things, including a magnificent throne.
I found her and her people praying to the sun instead of God."[251]

So Solomon sent the hoopoe back to Saba with a letter bidding the queen to come to Jerusalem and submit to the will of God. Instead, she sent back a gift of great value (spices and gold). "You send me wealth," Solomon exclaimed to her envoys, "but God has given me far better than what he has given you!" and he sent the men back to Saba with a threat of war. After they left, he summoned the jinn. "Which of you will bring me her throne before they return in submission?" An afreet from the jinn replied, "I will bring it before you rise from your seat. Indeed, for this I am strong and trustworthy." Another said, "I will bring it before you blink." When the throne was placed before him, Solomon ordered it disguised to test the queen. Upon her arrival he asked, "Is this your throne?" When she replied that it was, he said, "We knew beforehand because we have submitted [to God]." Later, when Bilqis entered Solomon's palace, she mistook the glass floor for water and raised her dress to her shins to wade through it. When Solomon explained her mistake, she agreed to worship the "Lord of the Worlds" as he did.[252]

> According to The Book of Jinn, Bilqis's father, known as Al-Hudhad, was one of Yemen's greatest kings, with a large, well-equipped army. "No king can approach my greatness," he would constantly remind his subjects. He refused to marry a Yemeni woman, but wed a jinniya instead, Rihana bint as-Sakan, who gave birth to Bilqis. Originally named Balqamah [others say Loukma], the child's origins were immediately apparent because her feet resembled devil hooves. As destiny would have it, the king died without a male heir and the people were misled into appointing a corrupt ruler. Mischief prevailed, until Bilqis, heartbroken for her people, proposed marriage to the new ruler.

---

251 Quran 27: 22–24.
252 Quran 27:27–44.

Thinking to solidify his claim to the throne, he agreed. On their wedding night, she plied him with wine until he passed out, then swiftly chopped his head off and hung it on her bedroom door. Amid much merrymaking, the people placed her on the throne and declared her queen.

Once the weakness of her pagan gods was revealed and Bilqis agreed to worship the One God, Solomon proposed to her. He ordered the jinn to bring pigeons and coat her with silver glitter [an old tribal custom still practiced in twentieth-century Egypt], but when they smeared the glitter on her legs, they turned to solid silver. After the wedding, Bilqis asked to be sent back to Yemen, and Solomon agreed, ordering the shayateen to build her forts the likes of which had never been seen before: Ghamadan, Naynawa, and others. It is said Solomon visited her monthly on a flying carpet. However, when he died the marvels he built for her vanished into the sands.[253]

The Quran also mentions Solomon's death to prove that jinn are unable to predict the future. Apparently, the Jewish king died leaning on his staff, but because he was propped upright, the jinn thought he was still supervising them and continued to work. Only when a creature gnawed through his staff and his body toppled over did they realize the truth. If jinn could see the future, they would not have continued to toil as slaves.

> When We decreed [Solomon's] death, nothing showed them he had died except an earthworm, which ate his staff. When he fell, the jinn saw that if they had known the unseen, they would not have remained in humiliating punishment.[254]

And so we arrive at the question of what the jinn can and cannot do. Apparently, they cannot tell the future. This is to be expected, though, since ignorance of future events is a prerequisite of free choice. Those whose future is not predetermined must expect to be bound by the fourth dimension of time. This is why clairvoyant humans are said to be tuned in to a divine frequency. Only those not bound by time may see forward. This is also why correctly predicting events is considered proof of a true Otherworld connection and prophetic status.

---

253   As-Shibli, *Akaam al-Murjaan fi Ahkaam al-Jaan*, 108.

254   Quran 34:14.

Modern Jinn

So far, I have shared jinn descriptions from the distant past by narrators with little or no scientific knowledge. But what about present-day jinn? Islam has certainly been in the news since September 11, 2001, when New York City's World Trade Center towers came crashing down. Were shayateen, souls who walk on the dark side, or other misguided Invisibles responsible for this and other current events? Or have Iblis and his followers been whispering into the hearts of the disenfranchised, harnessing pride, arrogance, and envy to make their deeds seem pleasing and righteous? If so, should this evil be attributed to an entire race? Certainly, jinn possession is still claimed to occur throughout the Muslim world. But are spirits really responsible for host suffering? Or, as with Muhammad, are they simply comforting the grieving and those without protection?

Before the codification of Islam, the jinn were fiery nature spirits that freely roamed the wild open spaces of Africa and the Middle East—regions where humanity was scarce. Tragically, many of these places are now crowded and polluted. Overpopulation, greenhouse gases, industrial chemicals, and the ultra-high radio waves of broadcast television and smartphones downloading the latest app have fouled their spaces and made separation from humans impossible. A constant haze of stray photons from streetlights has usurped the dark of night (once the sole domain of the moon), and a global network of electric cables radiates disruptive fields. Life on Earth isn't what it used to be for the jinn … and they are worried. Humans are defiling their home.

Orion Foxwood

When I was first confronted by the need to write this book, I discussed the jinn and the Invisibles in general with Orion Foxwood, a leading faerie seer and occult author. Orion's insights, along with those of Sethlan Foxwood, his companion, were pivotal in putting words to my disparate sensations, inner voices, and intuitions, and eventually in helping me interpret these things on my own. For this reason, and so many others, I asked him to write the Foreword to this book. In fact, he was, in essence, its Godfather, planting seeds and helping me find the proper place to bring it to life through Llewellyn. Now let me share some of his insights from our conversations.[255]

---

255 These conversations took place between 2011 and 2014, and I took copious notes. What I present here are excerpts from these notes.

As Orion mentioned in his Foreword, I introduced him and Sethlan to the jinn a number of years ago. At first, Orion was reminded of a Celtic expression, "spark of divinity." He found the jinn's energy contained a great deal of syncopation and counter rhythms, as opposed to the faerie folk, who were liquid flame. Jinn darted around like smokeless fire—flowing and wavering one moment, unexpectedly flickering and sputtering the next. It was haunting, ancient energy, he said, with traces from creation and the early universe. He was surprised to find how truly different these beings were from the angels and faerie folk he was familiar with.

Sethlan's impressions were more visual, and involved a ruby-red eye, trees and roots, and a red liquid pool impregnated by a unique (but not unpleasant) odor. Although he sensed the jinn occupied the same strata as other Invisibles, he felt they nevertheless existed in a different state, with a different elemental structure and language from the faerie, along a continuum of life that Orion calls "the visible, invisible, and intra-visible, or ... seen, unseen, and thresholds in between. Our senses encounter their presence in different ways, in different places even, and through different bodily expressions." Sethlan said that although the jinn seemed violent, this was only their fiery nature. When they first entered the room, Sethlan jumped, surprised by the sound of ringing bells (like finger cymbals). Drawn by Solomon's incense and the pressing issues at hand, this was their way of announcing their presence, before gathering around Orion to communicate their wishes ... It was the meeting that eventually led to this book.

One subject Orion continued to stress throughout our conversations was how to perceive the Invisibles through the "subtle senses." He felt our race has become terribly inexperienced in using, or believing in, the subtle messages we pick up from the environment:

> The five senses flow out and into one sense, which we call "aliveness." These senses,
> or departments of sense, have deeper and heightened octaves that most modern hu-
> mans rarely develop. This has left us with the uncomfortable feeling of disconnect-
> edness from life and/or terror of the invisible realm—because it "seems" unknown
> and menacing. When these senses are re-awakened, trained and integrated into
> our lives many of these fears and abandonment wounds are replaced with a sense
> of wonder, increased presence and aliveness. YES, there are dangers in the unseen.
> But there are also dangers in the seen. The only difference is that the invisible forces

cannot hide from our heightened senses the way embodied forces can hide within a shell or outer barricade.[256]

Orion also reflected on the need to "cultivate the heart that breathes," a positive attitude that facilitates interaction with the Invisibles. He described it as playful wonderment, the expectation that meeting the spirit world is fun, and that similar enjoyment will be had by the entity. "Permitting joy fosters a playground mentality." Orion has long felt that Invisibles want us on their wavelength so they can share human emotions and behavior (such as sexuality), while allowing us to experience their utter freedom. Ultimately, though, it comes down to a question of respect, he said; not worship, respect—for the myriad life forms on our planet. Orion also confirmed what I have felt from the start, that humanity must return to a cooperative relationship with the Invisibles and correct the environmental imbalances we have created before nature has to do it.

The jinn have communicated to me that they are concerned our increased dependency on the Internet, digital cloud storage, and electricity will be our downfall (besides polluting the planet and annihilating each other). Solar flares, gamma ray bursts, or other catastrophes can easily wipe out eons of accumulated knowledge in an instant if it is not stored in solid formats (books) impervious to magnetic surges that do not require electricity and/or complicated machinery to read. They have also shown me in chilling detail that humanity's brief window into our planet's timeline does not accurately reflect how fragile our ecosystem is, or the frequency with which it has been interrupted—only to start afresh with new life forms and another cycle. And of course there is Judgment Day, that time when our sun dies and the universe runs out of energy. Compared to that, humanity's petty feuds over land, religion, and resources seem as insignificant as an ant under Solomon's hooves.[257]

The Invisibles have far longer life spans than we do. Some live for thousands of years, a few for millions or more. Seen from their perspective, things look very different. Humans are useful to the jinn because we can manipulate solid matter. If an asteroid approaches Earth in the future we may be able to do something about it. Their plasmatic nature allows them far fewer options.

---

256   Orion Foxwood, personal interview.

257   Quran 27:18.

So far, our planet has been lucky. According to an article in *The Economist*, "For the first half of Earth's [4.6 billion year] existence, only the direct impact [of an asteroid] would have mattered, since there was no ozone layer to annihilate" (simple bacteria back then were adapted to UV and lived underground or in the water). "But once photosynthesis started (about 2.3 billion years ago), oxygen—and therefore ozone, the triatomic form of that element—began to accumulate, and living things came out of hiding and got used to living under its protection. From then on, a nearby [within 10,000 light-years] GRB [Gamma Ray Burst] would certainly have caused a mass extinction." In the past 540 million years, there have been five extinction events.[258]

Apparently, some regions of our galaxy are friendlier than others. Our solar system is at the edge, where stars are farther apart. At the center, the chances of being hit by a GRB are 90 percent every billion years. Complex life on Earth may be as ancient as is possible in our galaxy. And since complexity is necessary for intelligence, humans may well be the Milky Way's first intelligent (solid) life forms. But we are only as intelligent as our compiled knowledge. Take away the books and you have to start all over.

Figure 27: A jinni from Edward Lane's *The Thousand and One Nights*

---

258 "Bolts from the Blue," *The Economist*, 81. References a paper published on arXiv by astronomers Tsvi Piran and Raul Jimenez.

Homework: The Arabian Nights

Who or what the jinn or the Invisibles are, in general, is a question you will hopefully answer from personal experience by the end of this book. Nevertheless, the tales of others are instructive, so for homework please read jinn stories from the Arabian Nights (originally *One Thousand and One Nights*), a compilation of folktales in Arabic from the Islamic Golden Age. There are many translations, but look for the original tales, which were written for adults, just like most Bible stories were. Choose versions that have not been sugar-coated or edited down for children.

From Edward Lane's three-volume edition, *The Thousand and One Nights*, first published in 1840, read:

The Merchant and the Jinni
The Fisherman and the Jinni
The Envier and the Envied
The City of Brass
Jullanar of the Sea
Alladin and the Lamp

From Richard Burton's sixteen-volume edition, *The Book of the Thousand Nights and a Night*, including *The Supplemental Nights to the Thousand Nights and a Night*, published between 1884 and 1888, read (in addition to the tales mentioned above):

The Eldest Lady's Tale
Nour ad-Din Ali and his son Badr ad-Din Hasan
The Ruined Man who became Rich through a Dream
The Ebony Horse
Sinbad—the 1st and 7th Voyages
The Lady and her Five Suitors
Khalifah the Fisherman of Baghdad
The Larrikin and the Cook
The Tale of Zayn al-Asnam

The Adventures of Bulukiya
Tohfat al-Kulub
The King's Son and the Ogress
Ma'ruf the Cobbler

Figure 28: Jinn flying over the pyramids, from *The Thousand and One Nights*

7

·········

The Zar

Eugenie Le Brun described two zars in her eyewitness narrative: the private zar, presented at the beginning of Part Two of this book, and a public zar, which follows. This public zar was led by Cairo's leading sheikha at the time…

Sur Les Zars, *part 2*
Harems et Musulmanes d'Égypte by Eugenie Le Brun[259]

Remember I mentioned an old African woman, the ex-slave of a prince, who hosted the second zar I attended? Let me describe her gathering now. Certainly, my two experiences couldn't have been more different. I brought three other women with me this time—all disguised as authentic Muslim Turks, to force a door which would otherwise not be open to Christians.

What a maze of tortuous alleyways we passed through! What ponds of mire and mounds of debris we had to lurch over before we could finally descend from our carriage! Eunuchs led us into a courtyard pitched with multicolored tents festooned with streamers. We were expected, our seats were reserved, and the mistress of the house herself came to greet us. Comparing this house to the previous one, I was forced to admit that the *afareet* could not be held responsible for the laziness of the possessed.

Cheerfulness was in the air. In fact, the gathering felt more like a wedding than a meeting of the possessed! When I mentioned this, I was told it was the

---

259   Le Brun, *Harems et Musulmanes d'Égypt*, 275–98. My translation, edited for length.

last day of their weeklong *moulid*, the cult's annual pre-Ramadan festival. The workers were all looking forward to a month's rest. Today was the final ceremony, which included a sacrificial parade. The animals, brought as presents or offered by the kodia's farmers, had been saved for last: sheep, goats, buffalo calves, even a young camel, and numerous poultry. All were to be ritually purified and put to death, cut into pieces, cooked in giant stew pots, and then served to this large family of Possessed. Meanwhile, the *afareet* were invited to feed at the banquet of their choice. The screams and spasms of the slain, the stench of pulsating entrails, the howling icy gasps of death, and the blood baths all belonged to them.

At last, the canon announced the noon hour. This signaled the musicians to begin chanting magic incantations to the beat of muted tambourines. Eight African matrons moved to the assembly's center. All were professional kodias, each with her own public zar, invited to officiate the ceremony by the mistress of the house, their colleague and for some, their teacher. Today was reserved for the antics of the high priestesses and the animals. First the beasts were presented, one by one—a process that took over an hour. While four of the kodias washed the animals' heads and sense organs, the other four fumigated them with incense. The poor creatures, bewildered, asphyxiated, almost mute from bellowing, limply abandoned themselves to the women's bruising palpitations.

The censing finished, the kodias took off their aprons and mingled with the crowd. The choir, which had stopped, now resumed even louder with a change of key. Strange, violent, intolerable fragrances from strategically placed jars added to the nerve-wracking atmosphere—ideal for pushing overstimulated nerves and unbalanced brains into ecstasy.

Turning heads guided my gaze toward the dance circle. One of the matrons sat on a chair, eyes closed, limbs limp, seemingly asleep. Gently, someone replaced the scarf wound around her head with a tasseled, gold-braided tarbouche. Eyelids closed, lips coated with foam, her arms beating the air, the kodia rose and edged her way inside the dance circle—without bumping a soul.

As the high priestess performed her choreographed frolic—which later turned clownish—the choir summoned other well-known spirits. Their "mounts" quickly appeared. Minute by minute, the possessed descended into the arena, until there were eight—the eight from the fumigation ritual. Those around me called them the "grand pashas of the infernal world." Each wore a tarbouche and a scarf and brandished either a cane or a sword. They moved in cadence on the narrow stage, some with eyes closed, others with eyes open—their wild, glassy stares fixed on the multicolored hangings overhead. Incoherent words, raucous exclamations, a dog's bark, all came tumbling from their foam-coated lips. Menacing gestures seemed poised to strike, but touched no one.

Hovering near the Infernal Eight stood a tall, thin African woman, her face frozen in a sardonic grimace. Acting as stage director and dresser, she changed their costumes, fixed their hair, and organized accessories passed to her from the prop room. But when the drums beat her spirit's rhythm, she suddenly dropped cataleptic to the floor. Without a fuss, someone else took her place and the show went on as before.

Eventually, the "rides" began jumping higher than a meter, then flopping heavily down, legs extended forward. Folding their appendages under them, they jumped again, followed by more falls. In an apparent blind, self-destructive fervor, they frenetically rolled on the ground, pounding it with their foreheads, elbows, and knees. Straightening, arms stretched out like pendulums, they hurled themselves sideways onto their right hands. Head down, feet in the air, spinning like large cones, they continued this foolish savagery until exhaustion overcame them. In the end, all eight collapsed into waiting gilt armchairs.

Once they were seated, the guests threw themselves at the kodias' feet, humbly kissing their silk coat hems and begging for miraculous benedictions—"healing touches" that resembled a massage. It began by a high priestess squeezing the supplicant's head between her hands. Then, as they lay face down on the floor, she pressed on their shoulder blades and pulled their arms and fingers, rotating them in the joints—until the whole thing ended with a vigorous hug.

This was only an intermission, yet the stage remained occupied. Two African women danced solemnly face-to-face; one as tall as a monument with innumerable plaited braids, the other as fragile and thin as a straw. They were very wealthy freed slaves from Constantinople who came to Cairo every year for the zars. They executed similar jests as the kodias with indisputable skill; the same stupendous leaps, the same resounding body blows, the same frenzy. They wildly beat themselves with heavy gold and silver inlaid wooden cylinders, occasional brief roars escaping their foaming lips. At any moment I expected them to tragically sink to the ground, so bloody and insatiable was their satanic ardor. Yet, as soon as the drumming ceased, their murderous rage disappeared, as if by enchantment—replaced by a saintly aura of benevolent charity. They, too, massaged the sick, made prophetic predictions, and sat among the kodias in sumptuous armchairs—until new rhythms summoned different spirits and the dance began again.

This continued until dawn. Finally, everything ended in another parade. A table laden with offerings and candles was carried to the center of the courtyard and the purified animals were led around it. Once again the rabbits, pigeons, and chickens were blinded by incense and palpitated by a hundred brutal hands. The sheep, goats, and buffalo calves trampled each other, frightened as much by the frenzied singing as by the silk lamee blindfolds wound around their foreheads and lashed to their collars. The camel followed, pompously decked out with silk scarves, loose coats, braided tarabouches, and all the other costumes. The kodias followed it, exhausted I imagine, throwing handfuls of almonds, hazelnuts, dates, raisins, and candy with every step. The treats clattered against the walls and struck people as they rebounded. This was the sacred share for the spirits who loved sweets. No human was allowed to touch the offerings, under pain of immediate revenge, most likely the breaking of furniture.

In the end, the unhappy animals were led away to sacrifice while the kodias completed the final incense ritual, the supreme exorcism—without smearing themselves in blood—and brought the proceedings to a close.

Comparing this zar to the previous one, I left with a completely different impression. This one had been well organized, like a theater production. The kodias were obviously pontificating with their fortune-telling and the laying of hands and their acrobatics revealed years of practice with a marked taste for exhibitionism. Even so, it felt as if an ardent gust of madness had just blown over these women so desperately seeking a union with the Divine.

From a twenty-first-century point of view, Eugenie Le Brun's "ardent gust" seems less like madness and more like a blast of clarity into a quickly receding past. Ceremonies of this magnitude are no longer held in Cairo today. Putting aside religious considerations, people now balk at spending so much money for something so … nebulous. They are more concerned with feeding their families or saving for a down payment on a home than in pleasing spirits. Egyptian society, religious tolerance, and the world in general have changed. Surprisingly, though, zar trance induction techniques have not. They have remained the same for centuries—actually since antiquity, if you compare them to the induction techniques of the Greek maenads, which are strikingly similar (see chapter 2).

To Western psychiatrists, the zar is simply a "dissociative identity disorder" found in traditional African and Middle Eastern cultures. It is:

> A general term applied in Ethiopia, Somalia, Egypt, Sudan, Iran and other North African and Middle Eastern societies to the experience of spirits possessing an individual. Persons possessed by a spirit may experience dissociative episodes that may include shouting, laughing, hitting the head against a wall, singing, or weeping. Individuals may show apathy and withdrawal, refusing to eat or carry out daily tasks, or may develop a long-term relationship with the possessing spirit. Such behavior is not considered pathological locally.[260]

---

260 American Psychiatric Association, *The Diagnostic and Statistical Manual of Mental Disorders*, 4th Edition. In the 5th edition, "zar" was rolled into the Dissociative Identity Disorder category.

Those who have experienced a zar visitation, however, find the initial experience disorienting and utterly exhausting, both mentally and physically—and a cathartic relief after that. To cult members, the zar is where the visible and invisible worlds meet, for better or worse; where just the right rhythm dissolves the ethereal veil and all manner of Invisibles come tumbling out.

But before we dive into the trance dance possession cult that led me (and many other belly dancers) to the fire spirits, let me quickly explain how I came across the zar, or more aptly, how they came across me. Early in my career as a Middle Eastern belly dancer, I was drawn to the ritual's wild head tosses because the movements looked dramatic with my knee-length hair. When someone finally told me what the dance was for, I guiltily realized I really should research the belief system I was profaning—at the very least to prevent other foreigners from committing the same *faux pas* as I had. This was in the early 1980s, around the time Anwar Sadat was assassinated. I was a full-time professional dancer in Cairo and my bandleader's family was (and still is) involved in the zar. Eventually, after much coaxing, he arranged for me to attend a number of rituals (zar, zikr, and Mevlevi Sufi whirling). I had no idea I was opening Pandora's box!

In the 1960s and 1970s, Egyptian culture was far less constrained by Islamic conservatism than it is now, and the zar, as a healing ritual, was well established in all strata of society. As Eugenie Le Brun's descriptions imply, African servants and slaves introduced the cult into Egypt's wealthy harems during the 1800s. A century later, even superstar Middle Eastern singer Om Kalthoum hosted several rituals as a last resort to cure her health problems. While the rituals were not approved of, religious clerics tended to turn a benign eye to it. But after Sadat's assassination, the winds of change blew in a new direction and the imams began to crack down on anything that even remotely resembled "pagan practices" (which sadly included belly dance). Today, belly dancing is hardly tolerated and the zar ekes by "underground"... for how long is anyone's guess. Yet in spite of this general narrow-mindedness, both dance forms have deeply influenced Egyptian society.[261] And while the zar is less well known to foreigners, it offers the region's women an important physical and emotional escape valve—whether they believe in the jinn or not.

261　For a complete view of the ambivalent role belly dancing plays in Egyptian society, I highly recommend Karin van Nieuwkerk's excellent book *"A Trade Like Any Other."*

What Is a "Zar"?

To Egyptians, the word "zar" has several meanings: a ceremony to placate possession spirits; the name of the spirits themselves (*zar* singular, *zayran* plural: a subspecies of *jinn*, the blood-loving red tribe); the cult that believes in these spirits; and the dance done to communicate with them. *A Dictionary of Egyptian Arabic*, the definitive source for Egyptian Arabic translations, defines *zar* as "a ritual of sacrifices, incantations, drumming and dancing performed for the purpose of appeasing any number of spirits by which a person may be believed to be possessed."[262] Cult members occasionally call their spirits a jinn or shaytan, but not *rouh*, afreet, or marid (popularly depicted as giant ogres in Egypt). The name they usually use, though (besides *zar*), is *asyad,* or "masters" (singular *sayed,* "master").

As to the word's origin ... one school of thought is that it was derived from *za'ir al-nahas,* or "bad luck visitor," from the Arabic root *za'er,* "visitor." *Zar* in Arabic actually means "visited," the past tense of *yazour*—"to visit." This is thought to stem from the popular belief that these spirits, when in human form, cause mayhem for whoever offers them hospitality. Others believe the word is a variation of the verb *zahr,* "to become visible, perceptible, or to manifest." Nevertheless, most zar scholars hold that the word isn't Arabic at all, but Amharic, the language of the Habashi, or Ethiopians. To them, *zar* designates either "the evil that hits humans" or the almighty god of the Koshiyeen al-Wathaneen (one of the country's pagan tribes) who was named Zar. An Amharic root would make sense since the cult's point of origin is thought to be the Ethiopian city of Gondar, where many legendary healers once lived in the surrounding hills. *Women's Medicine*, a compilation of research papers about the zar, has several excellent articles about the cult's origins for those interested in the details.

Nevertheless, no one is truly certain where this belief system came from. Some Egyptians maintain it originated in pharaonic Egypt, while anthropologists steadfastly insist it came from East Africa, specifically Ethiopia and Sudan, and then spread to the Middle East via pilgrims, slave traders, and prisoners of war. The hadith reinforce this idea. Even in Muhammad's time, Ethiopian women were associated with the jinn:

---

262   Al-Said Bedawi and Martin Hinds, *A Dictionary of Egyptian Arabic.*

The Messenger of Allah was sitting and we heard a scream and the voices of children. So he arose, and saw an Ethiopian woman prancing around while the children played around her. He said: "O Aisha, come see." So I came, and put my chin upon his shoulder and watched her from between his shoulder and his head. He asked me: "Have you had enough, have you had enough?" but I kept saying: "No," to see my status with him. Then Umar appeared and they dispersed. The Messenger of Allah said: "Indeed I see the shayateen among men and jinn have run from Umar."[263]

And yet the zar's presence in Egypt is hard to trace. Napoleon's *Description de l'Egypte*, compiled during his 1798 invasion, did not mention it, nor did Edward Lane's *Manners and Customs of the Modern Egyptians*. As a man, Mr. Lane would have been forbidden to attend this largely female ceremony, but his sister, Elizabeth Lane-Poole, visited Egypt in the 1840s and did not mention it in her book, *The Englishwoman in Egypt*, either. The earliest mention of an Egyptian zar I could find was by Lady Lucy Duff Gordon in 1869,[264] although the cult was described in Sudan and Ethiopia as early as 1839.[265] The most logical theory I have read is that the cult slowly migrated into Egypt from Sudan after the Egyptian ruler Muhammad Ali invaded Sudan in 1820.[266] Certainly, many zar traditions (musical instruments, vocabulary, songs, rhythms, etc.) are distinctly East African and the cult continues to thrive there. Furthermore, when Egyptian zar sheikhat or kodias, female shamans that lead the ceremonies, are asked about their heritage, most trace their roots back to their great-grandparents (the late 1800s), who were also sheikhat or kodias but in Ethiopia or Sudan. The kodias, in par-

---

263   Hadith *Jami at-Tirmidhi* (#4055), narrated by Aisha.

264   Lewis et al., *Women's Medicine*, 178.

265   Charles William Isenberg, a missionary, observed a ceremony on October 1, 1839, in Ankobar, Shoa, Ethiopia/Abyssinia. Lewis et al., *Women's Medicine*, 250.

266   Brenda Seligman originated the hypothesis that the zar was imported into Egypt from the Sudan after Muhammad Ali's conquest. She noted that women of every social class participated in the zar, but particularly Negro slaves and freed African women and that the ceremonies were run by "freed Negroes." She also witnessed rituals in the early 1900s in the Sudan among the "black battalion," the impressed Southern Sudanese troops of the Turkish-Egyptian army. Lewis et al., *Women's Medicine*, 84.

ticular, were from Sudan. Whatever the zar's roots, though, its recent development (during the nineteenth and twentieth centuries) appears to have been triggered by the social upheaval Muhammad Ali instigated, particularly by the cultural restrictions imposed on women. Even today, the zar spirit pantheon reflects its former role as a nineteenth-century coping mechanism, as you will see when you meet the individual entities later in the chapter.

Who Holds a Zar and When?

What we do know is that today, thousands of women in Egypt still turn to the zar when modern medicine fails them. If doctors cannot find the cause of their physical or mental ailments, they assume supernatural forces are involved. Their first impulse is to consult a male Islamic healer, a *faki Islam,* who will attempt a minor exorcism if the jinn (rather than sorcery or the evil eye) are suspected. The only jinn able to resist these banishments are the zar spirits. Therefore, if a woman's problems persist after an exorcism, her sickness is assumed to be the work of zayran. To be certain, however, she must seek the opinion of a sheikha or kodia. Zayran are believed to invade humans during a "crisis point" in the individual's life[267] but manifest only when they want something. Hence, if someone is diagnosed as *malbusa* ("clothed"), *milammisa* ("touched"), or *ma'zura* ("excused")—the Egyptian terms for "possessed"—it is essential to know who the mischief-making spirit is and what it wants, because only when its demands are met will a host's suffering go away. (As an aside, a number of researchers have observed that zar hosts tend toward disassociation and hysteria and that they have eating and sleeping disorders typical of anxiety-induced neuroses. The zar often cures hysteria paralysis, for example.)

To test the waters, a sheikha may suggest the patient attend a weekly hadra, similar to the one I described in chapters 1 and 3, to see if the spirit manifests on its own. But even if it doesn't, once a sheikha determines a woman is possessed, she will organize a diagnostic ritual (if the patient can afford it) to coax the intruder out into the open and

---

267 Crisis points, the psychological shock or meltdown that allows a spirit to enter a patient's body, occur at times of extreme weakness: during severe life-threatening illnesses, the loss of virginity, sexual domination, sentimental deception, forced marriage, natural abortion, stillborn birth, the death of a child, etc.

hopefully negotiate a truce with it. Its identity will depend on which song the patient feels compelled to dance to (in Egypt, it's called *daqa*—Arabic for beat; in Sudan they use a different word, *khuyut* or "thread"). The belief is that each entity or tribe responds to a specific chant or rhythm, so the sheikha will cycle the musicians through their repertoire until the woman feels an uncontrollable urge to move. Once she selects a rhythm, the musicians then play it until she dances herself into a trance. The spirit then descends into her body (*ninzil* in Egyptian Arabic), seizes her consciousness, and, using her vocal chords, negotiates its demands with the sheikha.

Diagnostic zars can last anywhere from a day in Egypt to a week in Sudan and Ethiopia. Each region has its own traditions and rituals, but all take time. Most first-time patients have never experienced trance before, so they only relinquish consciousness once they are completely exhausted. After that, they have reference points or "keys" and eventually learn to descend within minutes of dancing. But in the beginning, the "brides" are "virgins" and take longer. Yet it is a skill they must learn, because once they agree to terms with their possessors, their *sayed* ("master") will expect to regularly manifest in their bodies and ride them. If they can't, they will take revenge and make their mares sick again.

Sadly, in addition to physical or mental ailments, many zar patients also suffer from poverty and the cultural limitations imposed on their gender. Women from the lower classes lead difficult, stress-filled lives in Islamic Africa and the Middle East. Money is tight or nonexistent and usually only comes to them from men. They are under enormous social pressure to conform—to their family's expectations, their neighbors' ever-watchful eyes, and their religion's narrow role for women. Their movements are restricted, their marriages arranged, and many were circumcised when they were young. So when these women are confronted with sudden challenges, such as death, divorce, or a new wife in the household (Islam permits a man to take up to four wives if they are treated equally), their fragile psyches become quickly overwhelmed and susceptible to spirit invasion. Stress and grief often trigger low serotonin levels, but zar rituals offer the stricken a way to self-medicate. Difficult situations become suddenly bearable with regular neurotransmitter boosts and a physical outlet for repressed emotions. At the very least, the rituals allow participants to forget their daily lives for a few hours, change their environments, interact with other women, listen to emotionally charged music, and exercise.

In other words, zar participants often suffer from "melancholic" depression—exacerbated by learned helplessness, a sedentary secluded lifestyle, and a pessimistic outlook on life. Western medicine usually begins depression treatment with talk therapy (how to avoid excessive discouragement and self-blame by adopting a positive attitude) and behavior modification: thirty to sixty minutes of sunlight exposure a day, regular moderate aerobic exercise (such as jogging, brisk walking, or dancing to increase blood flow), and a consistent sleep schedule. Regular dancing at hadras certainly fits this prescription! But if symptoms persist, doctors then suggest drugs, mainly serotonin uptake inhibitors such as Prozac, and perhaps brief periods of total sleep deprivation (which alters brain chemistry). In extreme cases, they may attempt electroconvulsive therapy (electric shock to the brain). In Egypt, however, modern medicine often fails these women. Depression and other psychological diseases, while acknowledged in Africa, are hardly accepted in the mainstream. And so patients turn to the zar. Faith becomes their healer (a placebo cure), along with exercise, a healthy dose of neurotransmitters, and, in many cases, self-induced shocks.

Dancing is only half the story, though. Besides the ritual's physical effects, zars bring about important social modifications. Zar hadarat provide patients with human contact, people with similar afflictions to talk to. They also provide excuses. Once a woman is officially labeled as "possessed," a third party becomes responsible for her odd or unacceptable behavior, not the woman herself. She is allowed forbidden desires (like drinking or smoking cigarettes or partying) or to refuse sex with her husband. She has a reason, beyond her control, for why she isn't married or doesn't have children. She can dress up in her best clothes, put on all her jewelry, wear perfume, apply makeup, and flirt, all in the name of pleasing her possessor—hence the use of the word *ma'zura*, "excused," to describe those "with spirit."

Which brings us to the somewhat taboo subject of sex and the zar. When asked, women occasionally admit to experiencing an orgasm while "swaying"[268] (one reason among many they cover their heads and faces with a veil while they dance). This is not surprising. Trance dancing is enormously cathartic, physically as well as emotionally, and

---

268　"Swaying" is the English translation of *tafqeer,* the Egyptian word used to designate zar ritual movements. See also *takeer* and *takhmeer* in the glossary.

many zar participants suffer from sexual repression. The causes vary: large age differences between spouses in arranged marriages, female circumcision, apathy by husbands who may be absent, sick, or prefer another wife, or the utter boredom of sitting home alone all day in a cramped, dark, badly ventilated apartment.[269] You get the picture. When these women are finally allowed to let go … they do, completely.

And so there you have it. The zar is a complete world unto itself with unforgettable characters (the individual zar spirits) and a mystic supernatural setting. The music grows on you and the heavy smell of perfume and incense is intoxicating. The relief participants feel afterwards is real, albeit temporary, and the wellbeing that follows lasts for days—whether you believe in jinn or not. Are the spirits real, are the women possessed? The women believe that they are.

"Songs are the life of the soul, and music helps heal the sick."[270]

What Happens at an Egyptian Zar Ceremony?

As you have seen, the short answer is … a lot of dancing to live music by women over the age of thirty—who are generally *not* virgins, contrary to popular Arabic misinformation. This dancing, or "swaying," induces trance. Known as *faqqar* in modern Egyptian Arabic—"to sway or rock rhythmically, as during a zikr or zar, or from drowsiness or pain"—the word also means "to flicker," like a candle flame.[271] As a noun (*tafqeer*), it denotes a form of dancing where the body is "bent slightly forward, one shoulder a little higher than the other … with a turning movement"[272] of the torso. It is done either standing still by shifting weight, or with a forward "stumble" step circling the kursi (as Eugenie Le Brun described). Either way, the upper body is what matters, as it twists and bobs up and down and from side to side (I will teach you how to do this in chapter 12: How to Zar). Some zar spirit tribes, like the Saidi or the Saudi, have specific

---

269 Lower-class women who leave their homes without a male chaperone are frowned upon in Egypt.

270 An Arabic proverb often quoted in Sudan in conjunction with the zar. John Kennedy, ed., *Nubian Ceremonial Life*, 207.

271 Bedawi and Hinds, *A Dictionary of Egyptian Arabic*, 665.

272 Sengers, *Women and Demons*, 92.

steps, but most dancers do a general stomping shuffle. Eyes closed, breathing heavily, with strong emotions flickering across their faces, participants "sway" until they reach a "crisis point," when they either collapse in a trance or tire and sit down in exhaustion.

If a woman collapses during a hadra, the milder version of the zar ceremony, the sheikha will whisper in her ear and sprinkle rose water on her to bring her back. Open eyes signal that the spirit has either entered the body or left it (an event called *al-radwa*, or liberation). Afterwards, the dancer may be disorientated, and physically as well as emotionally spent, but she is calm and at peace. Unfortunately, this euphoric state does not last. The spirit has not been exorcised, only temporarily pacified. Zayran stay with their hosts for life, hovering around them and reentering their bodies at will. They may even be inherited! And although a victim upholds her end of the bargain, there is no guarantee she will remain symptom free. Zayran are notoriously fickle and often do not play fair or by the rules.

Not all women who participate in zar rituals (particularly hadarat) are possessed, though. Some are simply curious bystanders, drawn to the music. Others may be lonely or want to relieve stress through dancing. A few wonder if a spirit will call them. And rarely, one or two are even encouraged to attend by their families—because of their unusual behavior (like refusing to marry or have children) or socially unacceptable personalities (they are mean and grouchy or don't obey their husbands).

In general, African zar ceremonies, as opposed to Egyptian gatherings, are large group events attended by both children and adults. Women grow up watching other women go into trance, which is why they are not afraid to lose self-control; they have seen others do it and trust those present to keep them safe. They know the sheikha will help them navigate the treacherous zar universe and pull them back when it's time to leave. This could be one reason why possession ceremonies in Sudan, Ethiopia, and Nigeria are more intense than those of Egypt. African entities make their hosts do extraordinary things, such as speak foreign languages, act out events, and perform great feats of strength, self-mutilation, or self-harm. Egyptian ceremonies pale in comparison.

Islam could also be a reason. Sub-Saharan Africa is closer to its animist roots, compared to Egypt's stronger ties to the Muslim world—and its conservative requirements for female behavior. Egyptian women may be afraid of being labeled infidels. When not entranced, they often take great pains to prove they are not violating Quranic tradition by calling the spirits anything but "jinn": *asyad* ("masters"), *qurana*, *ahwat tahtiyeen* ("brothers and sisters underground"), or even *malayka ardiyya* ("earthly angels"). Nevertheless, as we have seen, one of Islam's Five Pillars is that "there is no god but God." Fundamentalists believe that entering into a contract with a spirit, any spirit, acknowledges its power. The orthodox establishment holds that only God has power and He has no rival; therefore, women who make contracts with spirits are violating an essential tenant. They are sacrificing to beings other than God.

Besides music and dance, other ritual components of the zar help participants enter trance. Panting from physical exertion (many of these women do not get regular exercise) and the pervasive clouds of incense and tobacco smoke cause hyperventilation and light-headedness. Drinking alcoholic beverages (forbidden in Islam, but requested by certain spirits) may also make them feel dizzy. And not all elements are physical. Some are psychological. These women want to let go. They feel safe enough to lose themselves in the moment. And they are not afraid to enter the realm of the jinn.

With that said, there are three main categories of Egyptian zar ceremonies: waiting rituals (or, more officially, "intermediary reconnection"), diagnostic rituals, and reconfirmation rituals. Each varies from region to region, sheikha to sheikha, spirit to spirit, and a patient's physical and economic conditions. Since I have limited space, I will only describe Egypt's rituals because I know them best, but check the bibliography for sources that provide vivid accounts of other cultures' ceremonies.

Waiting Rituals

These are the simplest of Egypt's zar gatherings, and include the popular weekly zar hadarat as described at the beginning of chapter 3. The word "hadra" is derived from the Arabic *hudour* or "presence," and was inspired by the Sufi zikr ritual of the same name (see chapter 8). In zar terminology, however, the name implies the presence of spirit masters and patients rather than the Prophet Muhammad and Allah. These relatively short rituals are generally held without elaborate fanfare or sacrifice on Fridays or Mondays, to the music of only one band—Saidi, Sudani, or Abou al-Ghreit, depending on the sheikha's specialty.

Zar hadarat are unique to Egypt. The tradition began in the nineteenth century when regular zar gatherings were held if not within, then close to, holy shrines to attract women attending weekly *ziyaras*. A ziyara, or "visit" (also from the Arabic root *za'er*), is in essence a pilgrimage to a holy place such as a saint's tomb, a Sufi practice introduced into Egypt after the Ottoman conquest of the 1500s. In the twentieth century, however, stricter Muslim opinions prevailed and the custom of holding zar gatherings near Islamic holy sites was frowned upon. Nevertheless, this is why the words "zar" and "ziyara" are associated in Egypt.[273] Nowadays, in the twenty-first century, *shaabi* zikrs are slowly replacing zar hadarat in popularity. Contrary to the zar, these mixed trance-dance gatherings are socially acceptable. Held near tombs or mosques, the faithful dance to popular music with Islamic lyrics instead of the zar's traditional African "beats." And dancers commune with Allah and the soul of the Prophet Muhammad instead of the jinn.

As recently as the 1990s, in addition to hadarat, women also attended longer waiting rituals called *daqa an-nahar*, "day-beats," or *daqa al-layl*, "night-beats," depending on preference or work schedules. Day-beats began around ten or eleven in the morning and continued until sunset, while night-beats started after dinner and ended at dawn. Special day-beats included all-day excursions, "sea zars" and "mountain zars," that allowed participants to breathe fresh air far from the dusty streets of Cairo. Sea zars involved large boats with one or several zar bands on board. The women would set sail down the Nile in the morning, dancing all the way, until they disembarked on an island between Rawd al-Farag and Waraaq al-Arab, where they would continue to dance until sunset. Mountain zars were held in al-Imam, near the mosque of Sidi oqba in Hosh Negfa, and included a stop at al-Soqia (a deep well among the tombs used for zar sacrifice remains) plus a visit to the tomb of Sitt al-Hadra—an entire day of singing, dancing, listening to music … and happiness.[274]

---

273   Lewis et al., *Women's Medicine*, 85 and 182–84.

274   Adel Al-Aleemi, *Az-Zar: Masrah al-Taqous* [The Zar: Ritual Theater], 52.

An Egyptian Diagnostic Ceremony[275]

This is the ritual most Egyptians think of when they hear the word "zar." But of the three types, these gatherings can be the most diverse! And since there is no central body that governs the zar or its practices, sheikhat are free to do as they please—meaning everything is increased or decreased according to finances. For example, poor zars tend to have only one band, simple sacrifices (rabbits, chickens, or pigeons), one box of low-grade incense, and few tips, while wealthy ones offer three bands, sumptuous costumes, plentiful high grade incense, a ram or cow in sacrifice, and enough tips to feed the sheikha and her musicians for a year.

Nevertheless, all Egyptian diagnostic rituals have certain elements in common: incense, trance dancing, and an animal sacrifice to the possessing spirit (which participants later eat in a communal meal). The center of attention, the patient or *ayana*—"the sick one"—is generally a married (or divorced) woman (spirits rarely ride virgins) who enters into an agreement with, i.e., "marries," her possessor during the ceremony. As the "bride" (*arousa*), she usually wears white, unless her spirit prefers otherwise.

The sheikha, the female master of ceremonies, is another shared feature of zar rituals (men do occasionally lead zar rituals, but in Egypt this is not the norm). And because the sheikha, too, is possessed, she is ideally suited to communicate with the Invisible world and mediate the tricky negotiations between unwitting host and disgruntled zar. The terms and conditions she arranges will be sealed in blood, so she had better know her stuff. She is also the ceremony's "producer" or organizer, and, as such, supervises preparations. During the ritual, she usually wears a simple, bright white embroidered galabeya and a white, heavily perfumed tarha that slightly covers her face.[276]

For those of you unfamiliar with Egyptian customs, wedding celebrations in Egypt invariably begin with an entrance procession called a *zuffa*, where family and friends usher the bride and groom into the reception hall, often led by a belly dancer. Special bands provide zuffa procession music (there is even a specific rhythm), and guests, with or without candles, will *zaghareet* (ululate) to announce their joy to the world. Egyptian diagnostic zars also use zuffas to escort brides into a ritual space—whenever a new

---

275 The following information is from personal experience, along with *Az-Zar: Masrah al-Taqous* [The Zar: Ritual Theater] by Al-Aleemi and *Women's Medicine* by Lewis et al.

276 For more information about the role and activities of the sheikha, please see appendix 3.

band begins their set—which can mean as many as three zuffas per ritual! Also similar to weddings is the great care expended in setting up and decorating the ritual spaces. But instead of constructing an elaborate "throne" and stage for the bride and groom, a zar's main focal point is the *kursi*, the spirit throne, where the Invisible "spouse-to-be" is expected to witness the proceedings.

The diagnostic zar often starts with the Harim Masri band, similar to the weekly hadarat I described back in chapter 3. The Harim Masri generally begin their set by singing *"Allahuma Sulli ala al-Nabi"* ("In the Name of God Pray to the Prophet") as the arousa, dressed in bridal white and covered in ornaments, waits outside. Carrying a *duff* (hand drum) upside down and full of tips for the band, she is paraded into the room by guests brandishing lit candles and zaghareeting, dancing, drumming, and singing. They accompany her three times around the kursi with the sheikha leading the way, swinging an incense burner as she recites the Fowatih:[277]

> In the name of God, I rely on God, all things are from the hand of God. The Fatihah to the Prophet, to those beloved of the Prophet, the friends of the Prophet and all who belong to the Prophet and pray to him. Oh my masters, hold my hand, for the sake of the Prophet, my guide. Take this incense smoke and give her a sign from the Prophet, may peace be upon him.[278]

The procession ends with the arousa center-stage in the middle of the dance floor, the sheikha's left hand on her head, the incense burner swinging in the sheikha's right. A heavily scented fog engulfs the patient and thoroughly infuses her clothes, hair, and skin with protective fragrance. Individual body parts are catered to next: right hand, left hand, feet, and under her clothes, until finally, after stepping three times over the burner, she is ushered to a seat of honor.

There is an established order as to how the jinn must be called. Zar have ranks, just as humans do, and tempers flare if the lowest are called first. The Elders must be respected before the arousa's spirits, or those of her relatives, can be called. After proper acknowledgment, the bands that are present at the ritual will cycle through their repertoires according

---

277   The Fowatih is the Egyptian zar opening, similar to the Quran's opening, the Fatihah.

278   Al-Aleemi, *Az-Zar: Masrah al-Taqous* [The Zar: Ritual Theater], 37.

to requests and the sheikha's recommendations. Many chants are call-and-response, so guests often participate as well. Each band specializes in particular spirits according to their origin, although the Harim Masri also sing chants for Bedouin, Arab, and Indian entities as well as those from Southern Egypt. Some of this group's best-known songs are for the spirits Mama Sultan, Ruma Nagdi, Abou Danfa, and Amir al-Hag.[279]

The tumboura band, which plays second, is also referred to as *al-Kheit*, "the strings," after its principal instrument, or *al-Baraabira*, because its Sudanese and Nubian members are dark skinned. They wear Sudanese thobes for formal occasions, but not for zar hadarat. They, too, begin their set with a zuffa, which is far more elaborate than the Harim Masri's. The group's dance leaders, the *sutari*[280] (or *sitri*) enter first (one or two), rattling mangour and *shakhaleel*, followed by three *afriqi* or "feathered ones." These two young women and a man dance naked except for multicolored feathers around their hips and multitudes of long necklaces hanging to their waists. The man also wears a gold crown and gilded metal pieces over his shoulders, knees, and the backs of his hands. The arousa follows them, traditionally in a cream-colored galabeya, again holding the tips duff, with the top of the tumboura (played by the musician behind her) resting on her shoulder. Then come the drummers and guests, all zaghareeting as the chorus sings:

> Celebrate, beauties ... Welcome to you ... celebrate ... We come to your home ... How lucky you are ... This happiness is your happiness, beauties ... We hold candles, oh beauties ... This happiness is yours ... Tonight is at your home, oh beauties ... [281]

---

279 Please see the spirit lists in appendix 4. I have recorded and translated many chants over the years, and on my album *The Zar: Trance Music for Women* (see bibliography), Ruma Nagdi can be heard on track 11. Abou Danfa is on track 1 of *Zar 2: Tumboura*. The lyrics of chants are often incomprehensible, even to ordinary Egyptians, since zar rituals are infused with vocabulary from across Africa and the Middle East, particularly Ethiopia, Sudan, and Nigeria, which is not surprising given the cult's origins and geographic diversity.

280 Each group has a dance leader who encourages participants to keep going until they reach trance. Traditionally, tumboura bands had two sutari, but nowadays, for financial reasons, one is the norm.

281 Al-Aleemi, *Az-Zar: Masrah al-Taqous* [The Zar: Ritual Theater], 38–41.

Cult members believe that Bilal, a former half-African slave during Muhammad's time,[282] used the tumboura to chant the Muslim call to prayer, the *adnan*. This band is therefore the highlight of the ceremony because it is believed the asyad (spirit masters) inspire the tumboura player, or sunjuk, directly. The lyre's strings are difficult to tune, however, so if the sunjuk is unskilled, they may be off-key or, worse, not strummed at all and simply used for percussion. Other group members play tabla sudani, shakhaleel, rattles made from empty aerosol cans filled with pebbles (or kashkash), and mangour. Men or women may play the mangour according to regional custom: the sheikha, the patient, or the sutari. Their sound is extremely effective at inducing trance.

The sacrifice, nowadays usually fowl, happens while this band plays. Once everyone enters, the feathered women and the musicians prepare the space by throwing salt on the floor. The sheikha silences the crowd and has the bride kneel before the incense burner. The animals are brought in for her to clean their beaks and wings, cense them, and apologize for their deaths. Circling the arousa, she will then chant:

"In the name of God the Almighty on High, God of the divine throne, obey him
you disbelievers, forgiveness is the family of forgiveness—they are good."[283]

Each zar spirit requires a particular animal in sacrifice, although the extended processions of sacrificial beasts described by Eugenie Le Brun no longer occur. Islamic fundamentalists put a stop to them ages ago. Yet the act of slaughtering to release a life force and its blood is still very much a part of the zar—and the Islamic faith, for that matter. Blood runs thick in Middle Eastern streets for Eid[284] when the faithful butcher sheep to honor Abraham. Pious Muslims share their animal's flesh with the poor, whereas zar sacrifices are cooked and shared with participants. The blood is left for the Invisibles. Today, the arousa no longer drinks some—even though, as you saw in Eugenie Le Brun's first story, this used to be an essential part of the ritual. Now it is enough to dab some on the arousa's forehead or smear her dress with it, a process called *tazfeer* in zar parlance, "to soil something with blood." The ritual is based on the ancient belief that God and other Invisibles require that food, or something of value, be given up in return for assistance.

---

282   Bilal's mother was a captured Abyssinian (Ethiopian) princess put into slavery.

283   Al-Aleemi, *Az-Zar: Masrah al-Taqous* [The Zar: Ritual Theater], 37.

284   Eid is the Islamic festival that commemorates God sparing Abraham's son Isaac.

After this prayer to God and ritual apology, the sheikha then has the arousa circle the kursi (or walk in front if space is limited) seven times while she beseeches the zar of honor to accept the arousa's gift. If Yawra is the possessing spirit, for example, the musicians will play his chant while the sheikha censes his two red pigeons, placing one on each of the arousa's shoulders, then both on her head, and finally one in each hand for the arousa to dance with. Afterwards, the animals' throats are ritually slit and their blood collected for smearing on the arousa's forehead, cheeks, and hands (sometimes even elbows, thighs, and belly). The slaughter complete, the incense burner is once again passed around the room and the spirits are invoked. Whiskey and cigarettes are shared (if called for) and the musicians play while guests enjoy the offerings and each other's company.

When the time is right, Sitt ak-Kibeera, the Great Lady, is honored. After the crowd is silenced, the arousa is brought center-stage and kneels in a prayer position on a white sheet. The sheikha then covers her with a black cloth and swings the incense burner around her head as she incants a prayer. The singer and sunjuk play the Great Lady's chant while the arousa's chest and shoulders are shaken in time to the music. Eventually, the arousa kneels upright and slowly sways to the beat until the black sheet is removed—and the afriqi pull her up to dance. This group's spirits are the zar's most well known: Yawra Bey, Roukash, Ad-Deir, Sitt-ak-Kabira, Gado, and Saleela. Yawra Bey possesses so many women in Egypt that it is rare to attend a ritual where he is not represented. His chant is usually sung in typical call-and-response fashion, while the arousa, wearing Yawra's clothes and imitating his gestures, dances and flirts with the audience.[285]

Simply sacrificing to spirits is not enough to cure a patient's ills, however. The sheikha must find the root of an entity's discontent before she can pacify it into agreeing to a cease-fire; i.e., get it to agree to stop torturing its host. Ultimately, she must find a compromise that everyone involved can consent to and abide by. This is the tricky part—getting the spirit to vocalize its grievances and eventually agree (via the host's mouth) to a truce before a room full of witnesses. And so the struggle to enter possession trance ensues—and the "swaying" begins in earnest.

---

285   To listen to Yawra Bey's call-and-response chant, go to tracks 4 and 20 on my album *Zar 2: Tumboura.*

The difficulty of relinquishing control and descending into trance is interpreted in a zar as a struggle between the arousa and her possessor. Initial facial expressions indicate resistance as her movements become more violent and union with the spirit approaches. Eventually, however, exhaustion and crises overcome her, she loses consciousness, and the spirit takes control. Once she opens her eyes again, she is calm and silent, but most importantly, possessed. From this point on, whoever speaks is not the arousa but the zar, and the patient cannot be held responsible for anything the spirit might say. The sheikha will swing the incense burner around her head, stare into her eyes, and urge her to confess everything. The spirit may not answer with words; it may use gestures instead—particularly if the host is shy, cautious, or a domestic abuse victim. For example, a woman may subtly turn her wedding band and grimace to indicate problems with her husband. But more often than not, the zar openly declares its rules and demands (such as sleeping alone on a certain day of the week—i.e., no sex that night). The sheikha then negotiates until the conditions are palatable to all concerned. When the parties finally agree and the spirit audibly accepts—an act witnessed by jinn and humans alike—the contract (*aqd*) is celebrated with great fanfare. The band, still playing the zar's chant, gradually increases their tempo and intensity as other women join the arousa on the dance floor. All become enraptured and, with a final bang on the drums, collapse to the ground unconscious. Swinging her incense burner in the ensuing silence, the sheikha walks among the fallen, rotating their heads with her hands, whispering in their ears, and sprinkling rose water on their faces and clothes. Afterwards, during a well-deserved intermission, everyone recuperates by sharing a meal made from the sacrificial animal.

Once an agreement is reached, the arousa is transformed—from miserable to happy. To celebrate and thank God, she will change into a green galabeya and dance with the Abou al-Ghreit band, or al-Ghreitaniya, a Sufi-inspired all-male group named after a saint buried in Shabeen al-Qanaater, a village north of Cairo where many zar musicians live.[286] Members also wear green to honor their patron saint. In accordance with Islamic tradition, their music does not technically evoke the jinn, but "spirit masters" and the Prophet Muhammad.

---

286   Shabeen al-Qanaater, "of the trains," is near Basous, toward Shoubra al-Kheema in the Qaloubia district.

In addition to tambourine-like frame drums and the traditional Middle Eastern tabla or *darabouka*,[287] members of the Abou al-Ghreit band also play two popular Sufi instruments, the nay (a reed flute) and hand cymbals, adapted into large dish-like finger cymbals known as toura. The cymbalist is also their dance leader. Their music is melodious and emotional, similar to Mevlevi Sufi compositions for "whirling dervishes." The toura player leads this group's *zuffa*, wearing a heavy, multicolored, floor-length *tanoura* skirt over his white galabeya. To everyone's delight, he spins Whirling Dervish style while removing the skirt. The arousa follows him, accompanied by a musician with an incense burner. Some group members have long hair that they whip around, imitating zikr or zar head banging. Others in white galabeyas, green *taraboosh*, and chest sashes carry white pennants inscribed with religious phrases in green.

One of the group's best-known chants is "Why Blame Me, my Friend?" (*"Bitlumni Lay ya Khali?"*).[288] When guests hear it, they often burst into tears, strike their heads, and wail as if a loved one has just died. The lyrics leave no sad thought or unhappy event unturned. And even if the words don't strike a chord, other people's wailing does. Emotional release comes in many forms. A few of the band's other chants are *"As-Salouwat"* ("Prayers"), *"Sayed Bedawi Sheikh al-Arab,"*[289] *"Abdel Salaam al-Maghrabi,"*[290] *"Sayida Zeinab," "Saly ala Mohammad"* ("[God] Protect Mohammad"),[291] and their namesake *"Abou al-Ghreit,"*[292] about a sheikh from the Qalubiya spirit tribe.

You can see how these modern ceremonies differ from the rituals of Eugenie Le Brun's era. Islam, represented in part by the Sufi-inspired Abou al-Ghreit band, has a much larger presence. And while the gatherings are still extremely theatrical,[293] they have been toned down considerably for twenty-first-century sensibilities.

---

287   A goblet drum stretched with fish skin on one side.

288   See Henkesh, *Zar 3: Harim Masri*, Track 12.

289   See Henkesh, *Zar 2: Tumboura*, Track 19.

290   See Henkesh, ibid., Track 18.

291   See Henkesh, *The Zar: Trance Music for Women*, Track 2.

292   See Henkesh, ibid., Track 4.

293   Zar researchers were struck by the theatricality of these ceremonies, to the point where they entitled books *La Possession et ses aspects théâtraux chez les Éthiopiens de Gondar* and *The Zar: Ritual Theater*.

A fourth zar band also exists, Rango, again with Sudanese roots, but it is not as popular in Egypt as the other three. It, too, is named after the group's principle instrument, the *rango*, a marimba or xylophone with wooden keys.

For all-night rituals, each band will normally play for about two to three hours, not including breaks and intermissions. Audience members show their appreciation by dropping *nuqtah* (tips) into the arousa's duff or hand it directly to a group's dance leader when requesting their spirit's "beat." Then, after the bands have finished, everyone will go home—except the arousa. Wearing an amulet the sheikha gives her, usually under her armpit, she will remain secluded, preferably in the same room with the spirits, for a week—on a "zar honeymoon." This means no sex with her husband. Once the week is up, the sheikha will remove the amulet, say a small incantation, and cense her one last time. In the old days, the arousa also marked the occasion by a purifying dip in the Nile.

And then the arousa begins her new life as an Invisible bride.

In Egyptian Nubia, zar traditions are more Sudanese in flavor. Only one set of musicians play and a ceremony's length varies considerably. If the hosts are poor and the occasion is a simple annual reconfirmation, a one-night celebration with a chicken or a couple of pigeons suffices. But if a seven-day diagnostic ritual is required, more animals must be sacrificed:

A white or black cock is killed over the patient's head on the third day at exactly noon and the blood smeared over her face, hands and legs. In the evening or the following day, the fowl is cooked and the sheikh shares it with the patient. On the seventh day the patient ceremoniously straddles the lamb or sheep holding the slaughtering knife in her hand. After five piasters are placed in the animal's mouth, the sheikh cuts its throat. The five piasters are then put in a cloth and tied around the patient's right hand. The hot blood is rubbed over her body and face and mixed in a potion with cloves, henna and water. After drinking this, the patient ritually steps across the dead animal seven times.[294]

Nubian audience members also participate. They, too, signal a spirit's presence by trembling in their seats, then make their way to the dance arena to sway to exhaustion and collapse. Nubian entities also request jewelry, new clothes, expensive foods, bizarre

---

294   Kennedy, *Nubian Ceremonial Life*, 210.

items, or out-of-the-ordinary behavior before they will depart.[295] When this happens, the dancer's loved ones will gather around to help pacify it. During extended rituals, Nubian sheikhs demonstrate their supernatural powers by hosting entities that diagnose illnesses, tell fortunes, or require elaborate costumes.

Once the principal sacrifice is made, the zayran are considered satisfied; however, the ritual continues until the animal is turned into the main dish of the final feast. Unpossessed guests don't eat any, however, for fear of attracting spirits. Afterwards, the arousa and other hosts bathe in the Nile, where any refuse is disposed of (downstream) to avoid spirit contagion. Strict tradition requires the arousa remain secluded forty days, similar to Nubian newlyweds.[296]

Reconfirmation and the Youm bi Leyla Ceremony

The initial diagnostic "marriage" ritual described above is only the tip of the zar cult iceberg. Once a woman sacrifices to her "master" and becomes a member, she must host a reconfirmation ceremony complete with sacrifice every year—a Youm bi Leyla, "a day and a night"—and attend those of others, in addition to weekly hadarat. Modern rituals usually begin after sunset and continue for twenty-four hours. The date is set in advance and participation is mandatory for friends, family, and those cured by the same sheikha. The first zar Eugenie Le Brun described was a reconfirmation ceremony.

Who Are the Zar? A Zar Pantheon

Finally, you get to meet the zar! Young and old, male and female, pious and pagan, aristocratic and simple, friendly or not, these entities are a strange mix of spirit and soul, of jinn and ancestor, of daemon and ghost. They assume many shapes—or no shape at all—when they ride the wind or their human hosts. In sickness and in health, until death do they part...

To understand who Egyptian zar spirits are, though, you need to know a little about where they came from—their African heritage—and, in the next chapter, their Islamic veneer. Africa is home to a number of ancient possession cultures; zar is but one of

---

295   Kennedy, *Nubian Ceremonial Life*, 207.
296   Ibid., 208.

many. And even though most modern zayran can be traced to three and perhaps four major traditions (Ethiopian zar, Sudanese tumboura, Nigerian bori, and perhaps the Yoruba orisha), it is possible that, once upon a time, they all had a common ancestor—similar to our human "mitochondrial Eve."

To test this theory, let's compare the African possession cults connected to the Egyptian zar. I mentioned earlier that researchers believe the zar originated in Ethiopia and Sudan, but that it was also influenced by West African traditions, notably the bori of Hausaland (the 75,000 square miles that straddle the Niger/Nigeria border) and the orisha of the Yoruba from coastal Nigeria, Benin, and Togo. Today, the Yoruba number about fifty million people and their possession spirits are perhaps Africa's best known, because of their influence on the New World religions of Santería, Umbanda, and Candomblé.

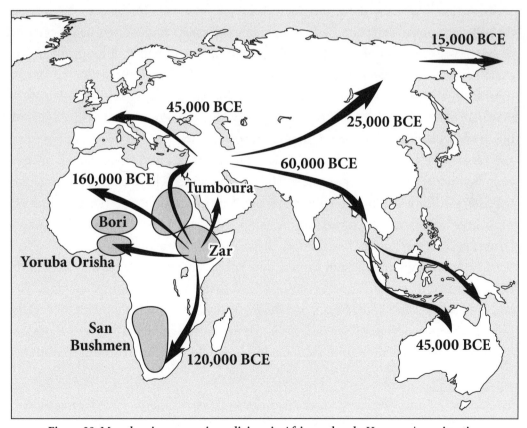

Figure 29: Map showing possession religions in Africa and early *Homo sapiens* migration

If all these possession cults share a common origin, they should share similar traits, right? And they do. To begin with, they all predate Islam and their members are mainly women. And even though names and ritual details vary, their underlying raison d'être is the same—healing. Patients enter these sisterhoods after being diagnosed "with spirit." And once initiated, they devote considerable energy into placating their entities: they wear their clothes, sacrifice to them, and allow them to manifest in their bodies. And most, from east to west and north to south, use some form of trance dancing to communicate with them.

Let's dig a little deeper to see if there are other similarities among Africa's possession cults.

Ethiopia/Abyssinia

Sadly, far less is written about the zar in Ethiopia—the zar's birthplace—than about other African possession cults. Besides *Women's Medicine*, I found only one other study, based on research from the 1930s–1950s, specifically dedicated to Ethiopian zar: Michael Leiris's *La Possession et ses aspects théâtraux chez les Éthiopiens de Gondar* (which translates to *Possession and Its Theatrical Aspects of the Gondar Ethiopians*). Of course, new books are released every day, so I may have missed recent publications. According to what I have read, though, Ethiopian spirits are divided into two main types: zar and *ganen*. The zar are not considered evil or murderous, but they do punish offenses by inflicting nervous or psychosomatic illnesses. Individuals have names, personalities, habits, and histories, similar to Egyptian zar, and are human in origin (ancestor spirits). Most believe in God. The *ganen*, on the other hand, are demons of divine origin, or "bad angels" as the country's Orthodox Christians call them.[297]

In practice, Ethiopian zayran include pure spirits, ancestor souls, and hybrids of the two, organized in social hierarchies according to their maternal lineages, religion, likes, and dislikes. Most live in the brush, particularly rocky or wooded areas, with the females being the more malevolent. Tradition has it that zayran descend from Eve. Apparently, she hid half her thirty children from God, fearing he would take them away. To punish her,

---

297   Leiris, *La Possession et ses aspects théâtraux chez les Éthiopiens de Gondar,* 12. My translation from the French.

God decreed that the hidden would remain so, with "brother governing brother."[298] This is why the zar are hidden and humans rule the Earth—*or*, why the zar rule invisibly over humans; it depends on how you interpret the phrase. A proverb takes the story further. Eve hid the fairest, brightest, and most pleasant, which explains why humans are disagreeable and the Hidden better in every way. This is also the explanation given when zar become difficult or hurt their "horses"—human cruelty is to blame, not the reverse.[299]

Zar and their progeny come in many shapes and sizes and are divided into two houses: right and left. The right house is composed of forty Amharic Christian males that spent fourteen years in Jerusalem for religious training. The right house rules over the left since it has the only entities strong enough to make the others obey. This is also why all great zar healers must be possessed by at least one of these Christian males. The left house has ninety-eight members, which include males "without pity" and females.[300]

Hybrid offspring between zar and *ganen* include the *welleg*, the *jenn* (evil water spirits), and the *kabere* from Tigre, which are the progeny of zar and *jenn*. Other entities are the *sotalay*, envious evil eye forces that cause spontaneous abortions, sterility, and the *ayna tela*, the "eye of the shadow," which obstruct diagnosis and drive hosts crazy. There are also the *buda*, evil entities that attack without provocation and invisibly drink human blood. Victims remain physically intact but their souls or life force are drained away. If *buda* choose to be visible, they appear either as humans during the day or as hyenas at night. All these entities are difficult to distinguish from pure zayran, however, because they invade when zayran invade, or possess zayran in the same manner that zayran possess humans.[301]

A few well-known individuals are:

Abaras: The mother of the *kabere* spirits from Tigray, the northernmost
region of Ethiopia. The Adwa *jenn* kidnapped her and forced her
to live with them in a lake. She began to manifest in the late 1800s,

---

298 Leiris, *La Possession et ses aspects théâtraux chez les Éthiopiens de Gondar*, 13, my translation from the French.
299 Ibid., 16, my translation.
300 Ibid., 13–14, my translation.
301 Ibid., 14, my translation.

around the time of the 1896 battle of Adwa, when Ethiopian troops defeated an Italian invasion force.

Sasitu, Enquelal, and Dira: Three female zayran who were once the daughters of Emperor Yasu (1680–1704), a great *dabtara* or "clerk," who could invoke spirits.

Zaba Esrael, Zaba Dawit, and Zaba Estifanos: The three sons of Emperor Kaleb, "sons of the night," who reigned humanely over men at Aksoum during the sixth century CE.

Waley: The spirits of Muslim saints.[302]

The pure, powerful males "from Jerusalem" are among the cult's favorites. They only cause minor illnesses in humans or livestock, intervene with other spirits on behalf of patients, and don't unduce trance or request sacrifices. Ethiopian zar may also be inherited. For example, certain powerful protector entities are passed down from mother to daughter for seven generations. The importance of women in zar beliefs is reinforced in rural areas where traditional gatherings are not always possible. A family's matriarch becomes the repository for the clan's zayran, which is why her spirits are consulted first when someone falls sick.

Even though zar are not maleficent by nature and their attacks are supposedly in retribution for human wrongdoing or trespassing, certain seasons, hours, places, and circumstances are propitious for possession. As the saying goes, zar are like bees—they hide in the rocks during winter but come out in spring. Apparently, they sting like bees, too! And even though these spirits travel and hunt throughout the warm season, two periods are especially dangerous: September, after the rainy season when yellow meskel bloom,[303] and March, when the first clouds of a new rainy season return. During the day, zar are active

---

302 Lewis et al., *Women's Medicine*, 38.

303 Meskel, or Yadey Abeba, are yellow daisy-like flowers that bloom in spring and stop growing in the dry season. Ethiopia, similar to Egypt, has only three seasons: dry, rainy, and growing. September to February is the dry season (*bega*), followed by the first of two rainy seasons (*belg*) in March and April. May is a hot dry month that preceeds another longer rainy season (*kremt*) in June, July, and August, which causes Egypt's annual Nile inundation. The coldest temperatures generally occur in December or January and the hottest in March, April, or May.

at noon, before sunset, and between midnight and three o'clock in the morning. They are drawn to rivers and bodies of water in general, reed beds, the brush, market places (sound familiar?), and enticing circumstances: traveling, defecating, proximity to someone being ridden by a zar, and any activity involving blood or incense.

The principle reason for possession is vengeance for an offense—and there are many no-no's. Contempt is high on the list, either direct insolence toward a spirit or a lack of respect for the cult or its members, and in the case of sect members, neglecting one's spirit. Hence, Ethiopian zar rituals are held to pacify an offended entity—similar to zar rituals in Egypt, Sudan, and Nigeria.

When a zar illness strikes, the Ethiopian equivalent of a sheikha will preside over a diagnostic ritual called a *wadaga*. Accompanied by chanting, clapping, and percussion instruments, she will encourage a patient to do the gurri, possession trance dance movements that signal a zar's presence or departure from a patient's body. Specifics depend on the spirit, but common movements are rapid head circles, sometimes including the rib cage, pendular back-to-front torso swings, and stylized Muslim prayer prostrations for Islamic spirits. When the healer feels a spirit is ready, she will urge it to reveal its name—a feat that usually requires numerous sessions. But eventually, in a choppy roar, the entity will recite a *fukkara*, or "war theme" (in zar parlance, an extended account of its qualities and accomplishments).

Once a zar publicly identifies itself, the healer will question it about the patient's wrongdoings, a process known as *falaffala*, "to flay or extract something from the flesh," or, in zar speak, "to interrogate." This is a delicate operation, since other spirits may also be present and evil entities enjoy making things difficult. Ultimately, though, the healer must convince the zar to peacefully coexist with its host in exchange for annual (at least) sacrifices, jewelry, regular opportunities to visit (i.e., "ride its horse")—and occasional gifts to the healer. She may also prescribe that patients adopt animals in their homes, such as chickens, for the zar to inhabit instead. And she may even attempt to transfer the entity to someone else or replace it with a benign one capable of fighting off the others.[304]

---

304   Leiris, *La Possession et ses aspects théâtraux chez les Éthiopiens de Gondar,* 15–22, my translation from the French.

Sudan

Far more has been written about the possession cults of Sudan than those of Ethiopia. Besides the multiple studies in *Women's Medicine,* other excellent sources are Janice Boddy's well-known book, *Wombs and Alien Spirits: Women, Men and the Zar Cult in Northern Sudan* and John Kennedy's compilation, *Nubian Ceremonial Life.* Before 2011, Sudan was Africa's largest country, encompassing nearly a million square miles (five times the state of Texas) until the southern portion seceded as South Sudan. The country still shares borders with Egypt and Libya to the north, Ethiopia and Eritrea to the east, and the Republic of Chad and the Central African Republic to the west. But to the south, where it once neighbored Kenya, Uganda, and the Republic of Congo, it now borders South Sudan.

Along with Egypt, Sudan is "the gift of the Nile." Most of the country's inhabitants live along the river's banks, or those of its tributaries, and drink its water. Sudan also shares Egypt's long history of indigenous civilizations, beginning with the Neolithic settlement of Nabta Playa in Egyptian Nubia[305] with its astronomical megaliths thousands of years older than Stonehenge.[306] The Nile River was one of two ancient trade routes between the East African tropics and the North. Sudan's religious beliefs reflect these ancient roots. Even today, they are split between ancient animism, particularly in the south, and Islam, which entered the country gradually during the Middle Ages. At first only the ruling classes and Arab foreigners adhered to Muhammad's teachings, but when Sufi preachers and their fraternities (*taruq*) arrived during the mid-seventeenth century, Islam gradually spread to the masses. The situation changed abruptly, however, in 1821 when Muhammad Ali and the Ottomans conquered the country. The new Turkish-Egyptian political framework splintered Sudan's traditional tribal hierarchies and a tsunami of imposed alien customs swept away eons of cultural stability. Sixty years of Ottoman rule followed, until an Islamic revolution, the Mahdiya, evicted the invaders in 1881. Not for long. Seven years later, the British claimed the country as a colony until 1956.

---

305   Nubia is the region between the first and sixth cataracts of the Nile. It begins just past Aswan in southern Egypt and ends after Meroe, but well before Khartoum, the country's capital.

306   Nabta Playa's astronomical megaliths are thought to have been erected around 6200 BCE. Stonehenge's megaliths are thought to date from 2500 BCE.

But what does all this history have to do with the zar?

The acute emotional and cultural upheaval that followed these nineteenth-century invasions ignited severe anxiety among the Sudanese. Zar healers suddenly found themselves treating far more than traditional fertility illnesses; women, in particular, desperately needed a coping mechanism to adjust to the severe new Islamic restrictions. Spirits reflecting this trauma began to manifest—and persist even today, almost two hundred years later. As a result, five different zar cults evolved: *zar-suakin* (a favorite of upper-class women with links to the Arabian Peninsula); *zar-bori* from West Africa; *zar-habashi* from Ethiopia and East Africa; the indigenous *zar-nuqara* from Sudan's southwest Azande tribe; and *zar-tumboura*, also from the south, practiced by slaves, concubines, and conscripted "pagan" soldiers forced into the Ottoman army.[307] Researchers now group tumboura and nuqara together as native branches of this ancient African cult. They hypothesize that Azande slaves transformed their native ancestor worship into a possession cult to treat the severe hysteria and mental illnesses (such as total paralysis and lunacy) that slavery induced.[308]

Today, zar-bori is the most widespread of the five. The Sudanese consider it feminine, cold, and white. Its main musical instrument is the *daluka* drum, chants are said in Arabic, and its leaders are usually female. Zar-tumboura, on the other hand, is male, hot, and black. Its musicians play the tumboura and mangour and sing in Rotona (a Nubian language); while "bori plays inside the house … tumboura plays in the sun, in the fire."[309] The cult has a hierarchical structure under a *sanjak,* an Ottoman military term for the leader of a detachment of soldiers. Zar-nuqara is less frequent and mainly practiced in South and West Sudan near Wau. Believed by some to be humanity's original possession cult, it is named after the group's large double-sided drums.[310]

Sudanese and Egyptian zars have much in common. Persistent nebulous illnesses (particularly mental disorders) or chronic bad luck are seen as the work of supernatural forces (the evil eye, sorcery, zar, etc.). Ceremonies loosely follow Egyptian formats—although, as

---

307   Lewis et al., *Women's Medicine*, 93.

308   Ibid., 112.

309   Ibid., 105.

310   Boddy, *Wombs and Alien Spirits*, 155.

Janice Boddy points out, there is no such thing as a typical zar ritual. Diagnosis begins when a religious figure—a sheikha/ummiya or a *sitt-al-ilba*, a "lady of the box" (a zar adept who uses incense and an *attar* to discover an entity's identity)—feels a patient's ills might be zar-related, which is verified through a ritual called "opening the box," *ifta-al-ilba*. For several hours, or even days, a sheikha will fumigate the patient with mixtures from her sacred tin box to see if any elicit a response.[311]

If uncertainty persists, the sheikha may suggest a *tajruba* to test the patient's reaction to different spirit chants, or "threads" (*khuyut*); when sung, threads are said to be "pulled." For three nights, experienced adepts accompany the ayana while the sheikha cycles the musicians through the main zar repertoire—in essence conducting a private healing session for her. Diagnosis is only complete, however, when the patient and her family publicly acknowledge her possession and pledge to hold a full-blown ceremony—when funds permit, which may take months.[312] By then, possession trance is almost guaranteed, since the patient will have already learned about her spirit and how to enter trance.

Traditional healing rituals last seven days in Nubia (northern Sudan), except Fridays, the Islamic equivalent to Christian Sundays. They may be shorter, though, depending on finances or the illness. As in Egypt, the arousa will be heavily perfumed, in white, and adorned with jewelry, henna, and khol. Up to a hundred women may attend, who all inhale heavy amounts of incense smoke.[313] The sheikh or sheikha, depending on the cult, is also possessed and may change costumes multiple times as her spirits manifest. An accomplished percussionist, she and other adepts play *dalukat* (earthenware drums stretched with goatskin), *nugarishan* (a brass mortar that sounds like a deep cowbell when hit), and upside-down metal washtubs called *tisht*. She may choose, to a limited degree, the order in which threads are "pulled," but she must adhere to the spirit hierarchy to avoid offending anyone. Southern sheikhat with slave ancestry are considered particularly powerful because of their deeper knowledge of (animistic) magic and sorcery.[314] The best are also gifted orators with a flair for drama and suspense.

---

311 Lewis et al., "The Story of a Tin Box," *Women's Medicine*, 100–117.
312 Boddy, *Wombs and Alien Spirits*, 154–56.
313 Kennedy, *Nubian Ceremonial Life*, 206.
314 Ibid., 212.

The Sudanese zar pantheon is quite rich. Similar to Egyptians, Nubians are devout Muslims and believe the jinn are as the Quran and the hadith describe them—extremely mobile entities partial to rivers, canals, mountains, deserts, dirt, garbage, and ashes. They inhabit empty rooms but prefer warm-blooded bodies, and reciting the first line of the Fatiha (the opening surah of the Quran) dispels them. The Sudanese divide the jinn into three subcategories: white, black, and red. All possess humans but cause different symptoms:

White: These good guys are mainly Muslim and famous for helping Islamic holy men. Their possession is not serious since they only cause quirky or eccentric behavior.

Black: These bad guys are mean and nasty and don't believe in Allah. They also smell bad. Hosting them causes painful, fatal illnesses or incurable madness. (Occasionally, a violent exorcism may expel them, but the trauma and injury this causes, if not outright death, makes the procedure extremely risky). These spirits work with *fakirs*, powerful unorthodox healers who deal in black magic, to find lost objects and see into the spirit world or the future.

Red: These are the zar, also known as *rowhan al-ahmar*, or "red winds." Pleasure-seeking and capricious, they like pretty things, the good life, cleanliness, and perfume. When they possess humans, they may cause mild illnesses but never death. They are neither good guys nor bad guys but—like humans—a bit of both. Red is also the color of blood, which attracts them, particularly menstrual blood, hence their preference for female hosts. Because of their bloodlust, they are often implicated in fertility problems—the inability to conceive, uncontrolled bleeding, miscarriages, etc. Zar are linked through the maternal line, the line of uterine blood, which is why they may be inherited from mother to child.[315]

---

315   Boddy, *Wombs and Alien Spirits*, 187.

The Sudanese believe in seven main zar tribes: Darawish, Pashawat, Khawajat, Habashi, Blacks, Arabs, and Sitat (Women). Individual members come and go, with newcomers appearing in dreams or with current events and old ones dying out as they possess fewer hosts. For a list and description of these spirits, please see appendix 4, A Zar Entity Compendium. It adheres to Janice Boddy's Sudanese hierarchy, although as she herself wrote, the categories are flexible.

Nigeria and the Bori

It is now time to leave the Nile and travel west to another African river and its basin: the Niger, homeland of the Hausa and Magawaza in the north and the Yoruba to the south (among many others). It is also home to bori and orisha, West African possession spirits. As I mentioned, zar-bori is considered the largest indigenous spirit-healing cult in Africa—where Invisibles from both sides of the continent unite to manipulate, or cure, their human "horses." I have not actually visited this region but have taken the following information from sources that have, mainly A. J. N. Tremearne (*The Ban of the Bori* and other books), the authors of *Women's Medicine*, and Adeline Masquelier, who wrote about the Mawri, a subgroup of Niger's Hausa, in *Prayer Has Spoiled Everything*.

Tremearne (1877–1915), the oldest of my sources, was stationed in Nigeria with the British army from 1903–1910 and spent considerable time researching the country's cultures and religions. He found no evidence that bori (which means "to boil," but how it became associated with spirits is unclear[316]) originated with the Hausa (now mainly Muslims) or the Magazawa ("fire-worshippers" or pagans),[317] but he did find that the cult existed prior to Islam's fifteenth-century arrival. Similar to the Oyo/Yoruba and other pagan cultures, the Magazawa believe in a supreme omnipresent and all-powerful Creator entity. They differ with monotheistic religions, however, in how this entity interacts with humans. To them, the Creator is remote (much like Einstein's God) and prefers to leave contact with Earth's inhabitants to the spirit world, the *iskoki* (pl. for "winds"), or bori. The Magawaza divide their spirits into two categories: tamed farm

---

316   Tremearne, *The Ban of Bori*, 24.

317   The Magawaza are non-Muslim Haussa, who are different from the non-Muslim Arna/Asna of Hausa-speaking Niger to the north. Lewis et al., *Women's Medicine*, 62.

dwellers, *gona* (or *gari* in Masquelier's Niger study), and untamed bush denizens, *daji*. The non-Muslim Hausa also recognize two types of bori: white urban Muslim spirits that cause mild diseases and black pagan bush entities that inflict serious illnesses or misfortune—much like the Arab distinction between Muslim and non-Muslim jinn.[318]

Tremearne hypothesized that bori were an amalgam of the region's ancient animistic deities[319] adapted to Islamic prohibitions—which included a ban on "frivolous" music and non-military drumming (hence the use of overturned basins [*calabash*] instead of drums for rituals). This certainly applies to northern Hausaland, near Ader in south Niger, where once upon a time mythic cave dwellers spoke to spirits and practiced an ancient religion called *azna*. Sometime before the 1700s, Hausa-speaking hunters adopted this belief system, and three centuries later the religion is still active.[320] During the late 1980s, Adeline Masquelier and several contributors to *Women's Medicine* studied bori worship in south Niger. They found that although the spirits and rituals differed from Tremearne's time, bori worship still bridged the gap between *azna* and Islam by incorporating entities from both.[321]

Figure 30: Bori

The rapid change that occurred during Tremearne's time was provoked by two factors: the spread of Islam and Europe's colonial aspirations, particularly those of England and France. England laid claim to Nigeria in 1885, while France made Niger a colony in 1922. Almost immediately, bori pantheons throughout the region began to reflect these national traumas—as can be seen in the spirit lists in appendix 4.

---

318   Lewis et al., *Women's Medicine*, 43.

319   *The Ban of Bori*, 294.

320   Lewis et al., *Women's Medicine*, 66–69.

321   Masquelier, *Prayer Has Spoiled Everything*, 125.

Political upheaval aside, the cult's basic concepts remained the same, however. According to Tremearne, the Hausa believe every human houses six ethereal beings that together create consciousness: the soul (*kuruwa*), which resides in the heart (although Masquelier was told the head); a life force (*rai*); a familiar bori of the same sex (similar to the Egyptian qarin) that mediates human and jinn affairs; a temporary bori of the opposite sex that leaves after marriage; and two angels (*malaika*)—one over the right shoulder, the other over the left—that record good or evil thoughts. The *kuruwa* and the *rai* join the fetus in the womb, while the familiar bori attaches after birth. The soul, the bori, and the two angels travel during sleep (separately), leaving only the *rai* to watch over the body. It is remarkable how similar these entities are to ancient Egypt's six familiar spirits. Pharaonic Egyptians believed the body (*khat*) was inhabited by the *ka*; its astral twin the *ba*, a life force that separates from the body at death (depicted as a bird with a human head); the *khu* and *sahu*, two parts of the immortal soul; the *khaibit* or shadow; and the *ikhu* or breath. All were expected to reunite three thousand years after death, barring catastrophe, to return to life on Earth.

In addition to these "familiars," the *Yan-bori* or "Children of Bori," as initiates are called, believe that multitudes of undetected independent bori known as *aljan* (Arabic for "jinn"), *iblis* (devils), or *iska* (the Ethiopian equivalent of the jinn) also permeate the space around us. Tremearne listed twenty-one Nigerian spirits in *The Tailed Head-Hunters of Nigeria*, sixty-five in *Hausa Superstitions and Customs*, and 241 North African "fusion" entities in *The Ban of the Bori*. As he points out, the bori of Tunisia and Libya (where Hausa were taken as slaves) differed from Nigerian entities because they were based on childhood memories, refined by homeland visitors, and superimposed with forced-fed Arab culture. *Women's Medicine* lists 138 newer bori from Niger's Ader region[322] and *Prayer Has Spoiled Everything* fleshes out prominent Mawri entities from the late 1980s—a pantheon reputedly over 300.[323]

Ultimately, these spirits reflect the cultures and issues, past and present, that have confronted their hosts throughout history. Hence, the bori have become an odd collection of marabouts (Muslim religious teachers), pagan ancestors, child-ghosts, hostile

322   Lewis et al., *Women's Medicine*, 71–80.
323   Masquelier, *Prayer Has Spoiled Everything*, 88.

foreign tribe members, Semitic jinn, nature gods, totems, and fetishes.[324] According to myth, many of them dwell behind the concealed red walls of Jan Gari, the Red City, in the Red Country between Aghat and Asben (legendary cities in Niger's desert). They emerge at night to roam with the wind, and occasionally to inhabit inanimate objects, *tsere,* or humans. During ceremonies, individual spirits are called with their favorite incense, colors, and sacrifices, similar to the zar. They announce their presence, when required, by a *kirari,* a boastful description of their merits and accomplishments, ride their humans with characteristic movements, and leave when their hosts sneeze (in some regions, not all). For a list, please see appendix 4.

The process of bori diagnosis is evolving. Recent methods, as described in *Women's Medicine* (from 1969–1972) and *Prayer Has Spoiled Everything,* differ—sometimes dramatically—from the methods Tremearne observed. He interviewed male healers, *boka,* who determined patients' illnesses for them while in trance. The modern Nigerian women described in *Women's Medicine,* however, provided their own diagnosis. Similar to their East African sisters, they showed classic zar possession symptoms: depression, withdrawal, listlessness, mobile pain, or other harbingers of intense psychological stress.[325] During three-day rituals, these women were encouraged to describe what had caused their initial possession (crisis point) by channeling family ancestor spirits. This enabled them to freely vent their complaints via a third party—albeit long dead. Village elders supplied additional testimony by channeling objective "guest spirits."

After an initial diagnosis, patients underwent three-week training programs to learn how to be possessed (by more than ancestor spirits). Seated straight-legged on the ground under a sheet with an incense burner, they inhaled smoke and listened to spirit chants (*wakansa,* from *waka,* "incantation") while rattles were shaken near their ears. The goal was to "feel possessed," an uncontrollable urge to dance. Minor entities were

---

324 Tremearne, *The Ban of the Bori,* 20 and 244.

325 Possession symptoms include fertility problems, accelerated heartbeat, headaches, loss of appetite, nausea, anorexia, dizziness, "mobile pain" (unspecific pain that shifts throughout the body), fits, nervous ticks, perturbed sleep (either too much or too little), coldness or shivering, fainting, lethargy or weakness, nightmares, uncharacteristic behavior, impaired personal relationships, deviations in role behavior, sadness or crying, manic peaks and valleys.

called first (contrary to East African practices): musicians, elephants and hyenas, Fulani pastoralists, serpents, and finally, for comic relief, town "Royals" with their exaggerated or ambiguous sexuality. Favorites included a ruler's over-sexed son, a homosexual Muslim judge, a pompous but insignificant local official, and a frenzied sex-crazed male. Training was only complete after five or six successful manifestations.[326]

Masquelier described a more traditional diagnostic process. Symptoms ranged from mild—stomachaches, headaches, pimples, and rashes—to severe—madness, paralyses, meningitis, etc., with prolonged dazed wandering being common. Possession invariably occurred because a spirit liked someone or it was offended. And similar to the process described in *Women's Medicine*, vocalizing the "offense" was a large part of a woman's therapy.

Masquelier's depiction of "initiation" ceremonies shows them to be almost identical to zar rituals. During extended dance sessions, patients called *amare*, or brides, married their possessors. Musicians cycled through the pantheon's repertoire to see which spirit(s) took control. The music was largely percussive, with singing and violins for melody. And trance occurred in three progressively deeper stages. Only one spirit at a time entered a host and mediums did not remember what happened or feel pain or emotion. Nor were they held responsible for their actions or words. Multiple sacrifices were made. Afterwards, initiates were expected to regularly allow their spirits to mount and penetrate them, buy them appropriate clothes and props, and devote their lives to their new partners.

As for the role of the sheikha, the closest bori equivalent seems to be the Tunisian *arifa*, Knowledgeable One, or *sarauniya*. But generally, a sheikha's duties were performed by two men: a Hausa master of ceremonies—an *uban mufane*, and a medicine dispenser—a concocter of potions or *boka*, who made diagnoses. Before Islam, Nigerian women were considered more potent sorcerers than men and often held positions of authority, even ruling as queens. But as the new religion spread, men took over the roles with power, including boka—even though this particular job had definite drawbacks. According to Tremearne, boka training is quite rigorous and involves copious drug ingestion:

> In order to attain to this position, the candidate must take medicines for three months from the other bokas, potions which will increase his capacity for understanding

---

326   Lewis et al., *Women's Medicine*, 52–53.

drugs, and also teach him how they should be prepared. After that, he offers up a sacrifice of a red cock and a white hen, or more, according to his means, and must then burn incense in the medicine-hut (gidan tsafi) for five nights running, taking care not to go to sleep. On the last night, his eyes are opened, and he sees an aljan without a head, and then various others..., of none of which must he show the slightest sign of fear. Next night he goes into the midst of the forest, and meets the dwarf, Gajere Mai-Dowa, with his bow and arrow in his hand. This bori asks what he wants, and he makes his request, and then Gajere will indicate certain roots which will give him special power in particular cases. He returns to the gidan tsafi, offers another sacrifice and incense, and is then a fully fledged boka.[327]

As you can see, ritual drug use, i.e., drinking appropriate "medicines," allows the Hausa to talk to spirits, but it has repercussions—impotence: "It is said that a proper boka is too full of medicines ever to wish for intimate relations with a female, and that if he did sleep with one he would be unable to complete the act."[328]

Mai-bori, trained male or female mediums, also diagnose possession, or rather their spirits reveal compatriots' misdeeds during trance, along with the necessary cures. But being a bori mount is not easy. Merriment or inattention brings immediate punishment. Alcohol and sex are also forbidden prior to ceremonies because they ruin receptiveness.[329] And some horses are even subjected to physical abuse...

Tremearne observed many bori rituals firsthand and described a few of them in his books. Generally, when the music started, dancers shuffled around in a circle, their hips swaying until the violin and incense took effect. Fixed, vacant eyes signaled "hysteria"; there was grunting, squealing, convulsions, and sudden rushing or crawling about as dancers mimicked their possessing spirit. The most extraordinary display was when they jumped into the air and landed flat on their buttocks, legs stretched out in front or with one crossed over the other. The dancer would remain rigid in that position until another participant lifted, then pressed down on, each of their arms. If the spirit spoke but was not clear, the chief mai-bori interpreted. Possession ended when the spirit was

---

327 *The Ban of the Bori*, 150.

328 Ibid.,150–151.

329 Ibid., 276.

expelled by sneezing. And even if the dancers clawed their chests, tore their hair, beat themselves, or even jumped out of trees in this state, they claimed they felt no pain. Nevertheless, it took days on a diet of kola-nuts and water for trance to completely wear off, even if no serious injury had occurred.[330]

Note the similarity of this to Eugenie Le Brun's "jumping" sheikhat at the beginning of this chapter. The former Turkish slaves she witnessed were faithfully reenacting traditional bori leaps.

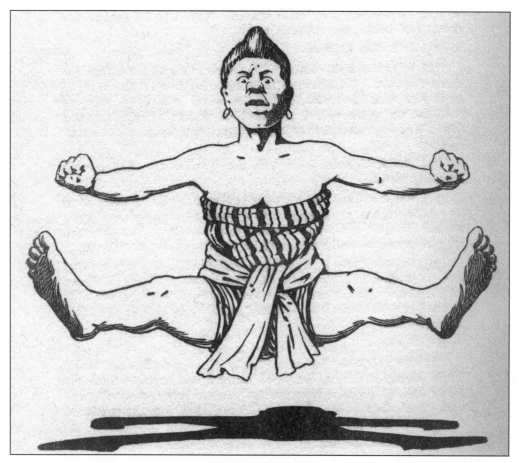

Figure 31: Bori leap

---

330   Tremearne, *Hausa Superstitions and Customs*, 530–32.

Nigeria and the Orisha

Now let's travel downriver to southern Nigeria, home of the Yoruba orisha. Yoruba is the name given to the West African tribes of Nigeria—and Nigeria's neighbors Benin (Dahomey) and Togo—that speak the Yoruba language. And while the orisha are not part of the Egyptian zar pantheon, I mention them because of their connection to the New World religions of Umbanda, Candomblé, Santería, and Voudun. And when you consider that African-American ancestry, and by extrapolation the New World slave population in general, was predominantly from Niger and Kordofan/Sudan (about 71 percent),[331] it is feasible that bori, tumboura, and zar influenced these New World religions as well.

Much like the *azna* and African pagans in general, the Yoruba believe in a remote Supreme Entity named Olodumare or Olorun, "Owner of the Sky" and Creator of the Universe. According to one creation myth (each tribe has its own), after Olorun completed our world, He[332] returned home for a well-deserved rest, leaving various species of Invisibles behind as guardians: the orisha as ministers, and under them lesser nature spirits, local place deities, humanity's "familiars," and later, as they accumulated, the souls of the dead or ancestor spirits.

According to one tribe's oral tradition, the Yoruba founded their capital, Ife, in the fifteenth century after conquering the indigenous inhabitants, the forest-dwelling Igbo. The conquerors adopted Igbo mythology but replaced their vanquished god, Obatala, with a Yoruba hero, Odudua, and revamped their creation myth. In the new version, Olorun still sends Obatala, his son, to create land, Ile-Ife or "Wide Earth," from the primordial waters by raking soil over it with a five-toed hen. And Olorun still tells his son to make humans out of clay, which his son does by shaping hollow Igbo shells for Olorun to breathe life into and assign each a destiny. But the revised story has Obatala becoming tired and thirsty and indulging in too much palm wine. When he finally returns to work, he makes figures so deformed that Olorun tells him to stop. The Supreme One then gives Odudua the job, and Odudua creates the Yoruba and their first

---

331   This is from the African genetic project I mentioned in chapter 2: Tishkoff, "The Genetic Structure and History of Africans and African Americans."

332   The supreme deity is gender neutral, but the literature uses "He" so I will stick with that.

kingdom, Ile-Ife. Jealous, Obatala and the Igbo rebel, but Odudua defeats them, and his sixteen sons go on to found the original Yoruba kingdoms.[333]

A key element of this myth is that Olorun, not the orisha, assigns humans their fates—the Great God may be distant, but He is not absent. Hence, the Yoruba religion serves two purposes: to communicate with (placate, ask for guidance, and seek protection from) the unpredictable orisha, but also to discover Olorun's wishes and the best way to fulfill them.

Worshipping a remote God is tricky business, though. How do you understand His desires if He rarely communicates? And so the Yoruba developed the fine art of divination, a system so unique that in 2005, UNESCO proclaimed it "a masterpiece of humanity's oral and intangible heritage." To discover and improve their destinies, devotees consult male diviners, *babalawo* or "fathers of secrets," who use a system of 256 divination characters (*odu*—a little like *The I Ching*) linked to a vast repertoire of poems. A client first whispers their issue to a ritual object on an altar out of earshot of the *babalawo*, then sits opposite the diviner to select a character in one of two ways:

By nuts: The *babalawo* shakes sixteen palm nuts *(ikin)* loosely in clasped hands, left hand below, right hand above, then abruptly tries to grab all the nuts with his right hand. Because of their size, this is impossible, so some are left behind. If one remains, the diviner draws two parallel lines on a tray covered with powder. If two are left, he draws one line. The process is repeated seven more times, with the outcome of each grab marked in two columns of four.

By divination chain: This shortcut uses eight seedpod halves (shaped like hollow bowls) strung loosely on a string. Held in the middle and thrown so that equal sections fall parallel to one another, pods falling concave-side up (like overturned bowls) are represented by one line, while pods concave-side down equal two lines each.

---

333   Benjamin Ray, *African Religions*, 43.

The 256 possible outcomes, or characters, are associated with four to eight poems (sometimes more) that the diviner has memorized and will recite for the seeker. But it is up to the seeker to decide which is the most appropriate—since only he or she knows the question. Besides, if the *babalawo* were to choose, that would interfere with his client's destiny.[334] Clarification can be asked for by casting lots (*ibo*) to yes/no questions. Ultimately, though, the belief is that destiny chooses for the client—a situation that encourages some to act with confidence, but gives others an excuse to do nothing.

The poems contain myths, proverbs, fables, and the notable results of when Invisibles or famous humans consulted the Oracle. These archetypal situations, along with their outcomes and the sacrifices made to ensure positive results, fall into categories: for good luck—defeat of an enemy, children, marriage, money, and long life, and for bad luck—personal loss, money problems, fights, illness, and death. Crucially, Ifa does not make absolute predictions. It only suggests possible ways to obtain favorable outcomes within a destiny's limits. If the results are disappointing, Ifa is not to blame; that particular destiny simply did not permit better results, or other powers intervened. And without specifics, considerable wiggle room exists for interpretation, particularly after the fact.[335]

Perhaps the most important difference between bori and orisha worshippers is their attitude toward possession. Hosting orisha is considered a privilege, not a necessary evil. These horses want to be ridden and often identify with their riders. They believe orisha guide them toward more balanced lives, restore their health, and transmit higher knowledge. New World religions believe lesser spirits descend on behalf of an orisha or that minute traces of the original entity infiltrate a host's body, its full presence being lethal for solid life forms. Either way, this enables a single entity to simultaneously possess thousands of worshippers at once.

Orisha medium initiations also differ from bori traditions. The Yoruba normally inherit their spirit affiliations from their fathers, but illnesses or serious problems are also considered signs that another orisha may be interested in the person.[336] Novices go

---

334   Ray, *African Religions*, 107.
335   Ibid., 109.
336   Ibid., 68.

through months of training—extended periods of seclusion, trance, instruction, and medication—until specific cues (a rhythm or a bell, for example) instantly bring about trance and an orisha's arrival.[337] New World practices differ slightly from African traditions in that spirit guides visit first. Advanced entities come later—one in Candomblé and one to three in Macumba and Umbanda. Only Temple Chiefs host more.[338]

The Yoruba do have something in common with the Hausa, though, and with the ancient Egyptians: a shared belief that multiple entities inhabit their bodies—souls, in the Yoruba's case. Olorun bestows the most important at birth: His life breath, humanity's vitality and strength. But its energy fluctuates because it takes nourishment from food, similar to the Egyptian *ba*. It also travels during sleep, but if caught and prevented from returning to its body (by a witch for example), both soul and body will die. A second entity, the shadow, resembles the ancient Egyptian *khaibit*, and a third, the "*ori* warhead," a twin being that resides partially in the head (the personality or ego) and partially in heaven (the alter ego or guardian soul), mirrors the Egyptian *khu* and *sahu*. According to Yoruban beliefs, the celestial portion of this entity, originally an ancestor's soul, chooses a fetus's destiny, or "lot," before birth—a personality, occupation, success level, and time of death—which Olorun then permanently attaches. The heavenly half is expected to help its terrestrial twin live with these choices, but it is often fickle and expects offerings—rituals called "feeding the head." Hence, the *ori* ends up being more important than the orisha because "what *ori* refuse to grant, orisha cannot confer." Nevertheless, an *ori*'s powers are limited. Once chosen, fates cannot be changed, even if selected by mistake—which happens regularly. Ajala, Heaven's Gatekeeper, makes faulty destinies that appear well made at their time of choosing but are doomed to fail.[339]

So who or what are orisha, besides being Olorun's terrestrial representatives? Simply put, they are advanced nature spirits that express energy *(axe)* as Earth's elemental forces: wind, thunder, lightning, rain, earthquakes, etc. They evolved without passing through multiple reincarnations and are both positive and negative; they destroy and

---

337   Ray, *African Religions*, 70.

338   Carol Dow, *Sarava!*, 23.

339   Ray, *African Religions*, 135–36; Dow, *Sarava!*, 21–48 and 177–85.

build, starve and nurture, smite and heal—and ultimately carry out Olorun's will.[340] They often channel their energy into objects, either naturally through plants or via humans through ritual. For a look at a few well-known Yoruban orisha and their New World descendants, please see appendix 4.

————

Africa is home to other possession cults besides the four just described—Tunisian *stambali*, *hamdasha*, and *guedra* and Senegalese *ndep* are only a few. They, too, share attributes, experiences, thought processes, and induction techniques that have not only survived since the dawn of time, but thrived—until the last century. Now science, education, and the major monotheistic religions are eroding their base. How long these ancient belief systems will continue to exist is anyone's guess—which is why we must study them now, before they disappear.

Homework: Dancing with Fire and a Rattle

Repeat the "Dancing with Fire" homework from chapter 1 and play a rattle while you dance. A child's toy will do, but South or Central American gourd rattles sound better and are not too expensive. Feel what it's like to dance and simultaneously make music. Did you listen to the music differently? Did the rattle affect you?

————

340 Dow, *Saravá!*, 21–23.

8

....

Allah

So far, we have talked a great deal about Middle Eastern and African spirits but little about their Creator, God, or *Allah* in Arabic. Within two hundred years of Islam's humble origins, its esoteric branch, the Sufis, developed techniques to channel this entity directly, to invoke His "presence," or *hadra*—the ultimate possession, if you will. They claimed evidence for their methods in the Quran itself.[341] Borrowing ancient shamanic practices from Anatolia and elsewhere, they developed zikr and whirling, the pinnacle of trance dance techniques.

I find it sad, though, that half the region's population, its women, was discouraged from using these techniques. The men probably didn't want their wives jumping around in public, foaming at the mouth. But as we have seen, the women invented their own methods to invoke hadra, although who or what is "present" is the million-dollar question…

Sufi trance dancing has changed little through the centuries, to the point where the following nineteenth- and early twentieth-century descriptions are still valid today:

---

341 Several passages in the Quran are said to mention zikr and encourage its practice, particularly "Verily! Only in the zikr of Allah will your heart find peace" (13:28). Other passages include Quran 3:191, 33:35, 87:14–15, 63:9, and 18:28.

Figure 32: Men at a nineteenth-century zikr in Cairo (with
extreme backbends that echo ancient Greek maenad poses)

Three Zikrs
Sufi Trance Dancing, from Edward Lane and Clay Trumbull

Cairo, Egypt—1836:[342] The ceremony started about three hours after
sunset and continued for two hours. Thirty performers sat cross-legged
in an oblong ring around three four-foot wax candles. Most were Ah-
medee dervishes, poorly dressed with green turbans. At one end sat four
poetry singers and a flute player. They began by reciting the Fatiha, out
loud and then silently. A slow chant of *La ilaha ill-Allah* followed for about
fifteen minutes, with participants bowing their heads and bodies twice per

---

342   This 1836 account is from Edward Lane's *An Account of the Manners and Customs of Modern
Egyptians*, page 439. Edited for length and clarity.

repetition. The pace quickened for another fifteen minutes as the singers joined in with an ode similar to The Song of Solomon.

When they finished, the men rose, still chanting *La illaha ill-Allah*, but in a deep, hoarse tone, emphasizing the first word *La* and the beginning syllable of the last word *Allah*. The sound resembled the *tac* of a tambourine rim being struck. Alternately turning their heads right and left with each repetition, the men stepped to the right, steadily quickening their pace around the circle. A tall, well-dressed black slave, one of the Pasha's eunuchs, joined the group and soon became *melboos*, or possessed. Throwing his arms about, looking up with a wild expression, he rapidly exclaimed: *Allah! Allah! La, La, La! Ya ami!* [Oh, my uncle!]. As his voice gradually faded, he fell to the ground foaming at the mouth, eyes closed, limbs convulsing, fingers clenched over thumbs—an epileptic fit, certainly. No one could witness this attack and believe it feigned. Undoubtedly, it came from a high state of religious excitement. No one seemed surprised; similar occurrences happen frequently at zikrs. The performers were now quite excited; rapidly chanting, violently turning their heads, and simultaneously sinking their whole bodies as some of them jumped.

The Issawiya, Moroccan disciples of Sidi Muhammad ibn Issa, performed the second zikr. About twenty dervishes sat close together in a ring, all but two beating large *tars*, frame drums more than a foot wide. The two exceptions struck a small ordinary tar and a *baz*, a little kettledrum. Six dervishes began to "dance"—exclaiming *Allah!* or *Allah Mowlana!* [God is our Lord] and behaving like madmen; bobbing up and down, spinning, gesticulating oddly, jumping, and sometimes screaming. In short, if a stranger were not told they were performing a religious exercise, he would think they were playing the buffoon; and their dress would reinforce this idea. One wore a caftan without sleeves, girdle, or anything on his head; another had a white cotton skullcap but was naked from head to waist, wearing nothing but a loose pair of drawers. These two were the principal performers. One, a dark, spare, middle-aged man, became wild and rushed toward the drummers, who surrounded a small, tinned-copper chafing dish full of red-hot charcoal. The dervish seized a lump of live charcoal and put it in his mouth; then another, and another, until his mouth was full. Then he deliberately chewed them, opening his mouth wide to show its contents. After about three minutes, he swallowed without evincing the slightest pain. The other half-naked dervish, in the prime of youth, became so violent that one of his brethren held him; but he freed himself, and rushing towards the chafing dish, put one of the largest coals in his mouth. He kept it wide open about two minutes; as he inhaled, the lump appeared almost white with heat and when he exhaled, numerous sparks blew out of his mouth. He then chewed, swallowed, and resumed dancing for half an hour, until the group paused to rest.

Cairo, Egypt—1907:[343] Standing or crouching in a circle, facing inward, the dervishes began their worship by repeating aloud the Muslim name of God, "Allah, Allah, Allah!" not twice, nor a score of times, but hundreds of times in rapid succession. The word itself was jerked out convulsively from the lowest depths of the lungs, with a terminal emphasis and prolonging of its peculiar hollow sound; at the same time, the whole body was swayed to and fro to put added force into the sepulchral ejaculations. The phrases were *Allahu Akbar*, "God is great," and *La illaha illa Allah*, "There is no god but God." The swaying increased in intensity as the rapidity of the utterances kept pace until the long hair of some worshippers alternately touched the ground behind their backs and before their feet, in almost lightning-like swiftness, and it seemed as if the very heads of the dervishes were flying from their shoulders. These invocations and bodily movements were continued until ecstatic exhaustion was attained and a final cry of *Huwwa* or "He" (God) terminated the devotions.

---

343   This 1907 account is from H. Clay Trumbull's *Oriental Social Life*, pages 258–59. Edited for length and clarity.

Figure 33: Nineteenth-century zikr dervishes pierced
themselves with skewers to prove their depth of trance

What Is a Zikr?

The first "divine presence" ritual the Sufis developed was the zikr. The name (also spelled *dhikr*) is taken from the Arabic root *z-k-r* (*thakara*), "to recollect, remember, or think about something." As a noun, *zikr* refers to the "remembrance" of God by repeated mention of his name. Most scholars agree that the practice began during Muhammad's lifetime. However, sometime between 800 and 1100 CE, the Sufis refined and formalized this act into two different types of rituals: silent versus vocal, and solitary versus communal. Both types, if practiced long enough, induce auditory and visual hallucinations—Divine Presence. The solitary silent form, *zikr khafi*, uses elaborate breath control. The other form, the collective vocal version, *zikr jali* or *zikr al-awaam*, engages group choreography so that many bodies may move as one and enter trance together. Members of a *tariqa* (plural *taruq*) or order (literally "path" or "way"), and sometimes members of the public, join together around a sheikh who leads them through the movements.[344]

Although techniques vary, most vocal zikrs share two things in common: "howling" God's name, i.e., controlled breathing through specialized pronunciation, and climax, God's presence ("hadra") during trance. Group rituals also vary by sect and leader, but generally follow a two-part format: seated and standing. In the beginning, participants sit on the floor (usually in a circle) and listen to readings and/or religious songs, chant prayers, and sway. This clears their minds of daily preoccupations to focus on God. When the sheikh feels everyone is ready, he signals them to stand for the zikr proper, an uninterrupted crescendo of sound, motion, and trance induction: hyperventilation, overstimulation of the auditory nerve, spatial disorientation, and disturbed equilibrium.[345] Yet, as Gilbert Rouget observed, not all participants enter trance, even though they do the same movements. As I said earlier, kinetically altered consciousness requires considerable mental preparation and unwavering intention, as well as physical stimulation.[346]

Zikr rituals haven't changed much since the eleventh century. Compare Lane's descriptions to zikr clips on YouTube. They are similar. You may also find clips of popular

---

344   Thomas Hughes, "Zikr," *Dictionary of Islam*, 708.

345   Gilbert Rouget, *Music and Trance*, 271.

346   Ibid., 304–06.

(shaabi) zikrs as well. These differ considerably from traditional zikrs in that musicians accompany a singer (given the honorary title of sheikh) who sings religious lyrics to popular melodies. In Egypt both women and men participate together (the women's bodies are well covered by long flowing *abayas* and headscarves). Similar to club dancing, everyone does his or her own thing, not group choreography—although some women clearly frequent zar hadarat as well because their movements resemble spirit dances. Nevertheless, most patrons are there to commune with God and be healed by his mercy, and often remain until the band quits (for hours).

Experiencing a traditional zikr, even as a bystander, is haunting. The incessant chanting starts as a hypnotic murmur; a throbbing undercurrent of syncopated voices, clapping, and frame drums, which swells to an urgent driving pulse, unyielding to pause or reflection. No thinking, only feeling, moving, and chanting. Breathe in, breathe out—expand your rib cage, collapse it, inhale, exhale—over and over and over. Shout louder, move faster, jump higher, bow lower—until your head spins. And underneath it all is respiration control, the zikr door to God.

Controlled breathing is the key ingredient to both silent and vocal zikrs for good reason. It is a powerful induction trigger. Why? The answer is camouflaged in semantics. "Breath control" is merely a catch phrase for what's really going on: hyperventilation, the intentional decrease of carbon dioxide in the blood through rapid exhalation. Three minutes and symptoms appear—dizziness, tingling, occasional tunnel vision, and most important, decreased brainwave frequencies. Yes, hyperventilation slows brainwaves—an effect first reported in 1924 with the advent of EEGs. It also induces something else—seizures in epileptics, which is why it is used to test for epilepsy, particularly in children. Perhaps this is why singing and chanting play such an important role in religious ritual. The mild hyperventilation they cause facilitates prayer and meditation, i.e., trance. Buddhist meditation, in particular, has developed chanting and breathing into a fine art. In fact, it is common knowledge that their respiration techniques reduce anxiety, tension, and out-of-control emotions within minutes. For example, a well-known trick to calm emotions is to inhale slowly for five seconds, hold your breath for two seconds, and then exhale slowly. Repeat ten times for an immediate shift in mind and body. See for yourself. I have included other zikr-inspired breath control exercises in the Homework section. A word of caution, though—try them sitting down first.

Whirl Dances

Curt Sachs published his groundbreaking dance encyclopedia, *World History of the Dance*, in 1937. He claimed that Mevlevi Sufi whirling was "something primitive, preserved from a period thousands of years before Islam, inherited from the shamanism of central Asia." Apparently, whirling has been used to contact spirits long before Sufi dervishes adopted it for their zikr rituals:

> Here the dance severs the natural bonds of human posture and motion. In dizziness the dancer loses the feeling of body and self; released from his body he conquers dizziness.... The whirling dervish, who extends his arms horizontally and turns his palm upwards, assumes without wishing to, the gesture of taking, of opening.... He awaits the generative force which takes possession of him, which removes the limitations of his body, extinguishes his consciousness, and pours divine spirit into him. The whirl dance is the purest form of dance devotion.[347]

Figure 34: Whirling dervishes

---

347   *World History of the Dance*, 42–44.

Curt Sachs listed many spinning examples, from a New Kingdom Theban tomb painting ("a negresse ornamented with vines"),[348] to traditional Jewish dances (*mahol*, or women's dances, derived from the verb *hul*, "to turn") and the frenzied escapades of the maenads. He should have included Brazil's Umbanda practitioners, since they whirl to enter and exit trance at gatherings called *giras* (from the Portuguese verb *girar*—"to spin, turn, or rotate"), but in his era, the Old World (he was German) was probably unfamiliar with this New World religion. Instead, he focused on the "Whirling Dervishes." To him and many others, this ceremony embodied the perfect combination of dance and religious worship. After witnessing several performances in Cairo, where "old men spun like tops for a full half hour,"[349] he noted that the Western physicians with him confirmed the dervishes were in a "yoga state"—i.e., trance.

Certainly, Mevlevi Sufi whirling is unique. Its haunting music, driving infectious rhythms, and modulating tempos are ideal induction tools—if you can get past the nausea and dizziness. But is it a remnant of "central Asia's ancient shamanic past"? Officially, it is a medieval Islamic ritual from Anatolia, institutionalized about a century after Al-Ghazali formalized his twelfth-century zikr hadra.[350] Is it older than that? Persia and Anatolia lie at the crossroads of prehistoric *Homo sapiens* emigration routes out of Africa. It could possibly go way back…

To investigate the origins of Sufi whirling, we must return to the thirteenth century, the heart of Islam's Golden Age (the ninth to fifteenth centuries). While Europe was foundering in the Dark Ages, Middle Eastern scholars were translating ancient Greek, Latin, and Aramaic texts into Arabic and using their newfound knowledge to make important scientific discoveries in mathematics, astronomy, chemistry, medicine, and engineering. The Black Death (1347–1351) was the beginning of the end for this extraordinary period, yet for six hundred years, Samarkand, Bagdad, Damascus, Cairo, Marrakesh, and Andalusia nurtured cutting-edge human intellectual prowess.

---

348   This is from Theban Tomb 113, belonging to Kynebu, who was Priest in the Temple for King Thutmose IV during the reign of Rameses VIII, Twentieth Dynasty, about 1140 BCE.

349   *World History of the Dance*, 41–42.

350   Al-Ghazali (c. 1058–1111 CE) was a twelfth-century Sufi master who popularized the mystic branch of Islam and established zikr and sema doctrine through his writings.

The original inspiration for the Mevlevi Sufi order, the first Whirling Dervish, was Muhammad ben Muhammad ben Hussein Bahi ad-Din al-Balakhi, better known as Mawlana Jalâl ad-Din Rumi. *Mawlana* means "our guide or master"; *Jalâl ad-Din* or "Majesty of Religion" is one of Allah's ninety-nine sacred names; and *Rumi* designates someone from the Sultanate of Rum, i.e., Anatolia. Most people, however, simply refer to this great Sufi Master as "Rumi." He was born September 30, 1207, in the Balkh province (hence the epithet "Balkhi") of Khorasan, a region now divided between northern Afghanistan and Tajikistan. At the time, it was a thriving center for Persian culture with its own brand of Sufism, "Khorasani." Rumi's father, Baha ad-Din, as his father before him, was a liberal Sunni Hanafi preacher and an Islamic scholar for the village of Vakhsh.[351] At Rumi's birth he was almost sixty years old. Frustrated with his circumstances, he soon uprooted his wife and young children and set off for Samarkand.

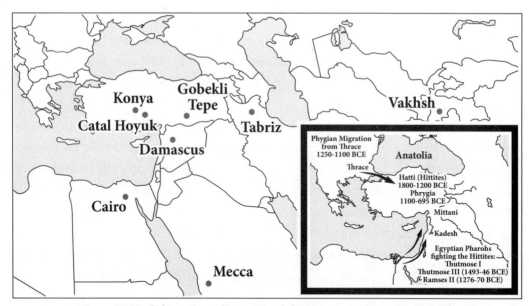

Figure 35: Neolithic points of interest and the important cities of Rumi's life
(with inset map of the Phrygian spread and ancient Egypt's conquering of the Hittite empire)

---

351   Vakhsh was a small town on a river by the same name, in what is now Tajikistan.

They did not stay long. In the spring of 1216, Baha ad-Din once again loaded everyone onto a caravan for a pilgrimage to Mecca. Rumi turned nine on the journey. Afterwards, the family went north to Larende (present-day Karaman) in Anatolia, a Farsi-speaking territory of the Seljuk Turks. There, Rumi spent his adolescence, married at age seventeen (in 1224 CE), and fathered two children, Celaleddin (known as Sultan Valad) and Ala-ad-Din Chalabi. He also lost his mother and brother—leaving him as his father's only heir.

In 1229 CE, Baha ad-Din, now close to eighty, was hired to teach in Konya, the Seljuk capital, seventy miles north of Larende. The Moroccan scholar Ibn Battuta, who visited the city a hundred years later, described it as a beautiful place to live.[352] Sadly, Rumi's father died shortly after the move, in 1231, but not before firmly establishing his son as a respected preacher and scholar. Such was the father's reputation and esteem that in spite of Rumi's youth, he was offered his father's jobs. Rumi accepted, but only after nine years of training. Two years after his father's death, Rumi's wife died as well, leaving him with two young sons. Lacking a woman in the house, he married a widow, Kerra Khatun, who bore him another son and a daughter. Rumor has it that she communicated with the jinn:

> On one occasion she supposedly complained that there were jinn (genies) living in their house and these genies had complained about her husband's habit of standing throughout the night until dawn reading the *Ma'aref* of Baha al-Din. The light from all the candles greatly annoyed the jinn and they hinted that some evil might befall the inhabitants of the house on account of their vexation. Worried, she approached Rumi with this tale, but he gave no answer and merely smiled. After three days had gone by, he told her, "Do not worry anymore, for the jinn have come to believe in me and are my disciples. They will not hurt any of the children or our companions."[353]

On November 29, 1244, the world as Rumi knew it came to an end. Shams-i-Tabrizi, a sixty-year-old wandering dervish from Persia, arrived in Konya. For a little over a

---

352 Gibb, *The Travels of Ibn Battuta*, 130. Ibn Battuta traveled to Anatolia in 1332–34 CE.

353 Franklin Lewis, *Rumi Past and Present, East and West*, 122, drawing from *Manaqeb al-Arefin* by fourteenth-century author Shams al-Din Ahmad al-Aflaki.

year the two men were inseparable, and Rumi, now an accomplished scholar and jurist, quickly metamorphosed into a joyful ascetic, much to the chagrin of family, friends, and students.[354] Rumi's disciples and his middle son, Ala' ad-Din, soon convinced Shams to leave town. Devastated, Rumi gave up writing poetry, neglected his disciples, stopped going to *semas*,[355] and withdrew into seclusion, all the while searching endlessly for Shams ... until, at last, he found him teaching in Damascus. Overjoyed, he sent his first son, Sultan Valad, to bring Shams back to Konya. Rumi's disciples and family had no choice but to relent. Whether the dervish was there or not, Rumi was a changed man.

The truce lasted less than a year. Shams married a young female disciple, who quickly died. Rumi's entourage blamed Shams for neglecting her, which quickly re-kindled their hatred. Finally, one night in December 1247, Shams disappeared again. Rumor had it he was murdered by Rumi's son or a jealous disciple, but this is doubtful since Shams is apparently buried in Khoy, Iran.[356] Khoy lies about one hundred miles northwest of Tabriz, along the medieval route from Anatolia to Tabriz. It seems more likely that the aging Sufi died on his wintery journey home. Again, Rumi searched for Shams, in Damascus and elsewhere, but never found him. Contrary to the previous disappearance, however, Rumi worked through his despair by composing epic works of poetry, the most famous being *Divan-e Shams-e Tabrizi,* in Shams's honor; the *Masnavi,* considered Rumi's greatest work; and a compilation, *Divan-e Kabi*r. Rumi died twenty-five years later, on December 17, 1273, in Konya, Turkey, at the age of sixty-six.

The year after Rumi's death, his followers, aided by his son Sultan Valad, founded what is now known as the Mevlevi Sufi order.[357] Rumi's message of peace, love, and tolerance lured many to his doorstep. The educated considered him a wise philosopher, while the uneducated saw him as a prophet. When Sultan Valad died, he was buried beside his father and a shrine was erected to both of them. It is now a popular tourist attraction, along with Shams-i-Tabrizi's tomb in Khoy.

---

354   Lewis, *Rumi Past and Present, East and West*, 274.

355   A *sema* is the Mevlevi Sufi group ritual where participants, or *semazen*, listen to emotionally charged spiritual poetry, Qur'anic recitation, and music, as well as whirl.

356   One tower of Shams's tomb still stands. The structure has been nominated as a UNESCO World Heritage site.

357   There are hundreds of Sufi orders, each centered around a different "saint" or leader.

Under the leadership of Rumi's grandson, Ulu ârif Çelebi, the Mevlevi Sufi Order expanded throughout the Ottoman Empire, so that by the time Ibn Battuta visited the area fifty years after Rumi's death, the order was well established.[358] Over the centuries, the ascetic Mevlevi lifestyle brought the order considerable social, economic, and political influence, either through members with government positions or who were gifted poets and musicians. All this screeched to a halt, however, with the Ottoman Empire's defeat during World War I. The new Turkish government of Mustafa Kemal Ataturk, "the Father of Modern Turkey," envisioned a secular republic for its citizens. So in 1925 they abolished outward signs of religion (including face veils for women and *tarboush* hats for men). They also declared the country's Sufi organizations illegal and either closed the *tekkes* (Sufi religious houses) or converted them into mosques and museums (including the main tekke, the *Mevlevihane*, in Konya where Rûmî is buried and the Galata tekke in Istanbul). The government later revived the Mevlevi order in 1954 as a "Turkish cultural heritage," to attract tourists, but never reinstated its religious status. Today, semas are performed throughout Turkey, particularly in Konya during their annual ten-day festival in December (December 7-17). Called *Sheb-i Aruz* (SHEB-ee ah-ROOZ), it celebrates Rumi's death—his so-called "wedding night," when the sheikh was finally united with his beloved Holy Spirit.

Remarkably, an uninterrupted chain of Rumi's direct descendants, the Çelebi family, has led the Mevlevi order for over eight hundred years. The present leader, Fârûk Hemdem Çelebi, succeeded his father, Celâleddin M. Bâqir Çelebi, in 1996.[359] He is the 22nd great-grandson of Mawlânâ Jalâluddîn Rûmî and President of the International Mevlana Foundation headquartered in Istanbul.

But all this history still hasn't answered the basic question of where all this whirling came from—"Central Asia's ancient shamanistic past"? The truth is, no one knows. Sufi whirling as we know it today is credited to Rumi. One story claims (and there are many, each more fanciful than the next) that while Rumi was walking through Konya's

---

358   Gibb, *The Travels of Ibn Battuta*, 130.
359   See the Çelebi Family website at www.mevlana.net.

marketplace, he heard apprentice goldsmiths chanting the Tawheed, "*la illaha ill-Allah*," to keep time as they hammered. Our hero was supposedly so filled with joy that he stretched out his arms and began to spin. According to Franklin Lewis, though, it was Shams who taught Rumi to whirl.[360] If this is true, then where did Shams learn it? Lewis writes a teacher taught him this meditation technique by "twirling me around" as a child.[361] In another passage he mentions the practice was widespread during Shams's time—and so effective that it was associated with "licentious acts."[362] It seems, then, that whirling was established in Persia and Anatolia long before Shams introduced it to Rumi. If this is true, then Curt Sachs's affirmation that the custom was derived from an ancient Central Asian shamanic practice suddenly doesn't sound so farfetched after all ...

If Rumi ritualized the practice of whirling, and his son Sultan Valad helped structure it and develop the order's philosophies, it was nevertheless his descendant, Pir Adel Çelebi (d. 1460), who is credited with refining the movements. But that's it. The only other changes happened during the reign of Selim III, from 1789 to 1807, altering the ritual's timing.

The Sema—Ritual Whirling

In my opinion, no one describes the essence of a sema ritual better than Rumi's descendant, the late head of the Mevlevi order, Celâleddin Çelebi:

> The aim of sema is not unbridled ecstasy and loss of consciousness, but submission to God ... It is a spiritual journey, an ascent through intelligence and love to Perfection. Turning toward the truth, the semazen grows through love, transcends the ego, meets the truth, and arrives at perfection. Then he returns, mature and complete, able to love and serve all creatures without discriminating in regard to belief, class or race.[363]

---

360 *Rumi Past and Present*, 171–72.

361 Ibid., 145.

362 Ibid., 171–72.

363 From the liner notes of *Wherever You Turn Is the Face of God* CD by the Mevlevi Ensemble of Turkey. Celâleddin M. Bâqir Çelebi was the twenty-first descendent of Rumi and head of the Mevlevi Order until his death in 1996.

Mevlevi Sufis believe that whirling is the essence of the universe; blood whirls through the body, the planets spin around themselves and the sun. Whirling creates gravity and magnetic forces. Even electrons whirl around their nuclei. All matter is engaged in sema. According to Rumi, "if sema stops, the order of the universe would collapse." The ecstatic state induced by whirling enables semazem to transcend their egos, experience God's perfection and Divine love, and transform their souls. Sema is kinetic prayer to music.[364] This may be a dilemma to Muslims outside the order, who are familiar with Islam's supposed interdiction of music, but not to Mevlevi Sufis. They believe religious music is an extension of God's essence, His Divine Love, and therefore a legitimate medium for contacting Him. In fact, the Quran does not directly forbid music at all. It can be argued that the ban is inferred in the hadith, but that depends on how you interpret the Prophet's words and actions. Al-Ghazali, Rumi, and his son Sultan Valad argued convincingly in favor of music and dance during worship.

Mevlevi dervishes no longer whirl in marketplaces. Long ago, they developed specialized light-filled pavillions for their rituals: *tekke* in Turkish, *sama' khaneh* in Farsi, *semhane*(s) *(samahane* [pl]) in modern Turkish, or *zawiya* in Arabic. Usually supported by eight wood columns, most accommodate up to thirteen whirlers, although the Mevlâna Cultural Center in Konya can hold up to two thousand spectators.[365] Typically covered by a dome, these semicircular or octagonal-shaped halls are laid with sprung wood floors for ease of movement. And like everything else, these floors are endowed with symbolism; the right represents the world of matter and what descends from God while the left symbolizes God's unseen world and what ascends back up to Him. Seating for onlookers is arranged along the sides. Occasionally halls also have second stories, private entrances for women, and reserved sections for musicians and order members.

Novices usually join the Mevlevi order as adolescent boys (the younger you are, the easier spinning is to learn) with a recommendation from an elder member.

---

364   The word *sema* (or "Mevlevi Mukabelesi" in Turkish) means "audition or attentive listening, i.e., the ear as the path to spirituality." It's from the Arabic root *s-m-a*, "to hear or to listen to." Technically, the sema ritual is a form of zikr, since participants silently repeat the name of Allah as they spin. As with other zikrs, the objective is union with God through divinely inspired trance.

365   Thomas Hughes, "Zikr," *The Dictionary of Islam*, 707–08.

Figure 36: Sufi whirling in a hall

They choose one of two paths: either to live in the tekke and undergo three years of rigorous training (to become a *chelle*, with the title of *Dede)*, or to remain at home as a nonresident lodge member without doing the three-year intensive program. *Chelles* are discouraged from marrying because women are not allowed to live in the tekke.

During a sema, the presiding elder or sheikh, a *postnishi*, reads the Quran and recites prayers. He remains stationary, either seated or standing, for the most part, although he may whirl at the end. He will nevertheless regain his place for the final Quranic recitation. Symbolically, he channels God's truth and Muhammad's revelations. Compared to a zar sheikha or kodia, both are masters-of-ceremony and spiritual intermediaries … but one communicates with God, while the other channels the jinn.

The sema is unique in that participants wear "uniforms," garments based on Rumi's thirteenth-century clothing. Of course, with the passing of time, the various bits and pieces have become endowed with spiritual meaning.

Hat: Mevlevi dervishes wear tall, conical, brimless brown felt hats known as *sikke* in Turkish or *kûlah* in Farsi. They represent tombstones for the human ego.

Cloak or *hirka* (Turkish) or *kesve* (Farsi): This voluminous black cape symbolizes the grave or worldly tomb. It is discarded before whirling to suggest liberation from worldly attachments and spiritual rebirth. A novice receives one from his sheikh after he completes the 1001-day initiation period, to mark his new rank of *chelle*.

Robe and jacket: A *tennure* (or in Egyptian Arabic, a *tanoura)* is usually a full-skirted, white sleeveless robe or gown worn on top of a white high-necked undershirt. A waist-length jacket of the same color is worn on top. The gown is the ego's death shroud (*kefen*). Nowadays, semazen occasionally wear different colors to honor Rumi's rose garden: red for dusk, dawn, and love; green for tranquility; yellow for unrequited love; and white for the Prophet Muhammad's exalted light.[366]

Belt and scarf: Black belts are wrapped around the waist to prevent the *tennure* from billowing too far out or up. Black represents pureness.

Shoes: Semazen do not wear ordinary shoes when they spin, but special boots with fine leather soles to reduce friction. Rubber or treads make turning difficult, similar to bare feet, while stockings or socks are too slippery.

As for Mevlevi music, there's certainly a big difference between the order's intricate compositions and the zar's raw percussive chanting—and yet both induce trance. Why? The answer is connected to how each stimulates the inner ear. During zars, women toss their heads with their upper torsos, whereas whirling involves the entire body. Hyperstimulation of the balance portion of the vestibulocochlear nerve means fewer auditory signals are needed to overload it. Of course, whirling is possible without music, but far

---

366   Dinç, Nefin. *I Named Her Angel.* Turkish documentary film about the Mevlevi sema.

more effective with it because it excites other critical brain functions, memory, and the primary emotions (see chapter 4: Trance Science).

The thing about emotions, though, is that they are partially dictated by culture and language. Words or lyrics from one culture (even translated) may not resonate with people from another. Yet the Mevlevi ritual has circumvented this problem with a universal emotional trigger—the "moaning" of a reed flute (a nay). No matter where you come from or what language you speak, a *nay taqsim* usually evokes feelings of longing and sadness. Its ethereal quarter-tone scales prompt spontaneous visceral reactions without words, hence its place of honor during a sema, after the initial prayer.

According to tradition, Rumi himself was a gifted musician who played the nay and the *rabab*, a spiked fiddle. In later centuries, Sufi composers wrote intricate hymns and suites (*ayin*) to accompany Rumi's poetry, that of Sultan Valad and Shams-i-Tabrizi, many of which are still performed today. Originally, the ritual had four parts: the opening prayer and flute taqsim, a processional march, the casting off of cloaks leading into the Four Selams (the whirling),[367] and a closing prayer.

Afterwards, the semazen file back to their rooms for quiet meditation. And even though the program was expanded during the Ottoman Empire,[368] this basic structure has remained the same.

––––––––––

And so we come to the end of Part Two, the Spirit section, and the end of the theory portion of the book. It is finally time to stop thinking and begin doing!

––––––––––

367   The Four Selams section is the heart of an ayin. The four vocal movements, called *selams*, are usually chanted by the *hafiz*. Semazen begin and end these movements in *alif* position in a salute to God's unity. Each section has its own symbolism, a four-part spiritual journey: 1. *Selam-i-Evvel*, Recognizing God; 2. *Selam-i-Sani*, Recognizing God's Unity; 3. *Selam-i-Salis*, Ecstasy of Total Surrender; 4. *Selam-i-Rabai*, Peace of Heart.

368   Later additions to the Mevlevi ceremony were the Son Peshrev, the Son Yuruk Semai, a taqsim, perhaps an *ilahe* hymn section, and another taqsim. Semazen continue to whirl during the two *sons* until the end of the first additional taqsim.

Homework: Breathing Exercises

Experiment with the different types of breathing outlined below. As always, use common sense and monitor your reactions.

Chaotic Breathing: Consciously alter the length and type of each inhalation for five minutes. This should completely focus your attention on breathing—an act we normally ignore and take for granted.

Circular Breathing: In through the nose and out through the mouth. Certain wind instruments use this technique to create continuous sound—Scottish bagpipes, the Australian didgeridoo, the Egyptian *arghoul*, and once upon a time, Plato's trance inducer, the Phrygian aulos. Maintain this for several minutes. You will discover that it, too, requires concentration.

Deep breathing: Completely fill and empty your lungs at a slow regular pace, about 20 to 25 times per minute. Do this for four minutes (about 100 breaths), then write down how you feel.

Counting Breaths: Think about something upsetting. Fully engage your emotions. Repeat the deep breathing pattern from the previous exercise. How many breaths does it take to calm you down? Write the number down.

Hyperventilation: NIH-sanctioned experiments determined that a respiratory rate of 30 per minute, plus a three-fold elevation of total expiratory volume per minute (VE) (i.e., exhaling three times as deeply as normal) for four minutes, are the optimum factors that produce EEG slowing.[369] This rate is slightly faster than the deep-breathing exercise above. You should begin to feel dizzy after about a minute, but continue for the full four minutes to truly experience the sensation. **Warning: If you have a tendency to black out or undergo seizures, this may set you off, so do not attempt it.**

---

369 T. Konishi, "The Standardization of Hyperventilation on EEG Recording in Childhood. I. The Quantity of Hyperventilation Activation." *Brain Development* 9(1), 16–20.

Zikr chants: *HAY Allah* and *Alla-HU*, inhalation versus expiration. The pronunciation of these two phrases is an excellent illustration of how vocalization supports breath control during zikr. Let's experiment with secular equivalents, "HEY you there" and "Come on HOME." Inhale while emphasizing the word "HEY" and exhale on "you there." You should fall into a two-beat rhythm of ONE-and-two. For the second phrase, inhale on "Come on" and exhale on "HOME." The rhythm changes to one-and-TWO. Chant each phrase for a minute and see how you feel … Now stand up and do it. And finally, bend over as you exhale and straighten as you inhale. This adds a whole new dimension to dizzy …

PART THREE

Kinetic Trance Techniques

9

·········

How to Prepare

Now for the practical portion of the book, where I finally get to teach you how to "feel the god within," as the Greeks put it. Remember what I mentioned in the introduction, however. "Possession" is not necessary to benefit from trance's healing and meditative properties. and because it is difficult to control, I will only cover techniques for milder "lucid" trances. Also, before you continue, quickly flip back and review chapter 3: the four stages of descent, how to recognize suppressed memories, etc.

As I mentioned previously, feeling safe is essential for trance dancing. If you are uncomfortable for any reason, you won't go into trance. Just like with hypnosis—if you don't want to be hypnotized, it won't happen. So, two ways to put yourself at ease (and set ground rules for your subconscious and the entities lurking around you) are preparation and ritual.

The Space

Let's begin by preparing the space you intend to dance in—the room that will soon become your sacred protective container. Ideally, it should be large enough for you to move about freely without disturbing others or them disturbing you—in other words, somewhere you can play loud music at night, year round, without interruptions, whenever the spirit moves you. And while the great outdoors may foster mystic connections with nature and sky, familiarity breeds subliminal triggers, meaning that consistent use of a space will help you go deeper into trance. Hence, inside warm and dry is far better than outside cold and wet. Obviously, the number of people participating will determine the room's size. Terpsichore Trance Therapy (TTT) allows 20 square meters per dancer. That's a lot. One person doing the movements in this book should find that 5' x 7'—the size of a dance rug—is enough. But check the periphery for sharp edges. You don't want to bump into a corner with your eyes closed. Obviously, the less furniture the better.

As for what time of day to dance, that's up to you. Some ceremonies, like the zar "day-beat" from chapter 7, are held during the day, but most occur at night, when the Invisibles are stronger. The choice is yours, though—whatever works best for your diurnal rhythms is what you should do. A word of caution, however. Don't dance right after a meal. As with swimming or any other strenuous exercise, wait an hour or so before you begin, otherwise you may find yourself extremely nauseous! Also important: no disruptions. Surfacing abruptly from trance can cause nausea, muscle cramps, and headaches, depending how deep you were. Block out an hour of uninterrupted time, turn off the phone, put a "Do Not Disturb" sign on the door, and warn your family and friends that you really do want privacy.

I prefer to dance on an Oriental carpet (except when spinning). It cushions my feet (or hands and knees) and the designs encourage visions. Carpets are personal, though, and should be chosen with care. Their colors, design, shape, and material will affect your journey—even smell, particularly if you kneel (yes, rugs have odors, some more noticeable than others). It doesn't have to be expensive. Machine-made from a hardware store or secondhand from a thrift shop will do, as long as it's clean. If you don't want to use a rug, make sure the floor is even, without grooves or bumps, and gives, i.e., has spring to it (wood rather than concrete or linoleum), to be kind to your joints.

Carefully chosen decorations also facilitate trance induction by creating a sacred atmosphere (whatever you feel that should be). But if permanently embellishing your space isn't an option, then a movable altar will do—any table or ledge where you can prominently display things: objects that make you feel safe, happy, and loved, and if you intend to invite the spirit world, candles, incense, and protective symbols. Since trance enhances creativity and/or problem solving, reminders of a task at hand or a query (if you have one) are also helpful. Plus, you will need a place to put water, a towel if you sweat, your dance journal, and a pen.

Next, consider lighting and music. Low light levels help minimize distractions and focus your attention inward, while flames act as hypnotic visual focal points. But fire attracts spirits, so use a dim electric lamp if you don't want visitors. The other major concern is music. You will need a sound system that plugs into an electric outlet (batteries have a way of dying at inopportune moments) and speakers rather than headphones or earplugs. The head movements you are about to do are incompatible with anything attached to your ears. Prepare your music ahead of time and make several sets with variable lengths. You may enjoy yourself more than you anticipated and want to continue, or have a sudden craving for something completely different. Also, once your brainwaves drop to theta and you enter trance, the music may seem louder or softer, so be ready to adjust the volume.

Personal Preparation

Personal preparation should also be thought through—what to wear, for example. The obvious answer is something comfortable, since you may be rolling around on the floor. I find that leggings or pants with a loose waist are best. I like to dance barefoot, but leather-soled shoes (not rubber) make spinning easier. Dancing in heels or socks, on the other hand, is dangerous (you may slip). Let your hair down, since these head movements tend to unravel braids and elastic bands fly off within minutes. Leave glasses off as well, along with long chains, floppy earrings, dangling jewelry, or anything else that could fly up and hit you. Many people wear amulets or spirit jewelry for protection, which is fine if it stays on. But the last thing you want is to lose something you care about or hit something with a flying object. Be objective. If it opens easily or comes off, it's best not to wear it. For women, no makeup is preferable, since it often runs when you sweat and stings the eyes.

Contraindications

It's important to be aware of medical conditions that could make trance dancing dangerous. If you have any of the following, consult your doctor. It's best not to take chances. Also consult your physician if you are not used to regular strenuous exercise. You should be able to sustain an elevated heart rate for at least twenty minutes, but preferably forty-five minutes or more.

Contraindicated conditions:

- Epilepsy—trance dancing is conducive to seizures
- Pulmonary problems, emphysema
- Cardiovascular problems—heart, arteries, clots, stroke, poor circulation
- Range of motion disorders, including joint, spine, or neck problems
- Psychotic disorders and obsessive-compulsive disorder
- Pregnancy or during a menstrual period
- Migraines
- Taking medication that makes you dizzy or nauseous
- Motion sickness or acute inner ear sensitivity

Pre-Induction Ritual

Once your space is arranged, your music organized, and your body ready, it is time to prepare your mind. This is where ritual comes in—that sequence of sensory cues that slows your brainwaves from beta to theta and triggers trance. A good ritual helps you focus on the present, not the future or the past. An excellent ritual inspires positive expectations. You must *want* to go into trance, *feel comfortable* with this decision, and *keep an open mind* during the experience. Leave apprehension, fear, and preconceived ideas at the door. As mentioned, reread chapter 3 to reacquaint yourself with possible trance symptoms, and always remember, YOU control what happens on your journey.

What follows is my pre-induction setup routine. I include it only as a template to help you devise your own. Experiment to find what works for you.

No interruptions—I turn off the phone, make sure no one needs me for a while, and then shut the door. By now, my household knows that when I disappear into the basement they better have a really good reason to bother me …

Turn down the lights—My first cue is a low light situation; I turn on special multicolored oriental lamps I only use for trance dancing.

Music—Next I head to the sound system and put on something slow, a haunting melody with not much percussion. Then I decide what induction music to play, depending on the time I have and the issues I'm mulling over. I usually create sets days in advance (a compilation of them will be released after the book), but sometimes I crave completely new music. My brain loves a challenge, and the intense concentration of dancing to unknown music deepens trance. I also organize what to play during cool down afterwards. Keeping everything next to the stereo avoids having to search for it later. Nothing kills trance like music issues!

Roll out the carpet—If it is not out already.

Light a candle—Do this if you want to invite the spirit world to your party. If you do, you will need matches, fresh candles, and a safe place to put fire while you dance. For important occasions, I light at least five candles, one for each cardinal point (north, south, east, west) and another for the altar. But for everyday exercise I just burn two, one on the altar and one next to my dance journal. As I lift match to wick, I stare at the flame and pray for guidance, clarity, and wisdom. It's not important whom you pray to—God, a prophet, the spirits, yourself, or no one in particular. The actual act of praying, of directing full attention to sending a message, triggers descent. I also focus on problems I want to solve, or creative projects lacking inspiration. I picture them in my mind, mull them over for a minute or so . . . and then let them go.

Incense—Invisibles find incense irresistible, so if you don't want visitors, don't light it. I keep a wide selection handy to satisfy urges (spirits making suggestions) and my everchanging moods. I light it with a short prayer or charm and inhale deeply while smudging my body. Then I circle the space with it to perfume the room and establish a perimeter. I invite, not invoke, benevolent spirits to participate—and warn malevolent ones they are not welcome if they don't behave.

At the moment, I am fond of a sixteenth-century charm Orion Fox-wood taught me:

> White spirits, black spirits, red spirits, gray
> Come ye, come ye, all that may
> Around and around, throughout and about
> All good come in, all bad stay out.[370]

Repeat this multiple times.

Then I set the burner out of harm's way, near an air current to keep it lit.

Switch music to a trance set—This set should begin with (at least) five minutes of slow music.

Deep breathing—I stand in the middle of the room and completely fill my lungs with air. No thinking, just feeling and listening to the music. Then I quickly exhale by sharply contracting my rib cage. Am I stressed or nervous? I recognize why and let it go. I breathe in again and feel the tension diminish. Exhale. After about ten of these I begin the warm-up exercises in the next chapter. But before you move on, please take time to do the homework.

Homework: Preparing Your Space

Set up your dance area. As you work, think of ideas for a pre-induction ritual and write them down in your journal. When you are done, bless your new space, particularly if you are open to spirit visitation. Now's the time to extend invitations to those you want and ward off those you don't. You set the ground rules, remember? Establish them from the beginning.

---

370   This is a loose adaptation of a well-known sixteenth-century charm cited in various sources: for example, *The Witch* by Thomas Middleton. Shakespeare also referenced it in *Macbeth*.

10

· · · · · · · · ·

How to Warm Up

Now we get to the physical exercise. But as any good coach will tell you, to avoid muscle injury you should warm up before doing any strenuous activity. And since the induction movements you are about to do are potentially risky, I *strongly* suggest you stretch beforehand—if not with the following exercises, then others, but do something, otherwise you could hurt yourself. The following stretches are uniquely adapted, however, because they are slow versions of the induction movements you are about to do. Half-time repetition promotes muscle memory—before full speed deployment.

As with other forms of exercise, avoid anything that causes sharp pain and build stamina slowly. If you are out of shape, start with ten-minute sessions, and then gradually prolong them. Be aware, though, that novices usually require at least 15–20 minutes of continuous "swaying" before trance sets in. You will also want to put on music—slower, melodic compositions for stretching, and then faster rhythmic tracks for induction. Try to avoid silences between pieces, so that your soundtrack is continuous.

Basic Stance

Before you learn to move, you must first master how to stand. Place your feet a little wider than your shoulders, toes pointing forward and knees slightly bent. Straighten and elongate your spine and adjust your pelvic bones so that the tops point up. No arching. Square and center your shoulders, then push them down. No computer slump. Imagine balancing books on your head. Elongate your neck and let arms hang loose. Now, shift weight from side to side, from one leg to the other, by bending the weight-bearing knee and leaning straight onto it (like the Tower of Pisa) without lifting your other foot (or heel) off the floor. If this is comfortable, you're in the right position.

Figure 37: Basic stance—shifting weight

Cosmic Hug

Tilt your head back and look up at the ceiling. Straighten and slowly lift your arms sideways over your head. You should feel a gentle pull along your upper arms and rib cage. Cross one arm over the other and bend both elbows until you can place flat palms on opposite shoulders in a giant self-embrace. Leave your hands where they are, bend your knees, and, with a flat back, lean forward from the waist until you can go no farther. This will pull on your lower spine. Release your back and collapse forward until your head is upside down, hands still on your shoulders. Hang there, and gently bounce your torso. This should separate and align your vertebrae. Next, release your hands and let them fall to the floor. Bounce some more. Slowly roll straight back up your spine into an upright position, arms dangling loosely by your sides.

Repeat this sequence three more times, alternating the top arm for the "hug." Breathe naturally but deeply. Fill your lungs as arms go up, exhale as you bend over. Inhale a second time while you hang upside down and exhale as you roll up. Do everything slowly.

Figure 38: Cosmic hug

Figure 39: Snake charmer—rotating upper body

Figure 40: Snake charmer—inverted torso

Snake Charmer: Cobra in a Basket

Begin by gently rolling your head around in a circle. Let it hang down in front like a tetherball and flop back in the rear. Complete at least seven revolutions before moving on. It's okay if you hear cracking. It's not okay if you feel sharp pain. Don't continue if it hurts; this induction method is not for you. As your head rotates, gradually include shoulders, upper torso, and waist until your entire upper body is involved. After two complete circles, end with your upper body upside down in front, head dangling towards the floor. Place hands on thighs for support and swing your inverted torso and head gently back and forth like a tetherball until the blood flows to your brain. Then center your head and once again, roll back up the spine. Repeat the entire maneuver, beginning with the head rolls, in the opposite direction.

The next two exercises actually belong in the induction category—but done slowly they are stretches.

Weaving 8's: The Zar "Sway"

Spread your legs slightly farther apart than your initial stance. As before, shift weight side to side, from one leg to the other, by bending the weight-bearing knee, leaning on it, and then pushing off to the other leg without lifting your feet off the floor. Once you transfer weight and balance to a leg, swing your torso forward and around it in a circle, allowing your head to gently roll. Then shift weight onto the other leg, by pushing off from the weight-bearing thigh, and trace a second upper-body circle in the opposite direction (clockwise on the right versus counter-clockwise on the left) over the new leg. When your torso swings to the rear, push off back to the first leg. Your chest will return to its original position to complete a figure eight. Do at least four, pushing from thigh to thigh and side to side, your head rolling with the momentum.

Figure 41: Weaving 8's—full-body, including head roll and arm toss

Once you master shifting weight, practice reducing stress on your neck. Your head should roll because your torso, supported by your thighs, rolls—not because the dead weight of your skull reels it around. By pushing from the thighs and aligning head with shoulders, rather than letting it flop uncontrolled or be jerked around by the neck muscles, you will relieve what could potentially become dangerous pressure on your fragile upper vertebrae. Head and shoulders should lead, while the torso plays "catch-up."

Figure 42: Weaving 8's—option from a sitting position

Figure 43: Zikr twist

Zikr Twists

Still standing, slide your feet back to their previous position directly under your shoulders and let your arms dangle by your sides. Posture is important for this exercise, so check that shoulders and pelvis are properly aligned along a straight spine with knees bent. With feet firmly planted, on the first count slowly twist your upper body to look behind you over one shoulder. Allow the arms to wrap around your torso, back hand touching front shoulder and front hand reaching behind to touch the back hip (note for dancers: the wrap completes on the syncopated back beat). When hands touch shoulder and hip, you should feel wound up like a spring. On the second count, slowly unwind in the other direction to face front. The arms will swing out and follow in delayed motion. Without stopping, on the third count continue twisting until you can see behind you over the other shoulder. Once again, the arms will wrap around, but with the other arm on top. As before, the back hand touches the front shoulder and the front hand reaches behind to touch the back hip. On the fourth count, switch directions and face front, arms following in belated motion. As the upper body twists, the head turns from side to side.

When done slowly, this exercise stretches spine and neck muscles and loosens vertebrae. When done quickly, it induces trance by agitating the inner ear fluid. Do at least eight slow twists, four on each side, in continuous motion. Never twist farther than is comfortable. If you are stiff, just swing your arms and turn your head.

As you move, focus on your body. Is anything stiff? Take extra care to stretch those muscles out. Listen carefully to the music. Find new things about it you hadn't noticed before. At some point during the Zar Sway or the Zikr Twist, the soundtrack should shift from "slow warm up" to "slow rhythmic induction" music. Trial and error will help you determine when that should be. The tracks should flow one into the other without breaks, and the beats per minute should increase gradually, not abruptly.

You can continue with Twists and Eights or switch to other techniques; that's up to you. Whatever you decide, though, start gently and pace yourself. Close your eyes. Concentrate on the tempo. At first, shift weight on the heavy downbeats, to "inhabit" the rhythm. Then move any way you want to, to whatever beat you hear. No one is watching. No one cares how you dance. Whatever feels good is what you should do—for as long as you want to do it. You don't have to please anyone but yourself. If you want to go down on your knees, dance on your back, squirm on your belly, go for it—do whatever makes you happy. In the coming chapters I have purposely given you movements that don't require much space. If you find a group to dance with where there's lots of room, so much the better, but most people aren't so fortunate. Remember, the goal is simply to keep your upper body and head in constant motion.

How to Fall

One last exercise before we switch to induction movements: how to fall. Not that I expect you will, but it's always good to know what to do, just in case. This technique is partly derived from Tae Kwon Do and partly my own. Falls usually happen during spins or head tosses because of dizziness—or because you trip on a rug or a piece of furniture when your eyes are closed. You never know. So … if you feel yourself falling, try to sink into a fetal position first. Collapse your knees and roll onto the floor. Obviously, the worst thing to do is topple from a standing position and break your fall with your hands and wrists. Instead, slap the ground with open palms aligned with bent forearms, then push into a roll. It's always better to distribute weight throughout the body than let one unfortunate bit absorb the entire impact. Proximity to the ground before contact also helps, which is why collapsing into a ball first is a good reflex to learn. Buckle your knees and roll onto your back a few times to get used to the sensation.

Trance in general, and kinetic trance in particular, is fragile. Much like sexual orgasm, it requires specific stimulation amplified by concentration and practice. When the stimulation stops, the state dissipates. In other words, during kinetic trance, once movement ceases, ordinary consciousness will slowly return. So if you are uncomfortable, for whatever reason, or feel you are descending too deep, stop moving. To resurface completely, lie on your back and bring your knees to your chest in a fetal position. When you are ready, slowly open your eyes and focus on the ceiling. You may feel dizzy at first, but this will pass. Don't try to get up right away, as your legs may be shaky. Give yourself about five minutes, and then another ten before trying to think clearly. Sip, don't guzzle, water, and no driving for at least half an hour. Some people need even more recovery time than that. "Fuzzy brain" is normal after trance, so don't be alarmed. It dissipates completely after a good night's sleep—which is almost guaranteed given all the exercise you've just done. Also, be prepared for vivid dreams as your subconscious works through whatever you dredged up in theta.

Possession

As mentioned previously, the techniques described in the following chapters are not intended to induce possession trance (in which a host personality steps aside while a spirit temporarily borrows its body). Nor will they enable uninvited entities to infiltrate, or worse, take up residence behind, your mental "firewall." They are simply designed to enhance receptivity—to new ideas, old memories, inner voices, and outer stimuli. Actually, the deep altered state possession trance requires is difficult to achieve. It takes weeks, if not months, of prodding, appeasing, and coaching before entities manifest— in cultures that believe in spirits. Mindset is everything, for good reason.

In the West, children are taught that the spirits they see and the voices they hear are not real, so as adults they no longer experience them. In cultures where spirits are a given, these mental barriers aren't erected. The Western mindset, with its scientific, cause-and-effect-based assumptions about reality, encourages its populations to only see, hear, or believe in what has been empirically proven to exist (except for God, of course). As a result, spirits have a much harder time convincing well-educated Westerners of their existence, or, even trickier, getting Westerners to let go of the reins and allow them to take over. This is why "ordinary" spirit possession (unlike demonic possession, which is extremely rare) requires a host's receptivity, if not permission, to occur. For the most part, if you don't say yes, it won't happen. This excludes, of course, abnormal physical states, particularly epilepsy, schizophrenia, and bipolar or obsessive-compulsive disorders. These are biological, chemical, or electrical malfunctions, not signs of the devil. And as I stated previously, if you have these sorts of medical issues, you should not try this method of trance induction.

Medical issues aside, you can see that attitude profoundly effects trance—and your experiences in it. Fear taints whatever it touches. But if you maintain a strong sense of identity and do not consider yourself a victim, interacting with whatever you come across shouldn't be a problem. Follow your moral compass, maintain a sense of humor, stand up for yourself, and you will be fine. You may even find that the beings you encounter are as curious about you as you are about them—and that they have a wicked sense of humor... the benevolent ones, that is. Those on the darker side, who make your compass spin, should be shunned.

For those who would like to experience possession, you too should begin with the techniques described, to see if you are capable of entering kinetic trance. Without trance there can be no possession, and not everyone is susceptible. Similar to hypnosis, results vary according to personality type and genetic makeup. However, if you do experience lucid trance and wish to go deeper, then the next step is to seek instruction from experienced individuals with proven track records. Also, think carefully about the spirits you would like to host. If you wish to experience a variety, I recommend contacting a Brazilian Umbanda temple. Their practices are full of positive energy and do not include animal sacrifice. If you want to communicate with human souls, visit the Spiritualists in Lily Dale, New York. And if you seek unity with the Holy Spirit (possession by God), try a respected Pentecostal congregation or Sufi sect—albeit if you are a woman, the Sufis might not be the best place to go. Women are not allowed to participate in public ceremonies or orthodox services, although attitudes are changing in Turkey (they now have female Sufi whirlers). Women do attend popular (shaabi) zikrs in Egypt, however, as I mentioned in chapter 8. In fact, shaabi zikr movements are so effective at altering consciousness that I have borrowed several for the next chapter. Before you discover them, though, please do the homework.

Homework: Muscle Memory

Practice a warm-up exercise routine until you can do it from memory. This will free you to close your eyes, listen to the music, and concentrate on your body.

> *"There is no path except by effort and practice at first;*
> *thereafter it becomes nature through custom."*
>
> —Al-Ghazali

11

·········

How to Zikr

Now that you're warmed up and stretched out, the next three chapters are dedicated to techniques that induce "flow," a mental state that sweeps you down a river of improvisation—much like rafting in a swift current. Eventually you will learn how to steer, but for now sit back, trust the process, and enjoy the ride. No planning, no performance, no worrying how you look, no outside world—just spontaneous movement to music.

Before we dive in, though, let me answer a frequently asked question: "to see or not to see?" Do you open or shut your eyes? Frank Natale, in his book *Trance Dance: The Dance of Life,* suggested dancers wear colorful bandanas to block out the world around them.[371] And in fact, Egyptian women do a variation of this. As mentioned previously, they drape tarha over their heads to reduce light and hide their inverted eyes and pained expressions. This is safer than a blindfold—but unnecessary if you are dancing alone in a darkened room. North African women use their long black hair, which is far more practical, since, when not covering their faces, it whips around at speeds that would normally send blindfolds flying. But honestly, if you dance alone, tying something over your eyes is dangerous. Turn the lights down instead. After all, no one is watching but the Invisibles. Most of these techniques are stationary anyway, so you don't need to see where you are going. Science also weighs in for eyes closed. Darkness triggers descent into alpha, which is another reason I encourage you to shut your eyes during warm-up (no matter what you do later).

---

371   *Trance Dance,* 39.

Group zikrs are different, though. Participants open their eyes when they stand, because jumping, spinning, and stepping require visuals to avoid a train wreck. The question then becomes, do they spot—i.e., fix their eyes on a specific point while they move? Spotting is one of the first tricks dancers, gymnasts, skaters, or other athletes learn when they spin to combat dizziness. But trance dancers want to be dizzy—so no, on the contrary, zikr participants maintain a fluid gaze. But I'm getting ahead of myself. Let me save the rest of this discussion for chapter 13, How to Whirl.

Instead, let's plunge in, sink-or-swim style. The zikr movements that follow, traditional and popular, are divided into three categories: seated, standing, and moving. Some are repeated because the farther off the ground you get, the better the results. But please remember—many of the movements are potentially dangerous, so it is important that you practice them slowly first, with the suggested modifications, before attempting them at full speed.

Seated Movements

These techniques are the easiest—and safest—to do. Sit however is most comfortable: cross-legged, legs straight in front, or kneeling on your heels. I find a modified kneel allows more range of motion, but this can be uncomfortable for anyone with knee problems.

Let's begin with methods to protect the cervical vertebrae at the base of your skull. But first, do several head rolls in both directions to stretch your neck muscles out.

Twist—Slowly twist your head to look behind you, left and right, without moving your shoulders. Feel the bones and muscles involved. Then include your rib cage, keeping shoulders and torso aligned. By engaging the back as well as the neck, you relieve pressure. Do about ten of these in each direction.

Nod—Drop your chin to your chest, then tilt your head back and look up at the ceiling. As before, do this a few times with just your head. Then, without moving your neck or shoulders, repeat the nod by collapsing and arching your rib cage, using your diaphragm and back muscles near your shoulder blades. Repeat this modified bob about twenty times to get the feel of it, exhaling as you look down and inhaling as you look up.

Crescent—Hang your head forward and with neck muscles alone, swing your skull from side to side like a pendulum. Then include your upper body by engaging your back muscles. Again, don't slump the shoulders, as this will make breathing difficult. Do twenty.

Forward-and-back bends—Still seated, support your weight with hands on thighs and lean to the front until your head flops forward. Then push off backwards until your head flops to the rear. Do this slowly several times to practice transitioning from front to back and back to front. Apply the "nod" modifications you just did. Keep a straight neck and move only your rib cage. Control how far forward and back you go with your arms. Either lean so far forward that pushing off your knees never takes you farther than upright, or catch yourself in the back with one hand on the floor behind you and then push off. Remember, the objective is to agitate your inner ear fluid, not snap your neck.

Figure 44: Forward-and-back bends

Figure 45: Torso twist

Torso Movements

Torso twists—This is an upper body zikr twist (since you are seated). Increase the warm-up tempo by swinging the arms faster. When looking behind you, include your rib cage and shoulders. The head leads direction changes.

Torso crescents or the crescent moon—Sit either cross-legged or on your heels with hands on thighs for support. This more-or-less horizontal sweep is generated from the waist and lower back and done with a straight spine. Sitting upright, lean to one side and let the weight of your torso pull you forward and down to your thighs, then around and back to upright on the other side. Now reverse the movement; right to left, then left to right. Your head will trace the shape of a crescent as it sweeps over your knees. The moon is a popular image in the Middle East because the Muslim faith is based on a lunar calendar. The crescent new moon heralds the beginning of a month, which is particularly important before and after Ramadan, the holy month of fasting.

Torso pendulum—This shaabi zikr movement is done kneeling rather than sitting. Similar to the Crescent Moon, it uses gravity and centrifugal force to swing the head. It differs in that the head traces a vertical upside-down path rather than a horizontal crescent. Again, when upside down, if needed use hands on thighs or floor for support. Start upright on your knees. Throw your arms in the air to one side and look up. Then collapse your torso, invert your head, and swing upside down from the waist to the other side, letting your arms sweep along the floor before righting yourself, rising on your knees again, and throwing your arms up to the other side. The higher you rise, the more room you will have to swing upside down in between. As your torso swings up, the arms go up and the head goes back (look up). As it swings down, invert your head and look at your chest.

Figure 46: Torso pendulum

Standing Movements

Use the same stance and posture from the warm-up chapter: feet planted slightly wider than the shoulders, bent knees, a long neck, and a straight spine.

Standing forward-and-back bends—This is similar to the seated version, only far more animated. You can still support your forward weight with hands on thighs, but in the rear arch there's nothing to catch you except your back muscles. This is a Sufi favorite, but it is not for the faint of heart—or the weak of spine (see the zikr illustration and Trumbell's 1907 description at the beginning of chapter 8).

Standing Zikr twist—This is the warm-up technique at full speed, with the same loose arms, upper body rotation, and pelvic twist.

Standing pendulum—This is the standing version of the kneeling pendulum described above. Since the head travels farther, the inner ear stimulation is greater. It is often used in zar hadras, particularly with the arm tosses.

Windmill—This vertical variation of the zikr twist has the arms circling up and down instead of wrapping horizontally around the body. The torso movements remain the same.

Moving, Turning, and Spinning

Now try covering ground with some of the movements; i.e., dancing!

Zikr stomp—Edward Lane gives a great description of this:

With extended arms and joined hands, the dervishes formed a large ring and turning their heads alternately to the right and left, repeatedly exclaimed, *Allah!* At each exclamation, they bowed head and body, and took a step to the right, so the whole ring moved rapidly round. Soon they jumped to the right instead of stepping, each placing his arms on the shoulders of those next to him, until finally they became quite excited, rapidly repeating their ejaculations, violently turning their heads, and sinking the whole body forward while jumping.[372]

Leaping and jumping in circles—Pulsing in the heels or leaping in the air imparts a sense of weightlessness, which further confuses the inner ear.

Moving Shaabi Zikr twists—These three twists produce serious inner ear stimulation without the excessive dizziness caused by lengthy spinning. As with the seated and standing versions, moving twists use the arms to rotate the upper body. Stepping or shifting weight happens in the beginning, with the arms wrapping over the weight-bearing leg during the stationary pause. A "step" can also mean simply shifting weight. **Step-Twist:** This is the easiest to do, with only two counts; one—two, right step—right twist, left step—left twist. Shift weight and then swing the arms. Switch directions by stepping onto the other foot. **The Pivot-Twist:** This movement uses four beats; one—two—3/4, right foot pivot to the left—step onto the left—torso twist to the left for two counts, left foot pivot to the right—right step (or just shift weight onto the right foot)—right twist for two counts, etc. Pivot the foot 90 degrees, either the ball or the heel. The third variation, the **Three-Step-Turn**, is by far the most complex technique in the chapter—a moving 360-degree turn (a complete revolution) spread out over three steps. It, too, uses four beats: one step—two step—three step—twist. Step 90 degrees to the side—step turn 90 degrees—step turn 90 degrees—plant the feet but allow the upper body to twist another 90 degrees propelled by the arm wrap. Repeat in the other direction. Eye focus remains soft, and you can pivot on either the ball or the heel.

---

372   *An Account of the Manners and Customs of Modern Egyptians*, 425–27. Edited for clarity.

Trance Symptoms

Don't stop because you're dizzy! Dizziness is the first milestone on the road to trance. The second landmark is "flow," when the autonomic nervous system (autopilot) takes over, often accompanied by a "second wind" burst of energy.

The third sign is tricky, a shift in body awareness and a disassociation of mind from body—"fly on the wall syndrome." Here you become an objective observer watching yourself through third-party eyes—and frequently, tunnel vision. For me, this phase is also accompanied by a subtle shift in timbre; the music becomes crisper, slightly more metallic, and all engulfing. Nothing else exists except what I hear and play (usually finger cymbals or a mangour). It feels as if someone else is playing for me. I become so tuned in to the music I anticipate what comes next, even to music I have never heard before. Everyone is different, though, so you must find your own landmarks.

The first time is always the hardest, so keep dancing even if you don't feel "different." Theta states aren't always sharply delineated. A clue you have arrived is that faces appear in the shadows and you start to "feel" others around you. Relax; allow the shapes to fill out, their personalities to unfold, and their voices to speak. Those eyes staring at you in the wall, that hunch you just had, or the whispering you thought you heard—will get stronger until you *know* something or someone is communicating with you, perhaps through metaphor. First visitations usually don't happen unless you *want* them to, though. But once the floodgates open, once the others begin to appear and you really see them, they will be with you, on and off, for the rest of your life. If this is what you want, keep practicing your visualization skills. After your first waking theta experience, you will be less apprehensive, more relaxed and open to possibilities most people spend their whole lives negating. Take that leap of faith, believe … You created the playlist, now it's time to follow the pied piper …

One last counter-intuitive suggestion: it doesn't matter whether you achieve an altered state or not. Exercise is good for you either way, and your body will reward you for it with a pleasant endorphin buzz and a rush of "feel-good" serotonin. Dancing and listening to music relieves stress; anything more is just icing on the cake. Adopt this laid-back approach and entering trance will become easier. There is such a thing as trying too hard.

Homework: Practice

Perfect the seated exercises until you no longer put pressure on your neck when tossing your head. Then try the standing movements, slowly, to see if any of them suit you. If not, there are plenty more in the next chapters—but these are gentler. The others are no-holds-barred.

12

·········

How to Zar

Hair flinging (or "head banging") is the hallmark induction technique of the zar—for the simple reason that it's the best method out there, besides whirling, to induce trance.

In fact, nearly every historic description of kinetic trance mentions wild head movements, from Plato and Euripides (in *The Bacchae*) to present-day Egyptian zar and zikr chroniclers. Certainly, witnessing trance dance frenzies can be shocking, given the extraordinary flexibility the state produces.

In Ethiopia, for example, the first European description of zar dancing (from the 1839 journals of two Christian missionaries) mentions a woman alternately singing, smoking, and moving her head "in every direction."[373] Michel Leiris reinforced these observations in 1931–1933, when he marveled at the dancers' "frenetic torso and neck movements, which entrain the head in vertiginous gyrations in every direction."[374] Zar induction in Somalia is similar. Instead of dancing, patients "went on hands and knees before the drums and shook their

BAKXAI.

Figure 47:
Maenad head toss

---

373 *Journals of the Rev. Messrs. Isenberg and Krapf, Missionaries of the Church Missionary Society*, 116–18.

374 *La Possession et ses aspects théâtraux chez les Éthiopiens de Gondar*, 43. My translation from the French.

heads from side to side."[375] But don't worry, not all zar induction techniques require wild head tossing or extreme elasticity.

How to Sway: Zar Faqqar Techniques

We know from the science chapter that head tossing causes trance by over-stimulating the vestibulocochlear nerve pathway—just like Sufi techniques. But unlike the Sufis, zar "swaying" does not follow predetermined rules or group "choreographies." Improvisation is the key to its success. Whatever works best, that's what the ladies do. Once entranced, however, they switch to specific steps and/or gestures to identify their possessing spirits.

Egyptian zar movements also differ from group zikr practices in that they are relatively stationary. Zar hadras are usually held in small spaces and the older or larger women who frequent them are unable (or unwilling) to jump around or spin like their male zikr counterparts. Furthermore, many women sway sitting down, since traditionally, only those who have sacrificed to their spirits dance on their feet. To counterbalance this, zar ceremonies use louder music, more frenetic upper body movements, and individual rather than group induction techniques.

On the bright side, this means beginners have a wide selection of seated movements to choose from. Collapse after climax is also easier. But dancers must take care, nevertheless. Seated or standing, you can still snap your neck from bad technique. Adepts may appear immune, but out-of-shape novices will quickly discover that over-zealous head tossing causes sore muscles and headaches. You can avoid these pitfalls by warming up beforehand and developing correct muscle memory by practicing the movements slowly. Supporting the neck with the upper torso also helps.

CAUTION: Head banging can be particularly painful for those prone to migraines. If you are predisposed to headaches, try whirling instead (the next chapter). Honestly, head banging is not for you. If, on the other hand, you can tolerate these movements, the next step is to push through the dizziness. Start on the floor, like zar novices, and build tolerance.[376] Once this is comfortable, kneel, and finally stand in a wide-legged stance.

---

375   Lewis et al., *Women's Medicine*, 170–71.

376   You don't want to become too tolerant, however, because induction becomes difficult. After forty years of spinning as a professional dancer, I am now almost immune.

Let's begin by reviewing the Weaving 8's warm-up exercise (which is not head bang-ing). The key points are to push off from the thighs and not whip your head around by just the neck. Use your upper back muscles. Done properly, this induction method is the only one you should need. But if your inner ears are desensitized or you are afraid of relinquishing control, more intense stimulation may be in order.

Spread your legs slightly farther apart than your shoulders. Shift weight from leg to leg by bending the weight-bearing knee, leaning on it, and then pushing off to the other leg with both feet parallel and flat on the floor. From the waist up, swing your torso forward in a circle over the weight-bearing leg (right clockwise, left counter-clockwise), allowing your head to gently roll. Egyptians turn their faces toward the direction they are moving but tip their heads away. Next, push off and trace a second upper body circle over the other leg in the opposite direction. The head switches and tips to the other side. As you finish, push off back to the first leg; the chest returns to its original position.

In summary, sway from the waist up, start slow, only go as fast as is comfortable, and, most important, don't whip your skull around by neck muscles alone. Continue for at least 15–20 minutes. If this doesn't work, don't worry. Zar induction includes many techniques, some quite extreme. Here are a few I have witnessed over the years. Experiment to see if any work for you:

Head Movements

Let's begin with the head—sitting down—*after* you warm up your neck muscles.[377]

Rolls or head circles—These are good to start with, slowly, which is why
I begin the warm-up section with them. They can be done upright or
with the shoulders and/or torso slumped forward. Ethiopian, Iraqi,
and Moroccan women do them quickly, either vertically or horizontally, to whip their hair around during folkloric dances.

---

377 To warm up, use slow circular head rolls, hanging crescents (swinging the head from side to
side in front and back), and twists (looking over each shoulder without moving for a minute
to release the muscles).

Crescent swings—This, too, is a fast version of a warm-up exercise. The head drops forward (or back) and swings from side to side like a tetherball on a rope.

Twists—This is the head portion of a zikr twist, the backwards glance over the shoulder. Be careful—when done quickly, the friction can be rough on vertebrae.

Backward head tilt—Here the head tips backwards until the skull rests on the shoulder ridge. Greek maenads were often depicted in this position. Done while whirling, it increases dizziness exponentially. It can also be combined with upper body zikr tosses.

Nods or head-banging—This is a sharp, abrupt jerking of the head forward and back or in a V pattern. Definitely practice this either sitting, kneeling, or on hands and knees first. When standing, dancers sometimes put their hands on a wall or hold their arms out like airplane wings for balance. In the movement's purest, most severe form, only the skull moves, double-time to the beat. For the V formation, the head makes a point in the middle, either to the front or back, with the ears perpendicular to the floor or tipped and angled toward the shoulders.

Figure 48: Nods or head-banging

Seated Movements

Sit comfortably on the floor (cross-legged, knees bent toward the ceiling, or legs straight out in front, etc.). Depending on the movement, some positions may be easier than others. The objective is to allow your upper body to move freely. Try the following to slow, rhythmic music:

Seated swaying—Close your eyes and sway to the rhythm, side-to-side and front to back.

Seated bowing or tossing—Eventually, swaying turns into rocking; side-to-side, forward and back, or both. Use your lower back muscles to change directions. As the movements grow larger, use your hands to push off and catch yourself on the floor.

Seated crescents—Fold your arms across your chest. Leading with the elbow or shoulder, dip your upper body toward your thighs and swing to the other side. Then reverse the motion, returning to an upright position after each swing. One variation is to twist back up to the starting position instead of swinging, which will make the dip one-sided and always in the same direction.

Seated torso twist—This zar version of the upper-body zikr twist uses both the head and torso, and is done quickly, double-time to the beat. The arms swing out straight if there's room or bent at the elbows if there isn't.

Seated figure eights—This seated version of Weaving 8's is often done with the arms in a unicorn position (see the standing version) or folded across the chest.

Kneeling Movements

Again, choose a comfortable position. If your knees hurt, try supporting your weight with your hands or going down on all fours. Kneeling generally allows more range of movement than sitting, yet keeps you close to the floor in case you topple over.

Figure 49: Rocking

Rocking—As with the seated version, push off with one hand from either your thighs or the floor, and catch yourself with the other hand in the back or on the opposite side.

Kneeling bounce—Bounce on your knees (double-time to the beat) during zikr twists or Weaving 8's. Complicated layering increases concentration, which intensifies trance.

Standing Movements

Those who sway standing up during a typical, crowded zar hadra use either a wide-legged stance or a stationary two-count step-touch.

Arms—When there is room, the arms swing loosely like a rag doll, with the shoulders generating momentum. One way to tell whether someone is entranced or not is by their arms (except while spinning). If they are carefully placed, their owner is usually thinking too much and not in trance.

Flailing arms—This Egyptian favorite often happens right before climax. It resembles overhanded rope climbing or the alternating swing of power walkers and cross-country skiers. The head tips back and the eyes fix vaguely on the ceiling.

Stooped arm swing—Here the upper body bends forward from the waist, as if hoeing, while the arms swing in unison.

Swimming—This gesture resembles a swimmer's overhead "crawl," where the arms alternately swing in circles. It is often accompanied by a double-time bounce in the feet.

Figure 50: Nubian arm cross

Nubian arm cross—This movement requires space. The arms swing out on both sides, cross in front, swing out again, and then cross in back, in typical Nubian folk dance style. The head rolls in a figure eight pattern and the feet shift weight.

Shoulder shrugs—These are layered on top of other movements, usually double-time to the beat; again, to increase concentration.

Bowing—As the name implies, these are rapid, two-count, up-down torso movements. Either the arms swing up in front and alternately touch the forehead or hang loose. The feet remain planted and when upright, the head tilts back to look at the ceiling.

Weaving 8's—There are many ways to vary the Weaving 8 technique, either by layering movements on top of it or by changing tempo (on beat, half-time, or double-time). See description and figure 41 on pages 257–58.

Back hair toss during figure eights—This is done standing, with the hands braced on a wall for balance, the head and torso tipped backwards, and the spine slightly arched. The hair swings from side to side across the back.

Figure 51: Rocking the baby

Rocking the baby—Standing or sitting, this version uses folded arms across the chest, as if cradling a baby.

The unicorn—Straighten your arms, clasp your hands together, and raise them above your head as you sway, to imitate a stationary "horn."

Zar twist—Here, basic step-touch footwork is combined with upper body swaying to make larger torso circles. Direction changes occur with the tap, and the circles begin as the weight shifts onto the foot with the step.

Tipping—Here the torso simply bends from side to side, instead of normal three-dimensional weaving.

Footwork/Steps

Egyptian zar footwork is quite basic and done mainly to keep beat. Nevertheless, there are a few traditional steps:

Step-touch—This is perhaps the most ubiquitous step, with a basic two-count rhythm: step Right—tap Left, step Left—tap Right. It is usually done in one spot, but can be used to travel.

Zar stumble—Eugenie Le Brun witnessed this two-count walking step during her first zar ritual, when the women circled the altar. It is done leaning slightly forward, with the weight on the balls of the feet. Participants use other forward-leaning walking or skipping steps when there is room.

Zar skip—This two-count step is skipping in place: and ONE—and TWO, Right ball-HEEL, Left ball-HEEL.

Double bounce—This movement falls into the layering/concentration category. The torso bounces double-time as the feet do a step-touch. This is actually quite difficult!

Hiking—This is enthusiastic walking in place, accompanied by swinging arms.

During Egyptian zars, hosts switch to their spirit's hallmark movements once in trance. Here, FYI, are a few of the many spirits who have their own dances:

From Egypt

Yawra: This spirit struts around the dance floor with an erect, aristocratic posture, smoking cigarettes, sprinkling cologne, and swatting imaginary flies with a fly swatter.

Figure 52: Gado—bouncing crawl

Gado: Since this entity lives in bathrooms and toilets, his hosts get down on all fours and alternately strike the ground to keep the beat and/or sweep the floor with a broom and a dustpan. The specific step is a bouncing crawl on all fours (knees and elbows), head lowered to the floor, that eventually turns into a straight-bodied, side-to-side roll on the ground.

Roukash: Yawra's six-year-old daughter does Middle Eastern dance movements similar to belly dancing, often while eating candy and carrying a doll.

Saleela: This vain, egocentric female spirit loves to admire herself in a hand mirror and apply makeup while dancing.

The Dier or Christian Foreigner: This zar wears priests' robes and shoves a crucifix in onlookers' faces while dancing. He appreciates good beer, white cheese, and black olives.

Al-Arabi: As this spirit dances, he waves a sword in the air like Don Quixote "fighting windmills."

From Sudan

The holy man: He causes a forward-and-back rocking step.

The Arab: This spirit inspires a two-count step-hop step on each foot. This is perhaps one of humanity's oldest dance steps, as it is used for the Old Kingdom hieroglyph for dance.

The Ethiopian or Habashi: This results in a swaying from side to side.

An old woman: This inspires a bent-over shuffle step.

Johnny (a white male): He strides forward and back, sometimes with a cane or a walking stick.

Homework: Practice

Try all the movements to see if any have an effect on you. Adapt them as you like; there is no right or wrong way to do any of them and only one Cardinal Rule: **Nothing should hurt.** If something is painful, don't do it. List preferred techniques in your journal and experiment with them slowly to build muscle memory.

13

·········

How to Whirl

Compared to the zar, whirling is like night to day: no wild frenetic movements, no fainting, no possession, and certainly no blood—just mystic communion with the Holy Spirit. Dervishes go deep into trance, yet show no outward sign or loss of control. Let's look at this miracle induction technique from a movement standpoint. Celâleddin Çelebi wrote:

> At the beginning of the Sema, by holding his arms crossed, the semazen appears to represent the number one, thus testifying to God's unity. While whirling, his arms are open: his right palm is directed to the sky, ready to receive God's benefi-cence; his left hand, on which his eyes are fastened, is turned toward the earth. The semazen conveys God's spiritual gift to those witnessing the Sema. Revolving from right to left around the heart, the semazen embraces all humanity with love. The human being has been created with love in order to love.[378]

Spinning is one of the hardest things beginning dancers learn; certainly, the younger you start the better. Spinning is easy as a child, less so as you get older. There's a reason Dramamine, an antidote for motion sickness, has become a household word in the United States—many people have sensitive inner ears. What I'm getting at is that whirl-ing is not for everyone. When I teach it, some students turn green after a few seconds,

---

378   From liner notes of *Wherever You Turn Is the Face of God* by the Mevlevi Ensemble of Turkey.

while others get the technique right away and whirl to their heart's content. There's no way to know how you will react until you try. So let's start. If spinning isn't your thing, you can always use techniques from the previous chapters.

The eyewitness accounts in this chapter contain clues to Mevlevi techniques. Their method is very specific; costume, foot placement, eye, arm, hand, and head positions were determined centuries ago. I do have one problem with their system, though—semazen only spin in one direction. To me, this is wrong on many levels, but particularly because stress repetition damages joints and muscles. By periodically switching weight and torque to the other side of the body, cartilage and ligaments are allowed to rest, even while you spin. For this reason, I have devised several alternative techniques to alleviate pressure on knees and hips—comfort over doctrine. But let's explore the traditional Mevlevi method first. After all, it too has been designated as a UNESCO "masterpiece of the Oral and Intangible Heritage of Humanity."

Mevlevi Sufi Whirling

Alif, the Beginning Posture—Stand tall with an elongated spine and feet
pointing straight ahead under your shoulders. Take one hand and
place it on the opposite shoulder, keeping the elbow close to the body.
Fold the other arm over top of the first, again with the hand resting on
the opposite shoulder and the elbow tucked in. Your forearms should
form an X across your chest. This is the unity position of the Arabic
alphabet's first letter, *alif*, and the numeral one, *wahed*. Close your eyes
and maintain this position for at least a minute. I always feel like I'm
in a cocoon, separated from the world. The focal points are the shoulders (pulled down by the hands), the heart (where the forearms cross),
and the feet, anchored firmly to the ground and the material world.
Now try walking in this position—first with the eyes open and then
closed. Can you keep your balance?

Spin direction—As I mentioned, the Mevlevis spin in one direction: coun-
terclockwise, towards the left. I believe this is easier for right-handed
people, but try both directions to see. You may be surprised. Each feels

different, perhaps according to which cerebral hemisphere has excess versus insufficient blood and/or fluid (from centrifugal force while spinning) or which part of the inner ear is stimulated. At any rate, good dancers learn to move and spin in both directions, left and right, to avoid becoming "one-sided."

Feet—According to Rumi, "my left foot is fixed on the pillar of sha-riah [Islamic law] while my right foot travels like a wheel all 18,000 universes."[379] As a spinning technique, this translates into "fixing" the left foot on the floor—i.e., shifting weight and balance onto the left leg, which is referred to as the "pillar" or *direk,* while the right foot, the "wheel" or *cark,* propels the spin by paddling around it in a circle. In other words semazen execute a 360-degree spin by pivoting around the left leg, towards the left. This is further transformed into a silent zikr, a remembrance of God, by thinking of His name with every footfall.

As you can see, footwork is the heart of Mevlevi whirling and the subject of much scrutiny. *The Dictionary of Islam* mentions that sema-zen turn on their left heel. Celâleddin Çelebi wrote that they revolve "from right to left around the heart." And above we learn from Rumi that "my left foot is fixed … while my right foot travels like a wheel." Importantly, the turn is *not* done in relevé, as in ballet, on the ball with the heels high off the floor. Instead, the feet remain flat with only a slight lift of the left heel or ball, depending on which part of the foot you pivot on. NOTE: Do try turning on the heel. It may seem counter-intuitive, but once you get used to it, it's actually easier.

The right foot, the paddle, takes large steps around the left, choosing one spot to land in and then returning to that spot after a 360-degree revolution. This is where the "zikr by foot" comes in. The spinner lifts the foot while thinking "al-," completes the turn, and steps back in the

---

379   From liner notes of *Music of the Whirling Dervishes* CD by the Gulizar Turkish Music Ensemble.

same spot on "-lah." The two syllables act as an internal metronome to regulate the pace. The right foot hits the ground as if striding, heel first, around the left "pillar" or wheel axel. Once you achieve a regular rhythm, you'll agree with Rumi; it really does feel like you are holding on to a wagon axel and walking around the rim of a wheel. The down side is that during the spin the right foot continually crosses over the left, stressing the entire left leg and ankle. The best way I have found to relieve this tension is to occasionally turn in the other direction.

Speed—A nineteenth-century writer reported that "after the preliminary prayer and prostration, they whirl around, ring within ring, without touching each other, for about an hour, until they are utterly exhausted … They made about 40 or 50 turnings a minute."[380]

This quotation was the only clue I could find about traditional spin speed. Obviously, rotation velocity depends on the music's tempo, which, similar to the zar, starts slow and gradually increases. In clips online, semazen generally take about two seconds to complete a revolution (i.e., a weight transfer from right to left to right again). That's about 30 spins per minute—a slow, steady pace. Forty to fifty per minute is quite brisk. Normally, Mevlevi whirling is not frenetic—because the music is not frenetic. Ultimately though, how fast you turn is up to you—to the music you choose and the speed you feel comfortable maintaining. That's the beauty of dancing in your own space. You decide …

Hands and palms—Most sources describe the semazen's ultimate arm positions, but few detail how they get there. From the initial *alif* position, whirlers drop their hands from their shoulders to their sides, join them in front at the wrists with palms out, slowly lift them over their heads, and unfurl them above their hats. The right arm remains almost perpendicular to the sky while the left drops slightly, but stays above the shoulders. The right palm faces up to receive God's illumination and the

---

380   Frank Dobbins, *Error's Chains*, 749–50. Edited for length and clarity.

left palm points down to transmit His celestial blessings to Earth. Centrifugal force helps the arms rise, but shoulder muscles maintain them in place, which is why they may be sore afterwards. If you switch spin directions, switch your arms.

Head tilt—Semazen tip their heads to the right, opposite the spin direction, sometimes almost until the right ear touches the right shoulder. Try it. It doesn't seem like much, but it certainly amps up the dizziness factor. Keep neck, shoulder, and head aligned over the torso and once in position, leave it there.

Trance deepening techniques—For those accustomed to whirling, here are a few tricks to increase the intensity of your experience. **Warning: These variations are *not* for the faint of heart and should be tried in a large empty space. They are geared toward experienced dancers unaffected by normal spinning.** While whirling, either roll your head in a circle, lower your chin to your chest, or look up at the ceiling (without tipping your head to the side). Maintain the position for several rotations to feel the effect. Next, try rolling your eyes into your head as you turn. This mimics natural eye migration during trance and encourages theta.

A semazen's objective is to allow a will greater than his own to take over—to surrender to the Autonomic Nervous System and whatever else guides it. You, too, can try this if you feel capable. While possession or "surrender" doesn't have to be the goal, it does add a totally different dimension to the experience.

Precautions and Practicalities

As we have seen, preparation is almost as important as the ritual itself.

Shoes and socks—I have already mentioned that it's easier to spin on a wooden floor than on a rug and that leather soles are better than bare feet or rubber, plastic, or tread-soled footwear. There's a fine line between too much and not enough friction; experiment to find your happy medium.

Nausea—There's no getting around it; adults usually feel nauseous and dizzy when they first learn to whirl. That's why it's better to start with gentle movements—such as zikr twists. On the other hand, those with a high dizziness tolerance must spin longer to feel an effect. Everyone is different and you won't know where you fall on the spectrum until you try. In either case, to avoid nausea and excessive dizziness, periodically spin in the other direction, particularly when you're finished and want to stop. The worst thing is to end "cold turkey." Your body may no longer be rotating, but your inner ear fluid doesn't know that. It keeps going—until you revolve at least once in the opposite direction—similar to swirling liquid in a glass. Another way to avoid dizziness is to use the delayed arm wrap technique. Plant the feet, but allow the upper torso and arms to continue twisting another 180 degrees before changing direction or ending a spin. NOTE: Stopping and starting too often makes nausea worse, not better.

Variations on Mevlevi technique—Pivoting for long periods on the same leg can twist the femur in its pelvic socket and cause repetitive stress. Turning on the heel, taking smaller steps, and rocking between feet to distribute the weight help prevent this.

Ball versus heel—Pivoting on the heel connects the pelvis directly to the ground, without the ankle or ball of the foot as unstable intermediaries. It also helps prevent the knee from twisting independently from the thigh.

Figure 53: Pivoting on heels

Pivoting vs. rocking—Gently rocking from right heel to left ball and back to right heel while whirling (or the reverse; see "spinning backwards") also helps eliminate torque on knees and hips by distributing the weight evenly between the legs.

Tanoura spin—Zar *tanoura* spinners also use modified Mevlevi footwork. They still spin on the left heel towards the left, but only twist the left foot 90 degrees before putting weight back on the ball again. Meanwhile, the right foot paddles behind the left in a "heel-toe" walk. It never crosses over the pillar and at most propels the spin 270 degrees, instead of a full 360 degrees, which greatly reduces pelvic torque.

Spinning backwards—Switching the weight-bearing leg mid-spin also helps relieve torque. While turning to the left in proper Mevlevi fashion, shift weight onto the RIGHT leg and heel, while continuing to twist the left foot 90-degrees to the left. This reverses the footwork; the right becomes the pillar while the left paddles. You still turn left with the head tipped right, but with the weight on the right leg, the spin feels backwards.

Spotting—I mentioned that one of the first tricks dancers learn when they spin is to "spot"—to focus the eyes on a specific point to combat dizziness. Stationary visual cues fool the inner ear into believing it is not moving. There are two ways to do this:

External focus—This is when dancers stare at something outside their personal space (delineated by the fingertips); the head turns separately from the body, as when ballet dancers whip their heads around faster than their bodies are rotating because their eyes are fixed on a spot in the audience.

Internal focus or "character turns"—This is when dancers' eyes focus on an object within their personal space; the head is fixed and revolves with the body. This is what Celâleddin Çelebi was referring to in the quotation that opens this chapter: "his left hand, on which his eyes are fastened." In other words, semazen spot on their leading hands. This is also how they avoid bumping into each other.

I came across a helpful article in a *Scientific American* blog that explains the neurological mechanisms for external spotting: "Dancers get very good at spinning because certain aspects of their brains *desensitize* to the turns. Specifically, the vestibular system, the system that controls your sense of balance and vertigo (dizziness), is desensitized…" Dancers "moved their eyes less as they whipped around…And they also felt the turning less than controls. More importantly, the dancers' sense of turning, and the vestibular-ocular reflex, were UNCOUPLED … So even though their eyes were moving in the reflex, they didn't feel it!"[381] Semazen train their brains to react to vestibular stimulation by inducing trance rather than dizziness. But for the ultimate altered consciousness experience, try not spotting at all. Stare straight ahead and watch the world whiz by, or better yet, close your eyes!

This completes my Middle Eastern trance dance induction compendium. Hopefully, a few techniques will work and you can enter trance. Personally, I use a combination of zikr twists, weaving 8's, and spinning—movements gentle on the neck. It takes me about five to ten minutes of steady dancing to reach a state of flow, depending on the music and how centered I was before I started. But then what? What happens next, once you've pierced the dizziness barrier and enter theta prior to climax/collapse?

Allow your thoughts to wander and remain objective about the subjects that pop up. If a flash of intuition or a memory surfaces, let it, but try not to dwell on anything too long. If you find yourself obsessively returning to an idea, particularly an unhealthy one, this could signal serious issues you may need professional help with. I have a rule of thumb, "The Twenty-Four-Hour Rule." If I'm thinking about something that happened within the past twenty-four hours or so, I consider this normal event-processing and let it take its course. But if I find I'm obsessing over events long past, unalterable situations, or unhealthy topics (against my moral standards), then after reasonable consideration I purposefully move on. Don't waste precious ritual time on negative, petty, or unworthy subjects. Remember, this is your party and you can do what you want! Don't let someone else ruin it for you. Refocus on the music, the shadows dancing around the room, a flickering flame. Think of someone you love, a pet, or a happy moment. Focus on a protective altar object, then let your mind free associate to change the subject, so to speak.

---

381 Scicurious, "Practice Spinning, Tiny Dancer," The Scicurious Brain, *Scientific American* blog, September 2013. Discusses a recent study about spotting by Nigmatullina et al., "The Neuroanatomical Correlates of Training-Related Perceptuo-Reflex Uncoupling in Dancers," *Cerebral Cortex*, 2013.

You'll be surprised at how many issues you cover during a session (one of the healing aspects of trance) and how fast time passes. You may also be surprised at how little you remember—unless your thoughts were emotionally charged. Before you know it, an hour will have passed and your embedded music cues will signal "time's up!" Later, don't be alarmed if this inner contemplation bleeds into your sleep. Trance dancers can have extremely vivid dreams after a session. This is normal and will pass. When the dark recesses of your theta world suddenly come under conscious scrutiny, your brain responds by processing what you dredge up—which takes getting used to. After you've been trance dancing for a while, there will be fewer secrets lurking in the murky depths, and so fewer nocturnal surprises.

More rules of thumb: First of all, thoughts dissipate rapidly, like dreams after sleep, so if you want to remember an idea, write it down quickly. Second, you will have body awareness but lack inhibition, which can lead to excess exuberance. Try to tone down violent gestures, rapid spins, or frenetic jumping until you are more familiar with the state, particularly if your dance area is limited. Everyone has his or her own style; please discover yours with care. Third, a frustrating fact about flow is that analyzing cool new moves will make you "choke" and the epiphany disappear. Instead, remain in objective observer mode and simply repeat the movement until muscle memory takes over. If you surface too soon, spin or revisit your induction moves. Eventually you can train yourself to interrupt flow, but re-entering it takes time, so only stop for something important. Later, with experience and longer sessions (mine last two to three hours), you can include slower interludes in your play list to drink, catch your breath, and write down ideas. Most experts agree, though, that thirty to forty-five minutes is sufficient for "emotional liberation"—when memories, personal issues, and/or creative theta flares emerge.

Stretching after physical exercise is important, but particularly after trance dancing. A ten to fifteen minute "cool-down" period acts as a buffer between theta's metaphorical universe and ordinary beta reality. It allows the brain to emerge gradually and sift through its experiences while you pamper overworked muscles. The next chapter contains my cool-off routine, which I include only as a template to help you invent your own. Even two to three minutes of calf flexing is better than nothing. But honestly, I look forward to stretching. It really does feel good and helps avoid sore muscles.

Homework: Pivoting and Rocking Spins

Try pivoting versus rocking spins. Do you like one better than the other? Start slowly and work up speed. (Don't eat anything for an hour beforehand. Seriously, I have had workshop participants lose their lunches and suffer through hours of nausea due to poor planning.) Experiment with where to put your arms. Both up? Like Sufis—one palm up, one palm down? Out to the side, pulled by centrifugal force? Down by the hips? When you're done, practice stopping with the arm wrap. Switch directions and rotate at least once in the opposite direction to avoid dizziness and nausea.

14
·········

How to Cool Down

After dredging up forgotten memories, hidden emotions, and flashes of inspiration (to say nothing of visits from the spirit world), it's good to reflect on what surfaced before you forget. This is why experts recommend at least five to fifteen minutes of quiet time after a session—to integrate the experience. Personally, as a dancer, I need to realign my body before my muscles cool off, so I came up with the following exercises. After stretching, you can lie down and meditate if you want. The dancing will have silenced your beta thoughts and flooded your body with adrenaline so you won't fall asleep. Many consider this the best part—when they can stretch out, relax, and go on a vision quest. Why waste a good opportunity to discover new frontiers? Try visiting the Shaman's Cave or another exotic place. At the very least, write down your thoughts, and then reread them twenty-four hours later. You'll be surprised at the insight a good night's sleep will bring. If it doesn't, wait a few days. Things have a way of explaining themselves sooner or later. And if you have a hard time resurfacing from "theta fog," sip water and eat a small piece of candy (preferably chocolate). The sugar will quickly bring you back to beta.

Stretches

Please feel free to modify these movements any way you like. They were designed with dancers in mind, but scaled back, they are suitable for anybody. At the very least, do five or six different static stretches for a minimum of ten to fifteen seconds each (although thirty seconds is better). Anything is preferable to nothing. Don't strain. With practice, your muscles and ligaments will loosen up and allow more range of motion. The goal is to prevent cramps and stiffness, not tie your body into knots (although the first time you try some of these exercises you may wonder). The movements are supposed to feel good, not hurt. Be gentle. Take your time. There's no rush. Choose music that's soothing, without a driving beat, that will help shift bones back into place, quicken brainwaves, and encourage mental processing.

Cosmic hug x 4—This is the same as the warm-up stretch. Standing with feet slightly wider than your shoulders and knees loosely bent, reach straight arms over your head, cross them, and try to touch your opposite shoulder blades. One arm will be over top of the other. Flatten your back and bend forward until your spine curls. Allow your head to hang toward the floor. With your head upside down, gently swing to and fro, first with hands on shoulder blades, then with arms loosely hanging to the floor. Knees bent, arms by your sides, roll back up your spine to a vertical position. Repeat this stretch three more times, alternating the arm crossed over top (right or left). For the last one, remain in the hanging position, then kneel and sit on your heels.

Prayer x 4—From this kneeling position, lift your arms straight over your head, palms facing front, and bend straight-backed from the waist until your hands touch the floor in front of you. This is a Muslim prayer position. Feel your spine elongate and stretch. Roll back up your spine, arms hanging by your sides, into the original kneeling position. Repeat this movement three more times.

Figure 54: Prayer—lifting arms over head

Figure 55: Prayer—hands down to floor

Rolling push-ups x 4—Still sitting on your heels, bend forward and place your hands near where your shoulders ended up during prayer. Lean onto your hands, unfold your pelvis, and arch your upper body gently down to the floor in push-up style. Once down, push your torso back up in a rolling arch. Bend your knees and fold your legs under you until, once again, you sit on your heels. Repeat this three more times, then lower yourself onto your stomach, legs together, arms stretched overhead, and lie on the floor.

Figure 56: Rolling push-up

Sphinx—Bend your elbows and fold your arms under you so your chest rises into a sphinx position, without moving the legs. Again, hold for thirty seconds.

Figure 57: Sphinx

Y—Open and straighten your arms to form a Y with your body. Raise your head again, still using the back muscles along your spine. Hold for thirty seconds, and then lie back down.

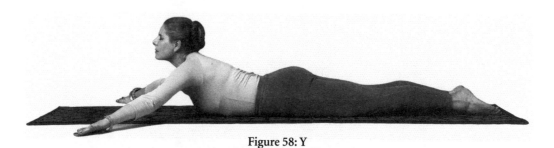

Figure 58: Y

Cobra—Place your hands near your shoulders and push up onto your arms. Your hips will come slightly off the floor. This will stretch the two bands of muscle that run up your abdomen, the rectus abdominis, and compress your lower spine. Hold for thirty seconds, and then gently lower yourself back to the floor.

Figure 59: Cobra

Cobra strike—Place your hands near your waist and push up one last time. Your pelvis should lift completely off the floor. After thirty seconds, bend your elbows and lie back down.

Figure 60: Cobra strike

Flying bow x 3—Still lying face down, move your arms overhead into a
V position and lift your rib cage off the floor, using the back muscles.
Shift your arms behind you, as if flying. Hold for thirty seconds, and
then relax back to the floor.

Figure 61: Flying bow—legs together

Spread your legs wider than your shoulders and repeat the upper
body lift. Hold for thirty seconds, and return to the floor.

Figure 62: Flying bow—legs apart

Lift your feet by bending your knees, arch your upper body, and
grab your ankles. Pull gently on your ankles to lift your chest higher off
the ground, making a basket shape. Hold for thirty seconds, then release.

Figure 63: Basket

Fetal tuck—Roll onto your back. Bend your knees and tuck your legs onto your stomach in a fetal position.

Figure 64: Fetal tuck

Pelvic rock x 4—From here, slightly straighten your knees, feet overhead, until your pelvis rises slightly off the floor. Hold for thirty seconds, then roll down your vertebra until your lower back returns to the floor. With each "rock," progressively shift your weight toward the shoulder blades by lifting your pelvis higher off the floor. For the second "rock," straighten your legs so that your feet reach farther over your head. The pelvic bones should rise completely off the floor until your weight shifts to just below the shoulder blades. Hold for thirty seconds and roll back.

Figure 65: Pelvic rock—straighten legs

The next two rocks may be difficult for some of you. If they are, simply repeat what you were able to do, or move on to the next exercise.

For the next rock, bring your knees to rest on your forehead. This will shift all your weight onto the shoulder blades. Hold for thirty seconds, and then roll down.

Figure 66: Pelvic rock—knees to forehead

Finally, for the last rock, bring your toes to rest on the floor behind your head. Separate your knees and allow them to fall next to your ears. Hold for thirty seconds. Your body weight will shift entirely onto your shoulders. This position, an inverted arc over your head, stretches the spine and separates the vertebra.

Figure 67: Pelvic rock—toes to floor

When time is up, roll gently back down, vertebra by vertebra, to an L position, with straight legs pointing towards the ceiling.

Figure 68: L

Victory V x 3—For this exercise, you will open and close your legs while lying on your back. With pointed toes, spread your legs as wide as possible. Put your hands under your thighs if you need support. Hold for thirty seconds.

Figure 69: Victory V—pointed

Bring your legs together and cross them, one on top of the other, while pulling your knees toward your chest to lift your pelvis off the floor. Hold for ten seconds.

Figure 70: Victory V—crossed

Open and straighten your legs again, this time with flexed feet. As before, you can support your outer thighs with your hands. Hold for thirty seconds. Cross your legs again with the other leg on top and hold for ten seconds.

Figure 71: Victory V—flexed

Once again, open and straighten your legs with flexed feet, but this time, reach up and grab your toes or ankles. Hold for thirty seconds. Release your feet and lie back on the floor.

Figure 72: Victory V—grab feet

K Twist x 2—Lie on your back and extend your arms straight out from your shoulders to form a T on the floor. Cross one leg over the other so that your foot rests below the opposite hand and your hip lifts off the floor. Turn your head and look away from the crossed leg. Hold for thirty seconds. You should feel a definite twist in your lower spine. Bend the knee of the uncrossed leg (the one aligned with your torso).

With the opposite hand (the hand you are looking at), grab the toes of your bent leg and hold for thirty seconds. If this is difficult, don't bother grabbing the foot. Bending the knee is enough. Release and switch legs. The previously crossed leg will now point down and you will look in the opposite direction. Repeat the two positions.

Figure 73: K twist

Pretzel x 2—After releasing your second foot, sit up on the floor. Bend one leg, cross it over the other, and rest the sole of this foot flat on the floor so that the knee is perpendicular to the floor. Take the other leg resting sideways on the floor and wrap it around your pelvis. Twist your upper body so that your shoulder rests on the far side of the raised knee. Hold for thirty seconds.

Figure 74: Pretzel—twisting

Take your back arm (the one touching the knee), lift it over your head, bend your elbow, and touch your opposite shoulder blade. Hold for thirty seconds.

Figure 75: Pretzel—touching shoulder

Release your arms. Keeping your legs in the same position, twist your upper body in the other direction, so that your back shoulder rests on the other side of the upright knee. Hold for thirty seconds. Switch legs, so that the leg underneath is now bent over top, and repeat the three positions.

Figure 76: Pretzel—reverse twist

Tortoise and the hare—After unwinding from the pretzel, still sitting, open your legs and bend your knees, keeping the soles of your feet on the floor. Let your upper body slump forward between your legs. With head hanging down, wrap your arms inside your legs—under your knees and over top of your shins. Hold for thirty seconds.

Figure 77: Tortoise

Feel your spine stretch. With knees still bent and feet on the floor, untwine your arms and place forearms on the ground in front of you, between your legs. Hold for thirty seconds.

Figure 78: Hare

Leg stretch x 4—Keeping your upper body and forearms in place, gently straighten both legs. If this is too difficult, take your forearms off the floor before straightening your knees and then put them back down. Flex your feet and hold for thirty seconds.

Figure 79: Leg stretch—middle

Slightly twist your upper body and arms to hang over one leg. Hold for thirty seconds. Then twist and hang over the other leg for thirty seconds. Once again, hang between your legs, but try to go lower this time, for another thirty seconds. Then gently release your legs by bending your knees. And you're done!

Figure 80: Leg stretch—side

At this point, you can either lie down for a vision quest (keep a pillow handy), or stand up slowly, curling up the spine, to end. Immediately write down your thoughts in your trance journal—whatever you remember—with the date.

And that's it...almost. It's important to (reverently) put your stuff away and close the space. This, too, should have a ritual, but less formal than the opening. What I do is leave the mellow cool-down music playing while I collect candles, store journals (I reread the session entry first), and turn off the lights. After the last flame is quenched (with a prayer) and the music silenced, I spend a few minutes in the dark with the spirits to say goodbye, but that's up to you. Since my studio is their home, I don't send them back anywhere. But if you dance in a space you also use for other purposes, you may want to come up with a sharing agreement...and a formula to evoke it.

"How long before I see spirits?" is a question I often hear, and the answer is always "It depends." You must learn to walk before you can run. On average, people take two to three sessions just to recognize waking theta. Yet I have seen people possessed by animal or other spirits on their first try (but this is rare). Please be patient. Everyone is different. What is commonplace, however, at least in the beginning, are vivid dreams afterwards. "Zar calm" is also a frequent sensation—an exhausted but happy lethargy that washes over mind and limbs for hours. Watch out for symptoms of repressed memories, though. If you feel severely stressed or depressed AFTER a session, something is wrong and you may want to seek mental health help. Your subconscious may be hiding banished traumatic events.

Exercise feels good...to a point. But if you over-toss your head, headaches and muscle pain will follow. Unfortunately, sore necks are a common side effect until dancers learn good technique. To help prevent aches and pains, avoid repeated stopping and starting, warm up beforehand, and cool down afterwards. Nothing combats sore muscles better than stretching. Warm showers or baths also help, as do neck massages!

Once your body becomes accustomed to trance dancing, you can ratchet up the experience. If you started on the ground, stand up, then move around, and finally spin. Changing music frequently also deepens trance, particularly if you include something unfamiliar. The brain loves a challenge. The mind wanders if it knows what comes next. Playing percussion instruments while dancing also helps concentration, although this can be difficult. Personally, nothing takes me deeper than playing finger cymbals and the mangour while dancing to new music—improvising with legs, hips, and hands, all to different rhythms. And of course, dancing to live music is the ultimate aid: group energy, emotional engagement, and not knowing what comes next, all at once—although performing for other people generally has the opposite effect and prevents decent!

Unfortunately, the body adapts (and ultimately habituates) to pleasurable sensations. Progressive desensitization to trance is a natural, although unwanted, side effect of intense neural stimulation. You may ask what remains, then, after the rush subsides? Theta flares, for one. Learned analgesia to pain is another (remember the dervishes eating hot coals?). Objective observer status, floating above the body while dancing, is a third—but without the adrenaline surge.

And if you establish relationships with Invisibles, these, too, will persist, but with a different intensity, more like a marriage or long-term friendship rather than a love affair...

Homework: The Ten T's of Trance

And so it is time for me to leave you—with a quiz this time, instead of homework. I call this the Ten T's of Trance. See if you can remember what the terms refer to...

- (Two) Types of Trance
- Tunnel: Trance's Four Stages
- Tether: the Music Lifeline
- Tosses: Tricks of the Trade
- Thalamus: Sensory Overload
- Theta: the Five Brainwave States
- Transmitters: Neural Stimulators
- Therapy: Dredging the Depths of Depression
- Temporal Lobe: The Spark of Divinity
- Training: Perseverance in the Face of Adversity

Conclusion

We have come to the end of our carpet ride together. I hope the journey has expanded your horizons, inside and out, and brought you much food for thought—about the Creator, human history, and the existential question of "Are we alone?" That's a lot for a dance manual. But dancing, or in this case kinetic meditation, is really only a means to an end: a method to contact the Invisibles, or, for those of you who don't believe in spirits or aren't ready to experience them yet, your subconscious.

For those of you who started off with the opinion that Creation is a random set of happenstances, that we are chaos synchronizing into order, do you still believe we are alone, with no other purpose in life than to reproduce? Or are you now open to the idea that our universe was intentionally created (possibly along with many others) by someone or something who set the process in motion? So far, science has no definitive proof one way or the other, so everything boils down to a simple question of choice: to believe or not to believe.

If you choose to believe in a Creator, then logic dictates there may be other entities that are similar in structure—entities I refer to as "the Invisibles." It is also possible that everything the Creator endowed with energy is interconnected with the Creator—through a "divine spark." This force, the essence of electricity, animates atoms and stars alike. And the more complicated or evolved a life form is, the more intricate the connection, to the point where humans have evolved a cerebral conduit in the right temporal lobe that brings us into direct contact. Furthermore, believing is not only a choice, but a skill (and an art) that is developed with practice. Tibetan monks are living proof of this. But you don't have to be a monk to enhance your connection. Praying, meditation, intuition, and sensory awareness are within the grasp of all humans.

I believe the universe's slower electromagnetic wavelengths hold the keys to these mysteries. Our world is constantly bombarded with all sorts of frequencies, perhaps even the elusive remnants of the Big Bang itself. Our brains evolved in this bath, adapted to it, and still require regular immersion during sleep. The biggest question is, what function do our brains perform? Do they transmit and receive external third-party communication (from our souls and other Invisibles, for example) like two-way radios, or do they actually create consciousness without input from the cosmos? Either way, our solid bodies translate into conscious beta the things that we learn unconsciously in delta, and subconsciously in theta. My personal opinion is that the Invisibles communicate through these slower wavelengths, amongst themselves and with us. We're just not very good at listening… yet.

There are probably innumerable species of Invisibles, just as there are innumerable solid species on Earth. I have discussed only one regional variety, the jinn—fire spirits created from smokeless flame and scorching wind, i.e., plasma. This little-understood fourth state of matter surrounds the Earth and protects our atmosphere, the air we breathe, from being blown away by solar wind. It forms fingers or tentacles in charged conditions, yet is invisible to our senses unless it is excited and emits light (the Northern Lights). Humanity is familiar with the jinn because they were immortalized "by the pen" in the Quran. And even though Islam's holy book only mentions a bare minimum about them, it does reveal several things: Both jinn and humans were given souls and the ability to make choices. Individuals of both species fall along a moral continuum bounded by good and evil, white and black, with infinite shades of gray in between. And it specifies that the truly evil beings, shayateen, are souls—both human and jinn—who have chosen darkness and hatred over light.

Most inhabitants of the Middle East or countries with a strong Islamic tradition consider all jinn to be evil, even though the Quran clearly states the opposite. According to its verses, Muhammad's first jinn contact was with the Nesabeen, believers in Moses and Allah, who immediately converted to Muhammad's message. These jinn appeared in his hour of greatest need—not to trick him, but to believe in him, and to carry his message back to their people. Sadly, many fanatics and charlatans manipulate the simpleminded or the undereducated by invoking these entities and the fear they inspire. Even today, violent exorcisms claim the lives of innocents who suffered more from physical or mental health issues and cultural prohibitions than possession. This is particularly true in cases of epilepsy, which is a neural malfunction, not the sign of Satanic presence. A clear line must be drawn between spirit contact and defective anatomy—a determination that should be made by a doctor in public, not family members in secret.

But what about the possession entities who invade in times of weakness and cause suffering when they want something? Are they evil? In reality, these entities tend to manifest when their hosts need help—similar to Muhammad when he first experienced the jinn. Possession illnesses often exhibit the classic symptoms of depression or hysteria. Yet, by forcing the issue of grief, fear, discontent, or abuse, these spirits become catalysts for change, sometimes on a grand scale. What is evil about that?

In Egypt the lives of the zar-afflicted are often riddled with stress, anxiety, boredom, repressed desires, and even physical or psychological abuse. Zar rituals often mirror Western psychiatric treatments in that they raise serotonin levels (through exercise rather than drugs) and release repressed emotions during trance (similar to hypnosis, another trance-induction method) in an atmosphere heavy with incense and camaraderie. The rituals even provoke shock treatments by short-circuiting the brain's electrical currents through sensory overload. But perhaps most important, these gatherings bring the isolated into contact with others who want to help them—including members of the spirit world, who, once acknowledged, are supposed to look out for the interests of their "horses."

What to believe? Are the spirits real? Do the jinn exist? Now that you have the tools and can see for yourself, you tell me! I would love to hear about your experiences. As I said at the beginning, what have you got to lose? And you may actually enjoy the process, but you won't know until you try...

Appendix 1
Surah Revelation Order

The revelation order of the surat of the Quran was first recorded in the early 700s CE, nearly a century after the Prophet's death, supposedly based on information attributed to Muhammad's companion Ibn Abbas. However, it appears the list was more a product of early scholars than the careful transmission of primary-source oral traditions. What follows is the chronological revelation order given by the 1925 Standard Egyptian edition of the Quran. This version does not correspond to any one ancient compilation, however, but several mixed together.[382] Surah positions are based on the revelation date of the first verses (ayat), not the whole surah, which may contain verses from several different occasions.

In this list, Surah that mention the jinn are in boldface, with an asterisk (*) beside the number.

	Revelation Order	Surah Name	Surah Number
610 CE	1	*Al-Alaq*	96
	2	*Al-Qalam*	68
	3	*Al-Muzzammil*	73
	4	*Al-Muddaththir*	74
	5	*Al-Faatiha*	1
	6	*Al-Masad*	111

---

382   Neal Robinson, *Discovering the Quran*, 69–75.

Revelation Order	Surah Name	Surah Number
7	*At-Takwir*	81 (only shayateen are mentioned)
8	*Al-A'laa*	87
9	*Al-Lail*	92
10	*Al-Fajr*	89
11	*Ad-Dhuhaa*	93
12	*Ash-Sharh*	94
13	*Al-Asr*	103
14	*Al-Aadiyaat*	100
15	*Al-Kawthar*	108
16	*At-Takaathur*	102
17	*Al-Maa'un*	107
18	*Al-Kaafiroon*	109
19	*Al-Fil*	105
20	*Al-Falaq*	113
21	***An-Naas***	**114*** (last line added later)
22	*Al-Ikhlaas*	112
23	*An-Najm*	53
24	*Abasa*	80
25	*Al-Qadr*	97
26	*Ash-Shams*	91
27	*Al-Burooj*	85
28	*At-Tin*	95
29	*Quraish*	106
30	*Al-Qaari'a*	101
31	*Al-Qiyaama*	75
32	*Al-Humaza*	104
33	*Al-Mursalaat*	77
34	*Qaaf*	50
35	*Al-Balad*	90
36	*At-Taariq*	86
37	*Al-Qamar*	54
38	*Saad*	38 (shayateen as Solomon's builders)

Revelation Order	Surah Name	Surah Number
39	*Al-A'raaf*	7*
40	*Al-Jinn*	72* (the Year of Sorrow)
41	*Yaseen*	36
42	*Al-Furqaan*	25
43	*Faatir*	35
44	*Maryam*	19
45	*Taa-Haa*	20
46	*Al-Waaqia*	56
47	*Ash-Shu'araa*	26
48	*An-Naml*	27*
49	*Al-Qasas*	28
50	*Al-Israa*	17*
51	*Yunus*	10
52	*Hud*	11*
53	*Yusuf*	12
54	*Al-Hijr*	15
55	*Al-An'aam*	6*
56	*As-Saaffaat*	37*
57	*Luqman*	31
58	*Saba*	34*
59	*Az-Zumar*	39
60	*Al-Ghaafir*	40
61	*Fussilat*	41*
62	*Ash-Shura*	42
63	*Az-Zukhruf*	43
64	*Ad-Dukhaan*	44
65	*Al-Jaathiya*	45
66	*Al-Ahqaf*	46*
67	*Adh-Dhaariyat*	51*
68	*Al-Ghaashiya*	88
69	*Al-Kahf*	18*

619 CE (at Revelation Order 40)

Revelation Order	Surah Name	Surah Number
70	*An-Nahl*	16
71	*Nooh*	71
72	*Ibrahim*	14
73	***Al-Anbiyaa***	**21***
74	*Al-Muminoon*	23
75	***As-Sajda***	**32***
76	*At-Tur*	52
77	*Al-Mulk*	67
78	*Al-Haaqqa*	69
79	*Al-Ma'aarij*	70
80	*An-Naba*	78
81	*An-Naazi'aat*	79
82	*Al-Infitaar*	82
83	*Al-Inshiqaaq*	84
84	*Ar-Room*	30
85	*Al-Ankaboot*	29
86	*Al-Mutaffifin*	83 (Last surah from Mecca)
622 CE 87	*Al-Baqara*	2 (Move to Medina [Hijrah])
88	*Al-Anfaal*	8
89	*Al-i-'Imran*	3
90	*Al-Ahzaab*	33
91	*Al-Mumtahana*	60
92	*An-Nisaa*	4
93	*Az-Zalzala*	99
94	*Al-Hadid*	57
95	*Muhammad*	47
96	*Ar-Ra'd*	13
97	***Ar-Rahmaan***	**55***
98	*Al-Insaan*	76
99	*At-Talaaq*	65
100	*Al-Bayyina*	98

Revelation Order	Surah Name	Surah Number
101	*Al-Hashr*	59
102	*An-Noor*	24
103	*Al-Hajj*	22
104	*Al-Munaafiqoon*	63
105	*Al-Mujaadila*	58
106	*Al-Hujuraat*	49
107	*At-Tahrim*	66
108	*At-Taghaabun*	64
109	*As-Saff*	61
110	*Al-Jumu'a*	62
111	*Al-Fath*	48
112	*Al-Maaida*	5
113	*At-Tawba*	9
114	*An-Nasr*	110

Surah *An-Naas*, the last surah of the Quran (revelation order 21, surah number 114), is often recited for protection against the jinn. It rhymes beautifully and is easy to say:

outh bi-rub an-naas
malik an-naas—
illahi an-naas
min shar al-waswaas al-khanaas
allathi yuwaswis fi sudour an-naas
min al-jinn wa an-naas.

I seek protection from Lord of the people
King (ruler) of the people—
God of the people
From the evil whisperings of "The One who Withdraws"
Who whispers in the chests of the people
From the jinn and the people.[383]

---

383   Quran 114: 1–6.

Appendix 2
Middle Eastern Trance Music

Below please find descriptions and explanations of musical instruments, bands, and various other musical subjects related to Middle Eastern trance dancing. For the zar and to a certain extent Sufi whirling, music is an absolute must, the invisible carpet that transports dancers to the ethereal world—yet still tethers them to the one they left behind.

Zar spirit songs (*daqa*, "beat," or *khuyut*, "thread") are based on heavy percussive skeletons, and range from simple chanting and clapping to haunting melodies interwoven with polyrhythms. Sufi compositions, on the other hand, rely more on melody. Zar rhythms are characterized by a "limping" syncopation (like a heartbeat) that unsettles the brain, which would rather find a regular pulse to entrain with. The music also builds in crescendos—within individual songs, a band's performance, and the ritual as a whole. A daqa may start slow and melodious, but it will end in a fever pitch. It usually has two parts: an introductory melody and a main musical phrase, which are easily repeated according to how quickly participants go into trance. For more about Mevlevi whirling music, please see the entry for *ayin*, below.

Abou al-Ghreit (also called *al-Ghreitaniya*): an all-male and purely Egyptian zar music band that takes its name from a Sufi saint buried in Shabeen al-Qanaater, a village north of Cairo where many zar musicians live. Members wear green and play instruments common in Sufi music. Their music is melodious and emotional, similar to the Mevlevi Sufi compositions inspired by Rumi.

Aulos: a double-reed flute from Anatolia.

Ayin: The structure of an *ayin* (the intricate hymns and suites performed at a Mevlevi ceremony) includes the ***Naat-i-Sherif, the Devri Veled,*** and ***The Four Selams.*** During the *Naat-i-Sherif*, participants sit on the floor in a circle and meditate for about half an hour, listening to the sheikh or lead vocalist, the *hafiz*, chant passages from the Quran or free-metered hymns, *naat*. This is followed by a short tympanic interlude of kettledrum strikes symbolizing divine order and Allah's creation command "Be!" (*kun* in Arabic, from the end of Surah 36:82, what Mevlevi Sufis consider "the Heart of the Quran.") A fifteen-minute *nay taqsim* follows the kettledrum strikes, evoking both the sadness of human separation from God and gratitude for His divine, life-giving breath. Then the *Devri Veled* begins: the semazens rise, bow, and walk slowly in procession three times around the hall (right step, pause; left step, pause) with arms in the *alif* position, robes pulled tightly around them and heads bowed. Each completed circle represents a phase of Allah's creation; after the third circle, the dervishes re-move their cloaks, re-cross their arms, and approach the sheikh to kiss his right shoulder. Then they whirl onto the dance floor, slowly un-folding their arms into their signature position. *The Four Selams* (vocal movements) follow, usually chanted by the hafiz. Each section has its own symbolism: (1) *Selam-i-Evvel* (Recognizing God); (2) *Selam-i-Sani* (Recognizing God's Unity); (3) *Selam-i-Salis* (Ecstasy of Total Surren-der); and (4) *Selam-i-Rabai* (Peace of Heart). (See also page 242.)

Bendir: This large frame drum, with snares attached to the inside rim, eventually replaced the *daf* (large tambourine) in *sema* (Mevlevi Sufi) performances. It is similar to the *tar* except that two or three gut strings [made from animal intestines] are stretched across the diam-eter inside the frame, touching the drumhead. These strings vibrate when the drum is shaken or struck and add an additional whispering sound to the percussive thump. It is played in the same way as the tar.

Daf: Rumi's thirteenth-century term for a large, round tambourine with five sets of cymbals; his original percussion instrument ("Do not visit my tomb without a daf" is carved on his shrine). Sufis generally consider the circle and spiral to be mystical shapes.

Dahoula: This Egyptian drum is similar to the tabla (see below) only larger, with a goat-skin or camel-skin head. Its loud, deep sound anchors the percussion section, along with the duff. It is played like a *tabla,* but without excessive embellishment.

Daqa: The Arabic term for "rhythm," or "beat." During zar rituals each spirit is represented by a unique rhythm that patients dance to (for example, *daqa Yawra Bey, daqa al-Jinn, daqa Roukesh*). In Egyptian "zar speak" the word is also used to signify a spirit "chant" in general, a call-and-response vocal format, instead of the Arabic equivalents for "chant" or "song."

Duff: The modern Egyptian term for a large frame drum, about eleven inches in diameter, occasionally decorated inside and out with small pieces of shell, white bones, or ivory.

Halile: These hand cymbals, each about a foot in diameter, are played in pairs during Mevlevi rituals, similar to ancient Egyptian or Hebrew use. (Remember David's musical procession into Jerusalem with the Ark?)

Harim Masri: The first musical group that performs during an Egyptian zar, usually four to six older women dressed in black who sing and play various frame drums. Their style reflects the group's combined Nigerian *bori* and Ethiopian (*Habashi*) zar roots (West meets East).

Jawqa: a choir or group of singers and musicians that perform at zars (*jawqit zar),* usually lead by a principal singer or musician (*rayes*).

Kanara: A five-stringed instrument, made from wood or metal, with a decorated sound box stretched with thin goat hide. It is played by holding it horizontally or vertically in front of the cest, hugging it to the chest with the left hand while the right hand strums using a plectrum (*al reesha*, "feather"). It is commonly found in Upper Saidi, especially in Nubia, and is also found in Sudan, where it is used in the Sudancese zar bands.

Kanoun: This seventy-two-stringed zither played horizontally on the lap or a table by plucking the strings with two plectra attached by wide rings to the first finger of each hand. It was introduced to the Mevlevi Sufis from Ottoman Art music.

Kashkash (or shakhaleel): Rattles made from empty aerosol cans filled with pebbles and shaken by members of a tumboura group.

Kemanga: Originally, this folkloric violin-like instrument had two or three strings and was played upright. With the influx of Western instruments in Egypt, the word also came to mean a violin.

Kemence: A short-necked fiddle similar to the *rebab*. This three-stringed bowed lute strongly resembles the Greek lira. It has a box resonator, carved in the shape of a trough and covered with a wooden soundboard. Its three metal or gut strings are played underhanded with a short horsehair bow.

Khener: Troupes of professional singers, musicians, dancing girls, and midwives who wore menat collars and carried sistra (both rattles) as tokens of their functions. They also wore dance belts (rattles) and played clappers. They facilitated birth, entertained the living, mourned the dead, and aroused procreative instincts—since sexual passion and energy were necessary precursors for birth and hence rebirth into the Afterlife.

Kudum: This pair of small copper kettledrums, of unequal size but similar proportions, was a fundamental percussion instrument for Ottoman Art music (see below). The heads are fitted with camel or sheepskin and played with wooden sticks.

Mangour: A large leather belt about twenty centimeters wide with cowrie shells sewn near the waist and hundreds of goat-hoof or sheep-hoof nails strung underneath. When fastened tightly around the hips and shaken, they rattle like a swarm of cicadas, or kashkash, but louder. Men or women may wear them. The sound is extremely effective at inducing trance.

Maqam: The Arabic term for musical scales with unique quarter tone progressions used in Middle Eastern music. Many are Persian in origin and were adopted after the Islamic invasion of Iran in 641 CE. The *maqam* of a piece is important to discerning Middle Eastern listeners because it elicits a host of emotions and/or cultural associations. For example, the *maqamaat* (pl) "Hijaz," "kurd," and "Iraq" were derived from the music of specific places. To compose a piece with one of them intentionally evokes memories or folklore from these individual regions.

Mazhar: This hand-held frame drum is similar to a *riq*, but larger in size. It consists of an undecorated wood frame with five openings cut out for ten pairs of brass cymbals (two sets per hole). The head is stretched with goat or camel hide, similar to the *tar* and *bendir*, and is played similarly.

Nay: A wooden flute made from hollowed cane or reed. The standard classical version used in professional orchestras has nine knotted sections, while those used in military or folkloric bands have only five; the five-knot version is used for the zar. Both types of *nay* are portrayed in the stone carvings of Egypt's Old Kingdom: the long version was played standing up while the shorter version was played seated on one knee. The *nay* is the principle instrument of the Sufis, who consider it a symbol of the human soul (it must be empty to resonate to God's breath).

Oud: Folklore has it that this variety of Middle Eastern lute originally had only four strings. Eventually, they were doubled to eight and a single bass added to commemorate the uniqueness of Allah. The Mevlevi

Sufis adopted this modern version during the twentieth century, although it was used by the general public long before that.

Phrygian music: This ancient Anatolian music is famous for its trance-inducing melodies, unusual musical scales or "modes," and unique instruments. The Greeks considered the Phrygian scale to be the musical mode of possession. The instrument it was played on, the *aulos*, is thought to have originated from Dionysus's homeland, Phrygia.

Rango: A zar band with Sudanese roots, not as popular in Egypt as the three other zar bands. It is named after their principle instrument, the *rango*, which is a marimba or xylophone with wooden keys.

Rebab: A common Middle Eastern spiked fiddle, strung with two or three animal-hair strings, that Rumi used for his original Mevlevi whirling rituals. The Ottomans later replaced it, however, first with the *tanbur* and *kemence*, then with the *oud* and the *kanoun*. By the nineteenth century, large Mevlevi ensembles also included European stringed instruments such as the violin and cello.

Riq: A frame drum with five openings for ten pairs of thin brass cymbals (two pairs per hole). It is played by holding the instrument in the left hand with thumb and first finger, while the middle and ring fingers strike the rim or cymbals. The right-hand fingers also strike it. In addition, the left hand may move or shake it.

Sagat: The Egyptian term for finger cymbals. These four round brass cymbals about six centimeters in diameter are pierced in the center so that they can be attached with string or elastic to the middle finger and thumb of both hands (see figure 23 on page 68). Originally, Oriental dancers (belly dancers) played them while performing, but recently their musicians tend to play them instead. Sagat may be used during zars, but not as often as toura (see below).

Samaee thaqil—of *Lama Bada* fame: This is the Arabic term for an Ottoman 10/8 rhythm adapted for *muwashahat* by Art *fasil* musicians during the 16th–17th centuries. The name comes from Turkish, *saz semai,* where *saz* is a musical instrument, a band or in this case, Oriental music, and *semai,* a traditional, irregular or solemn dance tune. *Thaqil* means "heavy" in Arabic. Belly dancers usually refer to this rhythm simply as *semaee.* It accompanies the Andalusian favorite *Lama Bada.*

Sunjuk: The leader of the tumboura group and the musician who plays the tumboura.

Tabla (darbouka): A Middle Eastern goblet drum, usually made out of clay, that rests on the thigh and is played with both hands. The striking surface, or head, is usually made from fish or goat skin. It is the basic/essential percussion instrument not only for the zar, but for Arabic music in general. To play it, a (right-handed) drummer sits with the drum on his left thigh, its head facing forward, and steadies it slightly with his left forearm. He strikes it with the index, middle, and ring fingers of both hands.

Tabla sudani: These drums are small tin barrels with a handle halfway down the body, covered top and bottom and stretched from end to end with freshly slaughtered camel hide.

Tanbur: This long-necked lute, preferred by Ottoman Art *fasil* music, preceded the *oud* (see above) as the Ottoman Empire's dominant stringed instrument. Its double courses of strings were plucked with a plectrum (*al-reesha* or "feather"), or, less commonly, bowed.

Taqsim: Literally "division," this solo improvisational style of musical performance is considered one of the oldest forms of traditional Middle Eastern music. In its purest state, a musician uses a maqam's core notes to explore a key signature according to pre-established guidelines. In practice, there are three different styles (a single instrument, the instrument with a drone, and the instrument with percussion). They are performed either to introduce a song, as an interlude within a melody, or as a stand-alone piece. In many instances, they are the glue that holds compositions together, either in folk or art music, from Morocco to Iran and beyond.

Tar: Called a *duff* by Egyptian musicians (or sometimes a *mazhar sada*, a plain *mazhar* without cymbals), this simple large wooden frame drum is about double the diameter of a *riq*. It is held in the left hand and struck with the right, fingers together. Hitting the center produces a lower tone while working near the rim gives off higher pitches.

Toura: These brass finger cymbals are thicker and larger than sagat (see above, and figure 23 on page 68), with a diameter of about ten centimeters. They are played during zar ceremonies by a member of the Abou al-Ghreit band.

Tumboura: The name for the second band that plays during an Egyptian zar and also for the six-string lyre the group takes its name from. This ancient Egyptian instrument appeared during the Middle Kingdom. The lyre's round sound box is stretched with goatskin, like a kettledrum, and pierced with two openings called "eyes," or *ein*. The strings are attached to a frame of wooden dowls decorated with ribbons, ropes of pearls, amulets, and cowrie shells (*wad'a*). The tumboura used in Egyptian zar bands is much bigger than the Nubian version, so the musician plays it sitting on the ground rather than holding it while standing or sitting in a chair. His left arm cradles the instrument, his left hand dampening or releasing the strings while he plucks them with his right.

Zuffa: The rhythm that percussionists play during an Egyptian wedding procession as friends and family usher the bride and groom into the wedding reception space. Also the name of the procession.

Appendix 3
The Sheikha and Zar Ceremony Preparations[384]

In Egypt, everything zar begins with a sheikha, and yet it is extremely difficult to become one. During the cult's golden age, professionals would gather from near and far for rare two-week extravaganzas called "Zars of the Belt" to test potential sheikhat. If found worthy, the sisterhood would wrap a white silk shawl around a newcomer's hips to welcome her into the ranks of the Chosen Few.[385] Today, these ceremonies have disappeared, but prospective applicants are still expected to have the right bloodlines (DNA), spend a decade or more in training, and be endowed with a phenomenal memory.

Heredity is foremost. Sheikhat and kodias, their Sudanese equivalent, proudly advertise themselves as "women of incense" from "strong houses," i.e., that they have inherited their zar expertise from grandparents whose homes were continually filled with zar incense. This is because jinn do not reveal their secrets to just anyone; they choose carefully! And breaking their oath of silence (spilling zar secrets) can be disastrous. Repercussions include madness, paralysis, and calamity to self or family.

As mentioned, training takes many years. Novices must learn to diagnose diseases, use herbs and incense, prevent curses, and make talismans and amulets. They must also memorize hundreds of spells, Quranic verses, hadith, the Prophet's biography, and everything jinn,

---

384   The descriptions are partly from my own experience, partly from videos given to me by others who attended rituals, and partly from Al-Aleemi's *Az-Zar: Masrah al-Taqous* [The Zar: Ritual Theater].

385   Le Brun, *Harems et Musulmanes d'Égypt*, 32.

including their types, lore, preferences, clothes, etc. Apprentices must also do long internships with established sheikhat (often beginning in childhood) and perform several verified cures on their own. No wonder sheikhat younger than forty are rare!

The same is applicable for Sudanese kodias, a word derived from the Amharic *kojak* or *kojek*—a "female tabla player (*tabaala*)." In Southern Sudan, zar leaders are also known as *ummiyat*. Either way, these women specialize in Sudanese traditions, whereas Egyptian sheikhat are familiar with many spirit types and work with the three Egyptian musical groups: Saidi, Sudani, and Abou al-Ghreit.

Although leading zar rituals is their most visible function, sheikhat also oversee their preparation, and even more important determine a patient's initial possession diagnosis. This she does through a process called "discovering [*kashif*] the atar." She requests a personal item (an atar), like a headscarf or underwear, to put under her pillow. If a spirit comes to her in a dream or presents itself through other signs, her diagnosis will be positive. Communication methods vary depending on the sheikha. Some hear words or feel the entities in their bodies. Others see them in dreams (or even while awake) or intuitively "know" their wishes via mental telepathy.

The process is slightly different in Sudan. In the south, a patient (*ayana*) will describe her symptoms to the ummiya and then bring her an *alaq* packet (requested objects folded in a cloth) to place under her pillow. If the ummiya's dreams do not reveal a spirit's identity within seven days, then the woman is not considered possessed.[386] In the north, a sheikha may bring her sacred incense box to the ayana's home, since zayran are notorious for responding to their favorite incense mélange. But even if they don't, the woman may still be possessed; silence among beginners is not unusual since verbal expression during trance is a learned process.[387]

Egyptian sheikhat customarily return a diagnosis within three days, with positive outcomes often attributed to violations of jinn space or broken rules. For example, a host must have thrown water on a threshold, showered or screamed at night, stood in front of a mirror, entered a dark room without first mentioning God's name, or something similar. And it doesn't matter if the patient didn't know her actions were forbidden! The

---

386   Lewis et al., *Women's Medicine*, 108.
387   Ibid., 128–29.

rules were established long before electricity was installed, so she should have known better. This also explains why women of previous centuries saw things when they stared into mirrors—the mirrors were illuminated by flickering gas lamp flames or candles (see chapter 5: Spirit Speak).

Given a positive prognosis, the sheikha must first decide where to hold the ritual— somewhere both affordable and spacious. The venue will then be emptied and thoroughly cleaned. Afterwards, the sheikha will burn incense, chant spells in the corners (jinn love corners), and throw seashells near a wall to test its "spiritual waters." If the results are favorable, logistics are the next concern: where to put the altars, dance area, audience, musicians, and chairs. Finally, the walls will be decorated, the carpets or straw mats unrolled, and the cushions and chairs arranged.

The night before the ceremony come the finishing touches: magical plants in strategic places (palm fronds, lemon or olive twigs, flower wreaths, barley, ein afreet, hebat al-baraka seeds, etc.) and two altars bearing candles and presents for the asyad (such as roses, henna, incense, and spirit-specific items such as alcohol or cigarettes). One altar will serve as the kursi, or "throne," for the jinn to congregate around. The other altar, the buffet, normally long and rectangular, will offer the zayran food and drink. Since each spirit requires special items, knowing the guest of honor's identity is crucial.

The presence of fire is also important. The kursi generally holds three candles: one for the zar of honor, a multicolored one for the other zayran, and a plain white one representing Sitt-ak-Kabeera (the zar mother spirit), the agreement and the purity of the souls involved, both jinn and human. During the ceremony, participants also carry candles, but their number and color depend on the spirits being called. Incense, too, is vital. As the favorite "food" of the jinn, its use is quite involved and deserves a book of its own (that I hope to write one day), but for now, suffice it to say that the main component of Egyptian zar incense is shaved sandalwood.

As for other preparations, the sheikha is not the only one busy the night before; so are the guests. While the non-possessed decide which brightly colored dresses to wear, the possessed apply henna and ready their spirit's dance apparel. After all, what is a ceremony without appropriate costumes, accessories, and props? Accessories and props are essential since, as during many African possession rituals, spirits signal their identity through their wardrobe. Guests will also prepare gold or silver jewelry to ward off undesirable entities, and tarha to cover their faces if they are drawn up to dance.

Arranging ceremonial containers for possession rituals takes thought, planning, and experience; these spaces cannot be haphazardly thrown together by novices or hostesses organizing social gatherings. They must be overseen by a literal master of ceremonies, a human arbitrator for the ethereal world—a member of "the Chosen Few."

Appendix 4
A Zar Entity Compendium

There is no better way to understand the zar than through individual spirits. Young and old, traditional or new, high-ranking or lowly, from Africa, the Middle East, and beyond, these entities tell a tale of the possessors and the possessed, of the lands where they emerged and the trials and tribulations of the humans they choose to haunt. Those found in Egypt differ from their cousins in Sudan and Ethiopia, or their distant relatives in West Africa, but all share an affinity for menstrual blood, incense, and fragile psyches. Let me introduce you to a few prominent characters that populate this rapidly vanishing world.

Egypt

Spirits of the Harim Masri

Mama Sultan: A zar elder, who requires a white galabeya and tarha.

Ruma Nagdi: A spirit soldier who wears an *aba'a* (cloak) and a *kofiya* (headscarf), as well as a galabeya.

Abou Danfa: A well-known Saidi spirit from the southern border of Egypt and Sudan.

Amir al-Hag: This spirit requires a galabeya, kofiya, and *aqal* (camel rope) and brandishes a sword as if fighting. He may request the "silent beat," where musicians keep time on cushions instead of playing instruments.

Spirits of the Tumboura (the Sudani Group)

Yawra: This *bey* or *pasha* (someone with authority and power) is the most
famous of the Egyptian zar pantheon. He is the son of Doctor Hakim
Pasha, another of the group's authority figures. He requires a tan (*su-kari*—brown sugar color) silk galabeya, a gold braid *tarboush* hat, a
red gold-embroidered *yaaf* for his chest, and either a (horse-tail) fly
swatter, a walking stick, a cigarette holder, or a bottle of cologne to
sprinkle on guests. This zar idol is the "hero of women,"[388] the "king
of lovers," and the epitome of an ideal partner. His sacrifice is a pair of
red pigeons, considered a refined, delicate food, and his alter candle is
red trimmed with gold.

Roukash: This six-year-old female zar is said to be Yawra's daughter. She wears
a pink dress and veil, carries a doll, and sucks on a lollipop or candy that
she will share with guests. Her hosts speak and act like children.

Ad-Deir: This foreign Christian authority figure is usually a priest or a
minister. He requests a wild rooster (*deek roumi*) as a sacrifice and
white cheese, black olives, beer, or other light alcoholic beverages for
his buffet. Pictures of the Virgin Mary, Jesus Christ, and Saint George
(Mari Girgis) or crucifixes are hung on the walls for decoration. Hosts
wear traditional priests' robes embroidered with crosses, and crucifixes
around their necks—that they occasionally wave in guests' faces. His
altar candle is white with crosses.

Sitt-ak-Kabira: She is the zar world's queen and mother, or "Mama," and
her chant is accorded special respect. If she is the possessing spirit, her
host wears a white galabeya under a white throw (*malaa*) covered by a
black one. Percussionists may also play the "silent beat" for her chant.

Gado: This spirit lives in bathrooms. He requires his hosts to wear a
hooded burlap cape (*burnous*), carry a broom and dustpan, and sit on

---

388 Yawra is often referred to as *Zeer an-nisa,* the hero of a popular pre-Islamic epic.

the floor and clean. He has a peculiar dance "step," described in chapter 12, and demands a simple black rabbit as a sacrifice; its color representing the darkness of bathrooms, particularly public ones.

Saleela: This young, narcisistic female spirit from Nubia is obsessed with her own beauty and often possesses pretty girls who like to show off. If she is the spirit of honor, the arousa will wear makeup and dance with a hand mirror to admire herself. The arousa will wear red clothes and makeup and admire herself with a hand mirror while she dances. Her sacrifice is a pair of hizaz pigeons. This possession state is similar to narcissism.

Sudan[389]

As-Sultan: This Sudanese spirit is the equivalent of a king. He wears a red *burnous* (a long hooded cloak made out of coarse woolen fabric), requires a rooster as a sacrifice, and generally possesses those who have a feeling of greatness or high rank.

Sitt Ak-Kabira: As in Egypt, she is the queen of zar spirits, but in Sudan she is also the wife of As-Sultan. Her clothes are white, but over them she wears two coverings, one white, one black. Her sacrifice is a black ewe, and her daqa, played by the tumboura group, is well respected. She usually possesses older women and confers prestige upon her hosts.

Wilad Mama (Children of Mama, vizier of the zayran): This group entity, a member of the Habish tribe, is a plurality of spirits. Threads addressed to it are for all zayran. It is called first to gather the others to descend and to receive the sacrificial blood on everyone's behalf. It also speaks for any horseless entity wishing to communicate with a human. Possession by it is mandatory for prospective sheikhat.[390]

---

389   These spirits were listed in Janice Boddy's *Wombs and Alien Spirits*, pages 274–301.
390   Boddy, *Wombs and Alien Spirits*, 232.

Darawish: These spirits are the zar equivalent of Islamic holy men and women. Chants are sung for the tribe as a whole and for individual spirits. Hosts generally dress in white. Well-known individuals are the zar counterpart of Abd al-Qadir al-Jilani,[391] Sayed Ahmed al-Bedawi, and Al-Jilani's daughter, Sitti Khudara, the Green Lady, who is pious, graceful, extraordinarily beautiful and the epitome of Sudanese femininity.

Habish, or Ethiopians: These are mainly Christian spirits, with an occasional Arab Muslim, and second only to the Darawish in importance. Besides Wilad Mama, other notorious individuals include Sitti Khudara's husband, Birono, and Lulilu, an uncircumcised female prostitute. The males request cigarettes and both sexes require red clothing: galabeyas, shawls, fez, etc.

Arab: These Muslim nomads from eastern Sudan's Red Sea region are generally fierce tribal warriors known for their aggressiveness, brute strength and fighting skills. However, small boys and a decidedly homosexual male, Sulayman Ya Janna, also belong to the tribe.

Khawajat (Foreigners): These European or Western spirits are mainly Christians, although the tribe is a catchall for anyone foreign. Its members symbolize wealth and power and request Western foods, clothes, cigarettes, and alcohol when they descend. Frankincense is added to their incense.

Pashawat: These are particularly powerful male Khawajat, i.e., pashas, Western authority figures, military officers, doctors, lawyers, and government officials. They, too, request alcohol, cigarettes, and Western food and clothes. Hakim Pasha (Doctor Pasha) and his son Yawra Bey, included in the Egyptian pantheon, are members.

---

391   Abd al-Qadir al-Jilani (1077–1166 CE) was the Muslim saint who established the first Sufi brotherhood and authored two books: *Sirr al-Asrar* (Secret of Secrets) and *Futuh al-Ghaib* (Revelation of the Hidden).

Sitat wa Banat, or Ladies and Girls/Daughters: This tribe is ladies only and includes the "angels or daughters of the sea/river," *malayka* or *benat al-bahr*, ancient benevolent entities that live in the Nile. In Egyptian Nubia, these spirits typically possess sheikhat, who hold hadra-like gatherings to help diagnose and cure the sick. Other female members of this tribe often request perfume or flowers when they manifest.

The next four tribes are traditionally combined under one category, "Black," but Janice Boddy found them to be distinct.[392] Please see her book for details.

Halib: These are tinkerers and gypsies from Aleppo, Syria (*Halib* in Arabic). The females are generally loose, uncircumcised women free from male control, who are known for their bold behavior and open, fearless attitudes towards men. Both sexes have a mobile, unfettered lifestyle.

Fallata: These spirits come from West Africa—Fulani, Hausa, Senegal, and occasionally the Darfur region of western Sudan. They are poor itinerant laborers, zealous Muslims rough around the edges who are working their way across Africa on a pilgrimage to Mecca.

Khudam, Abid, or Zurug (servants, slaves, or blacks): These are pagan zayran from the south who were enslaved by Arab Muslims. Members require black clothing or animal hides, heavy drum rhythms and props typical of Central Africa, such as spears or mortar and pestles. They cause serious prolonged illnesses and perform powerful magic.

Sahar: These Azande spirits from South Sudan and northeastern Zaire represent the dark side of the zar world. They make their hosts eat raw meat and go naked, and include cannibal sorcerers, alien spirits, and the Egyptian *ghoula*.

---

392   Janice Boddy conducted her Nubian research Jan. 1976–March 1977 and Dec. 1983–April 1984.

Nigeria and the Bori

Traveling west to the lands watered by Africa's Niger River, we have A. J. N. Tremearne's turn-of-the-last-century observations, populated with entities from the continent's traditional hunter-gatherer and pastoral lifestyles:[393]

Dan Sariki: The Prince, the spoiled son of a ruler.

Sarikin Rafi: The King of lakes and rivers.

Dan Galadima: The Supreme Appeal Judge of the Wanzimi court; during rituals, he hears cases and dispenses judgments.

Wanzami: The Barber, a lower-level judge of the Wanzimi court; he, too, hears cases and dispenses rulings during rituals.

Kure: The Hyena.

Malam Alhaji: The Learned Pilgrim, the "Angel of Death," the marriage officiator and the oldest Muslim bori.

Bebe: The Deaf-Mute.

Sarikin Filani: King of the Fulani, cow herding Islamic pastoralists.

Gwari: A pagan from southwest Zaria.

Sarikin Baka: King of the Hunters.

Tsuguna: The Squatter, either a dog or a monkey.

Birri: The Monkey.

Aradu: The Spirit of Thunder.

Kaikai: The Scratcher (from itch).

Kurama and Inna: The Hard-of-Hearing and the Stutterer.

---

393   Tremearne, *The Tailed Head-Hunters of Nigeria*, 254–57.

Mai Jan Chiki: The Snake and personification of the Evil Eye; he is fond of blood and among the first to drink from the sacrifice. During rituals, he makes his host slither along the ground.

Mai Jan Rua: Red Water or the Feverish One.

Kuturu: The Leper, Master of the Horse, and Gatekeeper of Jan Gari.

Janjare/Janziri: The pig; a filthy spirit that loves eating and rolling in dirt.

Now compare these entities to the recent ones mentioned in *Prayer Spoiled Everything* and *Women's Medicine*. Instead of by category, Masquelier, the author of *Prayer Spoiled Everything*, divides Mawri spirits by family or tribe:

Doguwa: These are local Mawri-Hausa entities, mostly specific to Masquelier's study region. This is also the proper name of Azane's wife (see below) or any tribe member without a name.

Zarma: These deities are from the western homeland of Niger's ruling minority after its independence from France in 1960. Descended from a noble family of nature spirits, the Tooru, these Invisibles are often referred to as "the black spirits" because of the black robes their hosts wear during rituals. Members control the Niger River, clouds, wind, rain, lightning, and thunder and usually demand red chickens as a sacrifice.

Baboule: These fire-eating, extraordinarily strong and violent spirits emerged during the local rebellions against the French during the late1920s. They are mainly foreign military spirits from the east that embody colonial powers. It is said they were brought by a Hausa WWI veteran when he returned from pilgrimage to Mecca. Hosts carry riding crops and clubs as props, occasionally beating each other with them.

Prominent Mawri individuals are:

Malam Alhaji: A religious Muslim spirit and a staple of most bori pantheons, past and present.

Kirai: The Red Sorcerer, the powerful, cunning leader of the Zarma spirits. He wears red and brandishes a hatchet to symbolize his control over thunder and lightning. His sacrifice is a red rooster and his mediumship is necessary to be a Sarkin bori, a regional cult chief. *Women's Medicine* lists his date of appearance as 1964.

Souleymane: Kirai's oldest brother and the most powerful Zarma spirit, according to Masquelier. Hosting him is also necessary to be a Sarkin bori. He appeared in 1954.

Gurmuniya: The Lame One, Kirai's Doguwa sister who cannot walk. During rituals she drags herself on the ground, legs folded under her. She lives in cemeteries and causes women to continuously menstruate. Her prop is an antelope horn with leather fringe.

Adama: A white Doguwa spirit that causes paralysis. *Women's Medicine* lists three different entities with the same name, one a Doguwa and another a Zarma that appeared in 1960.

Zanzana: The spoiled Doguwa child of smallpox and measles. During a ritual, she makes her host cry, whine, and constantly scratch herself. She wears a striped black and white wrapper and requests a speckled black and white hen as a sacrifice because the markings resemble welts.

Babai: An important Doguwa male spirit whose mediumship is also necessary to be a Sarkin bori. *Women's Medicine* lists him as from the *azna*.

Rankasso: A senior female Doguwa spirit who was prominent before colonialism. She has high standards of respectability, morality, and modesty and requires a black hen in sacrifice and a black wrapper for clothes. Her presence is also necessary for a Sarkin bori. *Women's Medicine* does not list her.

Mai Daro: The youngest and favorite sister of Rankasso, also not listed by *Women's Medicine*.

Mashi: The first son of Rankasso, listed in *Women's Medicine* as a native *azna* spirit.

Wankarma: A wife of Mashi. This jealous and cunning Doguwa spirit requires a black hen in sacrifice and a black wrapper for clothes. She hates Mashi's other wife, Bagurma. *Women's Medicine* lists her as a native *azna* spirit from the Lugu region of Arewa.

Bagurma: Mashi's other wife, who substituted her newborn girl for Wankarma's newborn boy and then presented him to their husband as her own. *Women's Medicine* lists this spirit, but as a male captive.

Azane: A strong bori not listed by *Women's Medicine* who makes hosts roll in the sand to "wash with dirt."

Magiro: A male deity invoked in times of epidemics, not listed by *Women's Medicine,* but who, according to Tremearne, is ruler of the North African bori (see next page).

Makeri: The Blacksmith, also not listed by *Women's Medicine*. He embarrasses the audience with crude language, sexual allusions, and explicit gestures.

Maria: A defiant, wanton, and sometimes vicious prostitute spirit who enjoys seducing males, humans, and spirits. Known for her generosity and love of sweets, cosmetics, and luxury items on one hand, and uncontrolled lust on the other, she is nevertheless extremely fond of her husband, Zahoho, whom she overindulges. She despises dirt and children, causes infertility in her victims, and only wears bright white dresses. Hosts demand sugar cubes and white kola nuts to eat and spend time admiring themselves in the mirror and brushing dirt off their clothes. *Women's Medicine* lists her as a recent Zarma spirit.

Zahoho: Maria's lazy unemployed husband, who is not listed elsewhere.

The following Baboule spirits were not listed:

Komandan Mugu: Commandant Evil, a spirit based on the historical figure Commandant Crocchichia. He shouts orders in Hausa and pidgin French.

Gwamna: Governor, another military spirit that shouts orders and blows a whistle.

Danne: A Mossi military spirit who supposedly eats dogs. Now his sacrifice is a white cock.

In *The Ban of the Bori,* Tremearne divided his North African bori into a number of categories:

The Great Ones (Baba): During the author's time North African bori were ruled by Magiro, the grandfather of all spirits, an evil pagan Hausa who demanded human sacrifices. As ruler of Jan-Gari, he prevented subjects from leaving by withholding permission from the Gatekeeper, Kuturu, to let them pass. Under Magiro were Malam Alhaji and Kuturu.[394] *Women's Medicine* lists Sarkin al-Jannu, King of the Jinn, as the bori leader.

Children of the Thobe (Muslim dress—Yan Riga): These spirits are all Muslim Hausa and more or less good. Some, the Malams, are marabouts (holy men/teachers), a few are ancestor spirits, but most are foreign jinn. Malam Ali and Sarikin Rafi are among the most popular.

Black Spirits (Babbaku): These are either pagan nature gods or ancestor spirits that farm or hunt in the forests. Their chief is Dakaki, the Crawler, in North Africa, or Mai-Ja-Chikki in Haussaland. Another favorite is the pagan Kuri, also once a chief of spirits. He is not cannibalistic, so does not drink blood. His wife, Doguwa, is venerated as the mother of all *masu-bori* (trained spirit dancers). Another particularly disgusting member is Jato, the equivalent of Egypt's Gado. This half Arab–half black spirit was once a malam who went mad from

---

394   Tremearne, *The Ban of the Bori*, 206.

excessive reading and too many forbidden pleasures. He is now this pantheon's filthiest spirit. He lives in drains, causes venereal diseases and fevers, and, while dancing, makes his host eat or roll in dung and simulate fornication.

Fighting Spirits (Yan Garke): These Children of the Shield are mainly foreign warrior jinn mixed with hero ancestor spirits. Their chief is Jaruma, Great Shield, a Gwari. Hosts dance with spears.

Youths (Samari): These are well-educated Muslim young people who read and write.

Little Spots (Yayan Jidderi): These are young spirits that cause rashes, eye infections, and smallpox. Thought to be the ancestor spirits of young children, their hosts behave like kids while dancing. A popular spirit is Nana Mariyamu, a child bride to Jato, despite her youth (she has not yet lived with him). She causes head colds and sore eyes and expects presents of sugar.

Forest, Water, and Grove Spirits (Children of the Grove, Yan Kurimi, Children of the Stream, Yan Rawa): These animal spirits were once totems. Forest bori include the lion, hyena, elephant, and dog. Water bori make their victims thirsty, appear as crocodiles and some control rain. Grove bori are a mix of totems and ancestor spirits.

Nigeria and the Orisha

Let's also look at a few well-known Yoruban orisha and their New World descendants, although out of West Africa's four hundred to six hundred deities, only several dozen survived the slave galleys across the Atlantic. For instance, the most recent Afro-Brazilian belief system, Umbanda, reveres sixteen major orisha organized into a cycle of four elemental quadrants—The Dynamics of Odudua. It begins at the South Pole and progresses clockwise:

- **Southern Fire:** Elegbara—Ogum—Oshumare—Shango
- **Western Earth:** Obaluaye—Oshossi—Ossae—Oba

- **Northern Water:** Nana—Oshum—Iemanja—Ewa
- **Eastern Air:** Iansa—Tempo—Ifa—Oshala

The following information is from *Religious Encounter and the Making of the Yoruba, African Religion*, and *Sarava!*,[395] along with an interview with leading members of the Washington, DC, Umbanda chapter of Templo Guaracy do Brasil.

Olorun, Olodumare, Oldumare, or, in English, God: This omnipotent yet remote Supreme Creator deity may rule the Heavens, but He is not intensely worshipped by Africa's traditional religions. Only prayers acknowledge His existence, not dedicated temples, festivals, or images. Nor do mediums encorporate[396] Him. Yet as the architect of universal destiny, He touches everything on the planet.[397]

Oxala or Oshala: In Yorubaland, this deity is Olorun's son and head orisha in his father's absence. Represented by the sun, his ritual day is Sunday. His persona is split into a noble young warrior and a frail old man who walks with a cane. The latter represents death, which is why his devotees wear white, the color of mourning. And while some cults consider him an orisha father figure married to either Nana or Yemoja, his mediums dress in women's clothing when possessed. Oxala begins and ends the Umbanda spiritual cycle at its southern pole, the last air spirit before Elegbara, the fiery spark of creation and renewal.

Nana: As Grandmother to the Deities, Guardian of Death's Portal, and Mother of Rain, this entity was the first, besides Olorun, to manipulate cosmic energy. When she encorporates, her mediums also hunch over and move with frail steps, similar to Oshala, and although normally calm and difficult to upset, she retaliates mercilessly once angry. As gatekeeper to the Afterlife, she and her female adepts are the only ones who

---

395   Peel, *Religious Encounter*, 107–114; Ray, *African Religions*, 56-71; Dow, *Sarava!*, 21–44.
396   The word "encorporate" is used by Umbanda practitioners to describe the process of spirit embodiment.
397   Ray, *African Religions*, 56.

know what lies beyond death's threshold. On Odudua's Dynamic Umbanda Wheel, she is due north opposite Oshala, the first water deity.

Yemoja or Iemanja: As Goddess of Nigeria's Ogun River, many consider this spirit to be the mother of all deities. Myth has it she had three sons with her husband Obatala: Ogum, Oshossi, and Exu. In New World religions, this Lady of the Sea and Mother of Pearls is the third Umbanda water deity and perhaps the most beloved goddess of Brazil. As the feminine principle of creation, gestation, and the hearth fire, she is linked to the moon. Her ritual day is Saturday and her sacred color is bright blue. While her feast day varies (December 31 in Rio de Janeiro), it is invariably held at the beach. Family and friends dig holes in the sand and fill them with lighted candles and flowers. At midnight or dawn, depending on the temple, they release decorated miniature candlelit boats into the sea and then dive into the waves to purify themselves.[398]

Ogun or Ogum: The eldest of Yemoja's sons governs iron, war (similar to Mars in the Roman pantheon), and agriculture. And while severe and controlling, he is also the most responsible orisha, who continually strives to keep his family united and safe—hence his reputation as a compassionate father figure.[399] He also protects military members and those doing battle, which is why his August festival is traditionally celebrated with military parades. His ritual day is Tuesday, and his sacred color is blue for Candomblé or green in Umbanda.

Ososi, Oshossi, or Oxossi: Yemoja's contemplative second son is the pantheon's hunting deity and Lord of the Forest. He, too, represents the fruits of agriculture, as well as positive energy, prosperity, and abundance—hence his epithet Lord of the Art of Living. He symbolizes freedom, optimism, and dynamism and as patron of the arts, creativity. On the negative side, he can be a dreamer, procrastinator, and careless worker

---

398   Dow, *Sarava!*, 26.
399   Ibid., 30.

who causes scarcity and starvation. His day is Thursday and his sacred color is green.

Esu, Exu, or Elegbara: In Africa, this trickster divinity receives a share of every sacrifice and is associated with entrances and crossroads. Nineteenth-century missionaries noted that the Yoruban festival season began in mid-July with the sacrifice of a human female to "appease the rage of Esu" to protect their farms. Afro-Brazilian traditions describe this deity as Yemoja's youngest son who fell in love with her and tried to rape her.[400] To them he represents universal libido and unbridled passion.

Obatala or Orisanla: According to African creation myths, this *orisha fun-fun* (white orisha) was responsible for fashioning the first humans out of clay, although his annual festival in Ife emphasizes his confrontation with Odudua: his rebellion, defeat, exile, eventual reconciliation, and return to Ife as its fourth King. During the reenactment, his statue, along with that of his wife, Yemoja, is paraded to his village of exile, where the current monarch, "the divine ruler, second to Obatala," presents the Igbo Chief with gifts in return for his annual blessing. This acknowledges Obatala as Ife's rightful ruler and guardian of its destiny, even though his people are no longer in power.[401]

Sopona/Omolu/Obaluaye: In Yorubaland, this is the smallpox deity. In Afro-Brazilian traditions he is either Nana's warrior son or an old man ravaged by smallpox scars. As Lord of Death, Disease, Health, Healing, and Rebirth, he governs the souls of the dead. According to myth, his mother abandoned him in childhood because of his scars, but Yemoja took him in, raised him as her own, and taught him to cure diseases.[402] His ritual day is Monday and his sacred colors are black and white or red and black.

---

400   Dow, *Sarava!*, 27.
401   Ray, *African Religions*, 70.
402   Dow, *Sarava!*, 32.

Shango: This fierce thunder deity originated with Odudua's tribe, the Oyo, who spread his influence as their political power grew. He was Odudua's grandson and Oranyan's son (the fourth Oyo King), and when it came time for him to rule he used lightning bolts to protect his kingdom—but also to punish disloyalty. In fact, myth has it he was so cruel that his subjects eventually deposed him, which pushed him to hang himself in disgrace. His worshippers disagree, though. They claim that as he aged, the stress of ruling sapped his strength and virility. To prove he still had what it took, he hurled his thunder ax from a hilltop, but it slipped, crashed into the palace, and killed everyone inside. He did hang himself, but from despair, not shame. His mediums demonstrate violent and erratic behavior while possessed and similar to Oshala's followers, dress in women's clothing.[403] In the New World, Shango is celebrated as the first African deity to debark on Brazilian shores. He is Lord of Justice, his ritual day is Wednesday, and his sacred color is red.[404]

Iansa: This strong-willed female divinity wields a flaming sword and horsetail hair whip as symbols for uncontrolled passion, orgasm, jealousy, and free love. She controls the wind, from refreshing breezes to cyclones, and energy, either electrical or sexual. She is the only deity able to control the Eguns, the spirits of the dead. In Africa, her ferocious nature is symbolized by a short beard hidden behind a face veil. Legend has it she was so thirsty for knowledge that she seduced all the male deities in exchange for their secrets. But Shango gave her far more than she expected—she fell passionately in love with him and gave birth to the Ibeji twins.[405]

---

403   Ray, *African Religions,* 70–71.

404   Dow, *Saravá!,* 44.

405   Ibid., 24–25.

Osun, Oxum, or Oshum: This gentle female river deity was originally from central and eastern Yorubaland. In Afro-Brazilian traditions, she is Oxala's daughter, the youngest and most beloved of Shango's wives. As the deity of fresh water, waterfalls, and brooks, she oversees the health of unborn children and the positive aspects of marriage. When possessed, her mediums behave like coquettish girls. Her father granted her the right to divine with cowry shells, making her worshippers the only women permitted to do so. Her negative side includes vanity, envy, and deceit, to the point where in some myths she is so vindictive she slices off a co-wife's ear.[406] In the Umbanda tradition she is also the goddess of money and love, her sacred color is yellow, and her day of worship is Saturday.

Ifa or Orunmila: "Heaven's Reconciliation," the male deity of divination, is Olorun's privileged messenger. In the Umbanda cycle his place of honor is in air next to Oxala.

Osumare or Oxumare: The Rainbow deity. Legend has it that Olorun created Earth in four days, and then made the rainbow to symbolize His alliance with it—a multicolored serpent arching across the sky to drink, with head and tail immersed in water. This androgynous entity is present wherever financial negotiations take place, including losses. And when it encorporates, mediums perform sinuous, contorted dances.[407]

The Ibeji twins: These cosmic mischief-makers embody the healing power of laughter and childhood innocence. They watch over all children, regardless of their family affiliations. In Afro-Brazilian myths they are the offspring of Shango and Iansa. Their day is Sunday and their sacred colors are blue and pink.[408]

---

406 Dow, *Sarava!*, 40.

407 Ibid., 43.

408 Ibid., 26–27.

Ossae: In New World traditions this son of Nana is the original healer and patron of doctors. An introverted plant-lover, he left home to live in the jungle, where he discovered the curative powers of all things green.[409] His African counterpart is Osanyin, the Yoruban deity of healing.

Aje: The Yoruban deity of wealth.

Oya: Or Oluwa, the river goddess of the Niger River.

---

409   Dow, *Sarava!*, 39.

Glossary

Afreet / afareet (pl): In the Quran, *afareet* refers to jinn of extraordinary strength or power. This word is also used to designate ancestor spirits, i.e., the souls of the dead, particularly those who died by violence and haunt the place of their demise. In everyday Arabic, it has also come to mean mischievous, sly, cunning, crafty, or naughty (as in children)—in a nod to the trickster, prank-loving character of many jinn.

Awlad al-ard: Children of the earth/ground. Spirits that live underground, either the jinn or qarin.

Ayah / ayat (pl): Verses (as in those from the Quran) or natural signs from God (divine coincidence).

Babylon: An ancient city or city-state located fifty-five miles south of modern-day Baghdad, Iraq, that rose to power from 1900 BCE until the Persians conquered it in 539 BCE.

Bakhour: "Incense," from the root *b-kh-r*; also "vapor" or "steam." As a verb, "to fumigate or cense." *Tabkheera* is an ancient branch of folk medicine that uses incense; burners (*mabkhara*) were found in Old Kingdom and other ancient tombs throughout the Middle East. Even today, special mixtures to prevent envy and the evil eye are popular in spice stores throughout the Middle East.

Dervish: "A member of a Sufi order," or in popular Arabic jargon, "a godly person."[410] The word is thought to originate from Farsi (the Persian language), where it means either "doorstep" and implies poverty, or "doorway" and refers to someone who has passed through a symbolic threshold into the spiritual world. *Dar* in Farsi means "door," hence a *dervish* is "someone who goes from door to door" or who opens one and passes through it. *Dar* in Arabic, however, means (among other things) "to circle, move in a circle, or to roam." Some believe the word came from the ancient Proto-Iranian *drigu-*, "needy, mendicant," via the Middle Persian *driyosh*. At any rate, the word now implies a religious aesthetic, the Muslim equivalent to a Christian monk.

Diana: In Roman mythology, Diana ("heavenly" or "divine") was the goddess of the hunt, the moon and birthing. She was associated with wild animals and woodland and equated with the Greek goddess Artemis, although her origin was purely Italian. She was considered the nearest Greek equivalent for Bastet, aka Hathor. There is an imposing statue of Hathor still present at the ancient site of Bubastis.

Hadra / hadarat (pl): Literally, "presence" in Arabic, but with a spiritual implication. The root, *h-d-r*, means "to attend or be present at." For the zar, presence implies the jinn or zar spirit masters, while in Sufi terminology it implies the presence of God. The word "hadra" also means either the tomb of a venerated Muslim religious figure or a specific type of formal group zikr that includes music, singing, chanting, and movement/dance.[411] When performed, this ritual is considered the climax of a Sufi gathering, regardless of the order's doctrine. The music can last for hours and usually includes singing, frame drum percussion, and melodic interludes on a reed flute, or *nay*. Participants' vocalizations, projected from deep within their chests, also contribute

---

410 Bedawi and Hinds, *A Dictionary of Egyptian Arabic*.
411 Ibid.

to the overall rhythm, as do the dancers' movements (bending forward while exhaling and straightening while inhaling). Climax is signaled by cries of *"Allah! Allah!"* or *"hu, hu"* (either the pronoun "he" or the last vowel on the word "Allah," depending on the method) followed by ecstatic silence. The Sufi order's sheikh or his representative will direct the ceremony and monitor its intensity and duration.

Hathor: The cow goddess of fertility, music, and the Afterlife. Her drunken festivals were a high point of Egypt's religious calendar and were celebrated until at least the Roman era. She has had many incarnations. Her first, during the archaic period, was as a cow. Since then, she has taken multiple shapes, most often as a beautiful woman wearing a solar disk on her head between two cow horns. She was a complex deity, both benevolent and destructive. In her role as mother, mate, and daughter to the original creator god, she helped women give birth, the dead to be reborn, and the cosmos to be renewed. The *Pyramid Texts* (the oldest surviving compilation of magic spells) of Pepi I refer to her three times.

Jinn (sometimes spelled *djinn*) and *jaan*: A fiery species of invisible spirit entities said to be composed of "smokeless fire" or the "tip of a flame," i.e., plasma. *Jinn* and *jaan* are used synonymously in the Quran as "collective plurals," meaning they refer to a group. *Jinni*, masculine, and *jinniya*, feminine, are the singular forms, all from the Arabic root *j-n-n,* "to cover, as in to shadow, hide or be hidden."

Khonsu: As the son of Amun and Mut, this god was part of the ancient Theban triad. He was also known as "the Traveler" because he was thought to cross the night sky as the moon-god. He issued prophecies and helped Thoth, the god of Wisdom. He was portrayed either as a man with a hawk's head or as a youth with a side-lock of hair.

Natufians: Mesolithic inhabitants of Palestine and the Fertile Crescent (13,000–9800 BCE), credited as being one of three cultures that independently developed agriculture (the other two were in central Mexico and along the middle Yangtze River in China).

Ramses II or Ramses the Great (1303–1213 BCE): He was the third ruler of the Nineteenth Dynasty and thought to be the first pharaoh of Exodus. His reign lasted for sixty-six years. He outlived most of his early wives and elder sons and married his daughters when their mothers died. He's believed to have had seven official wives, but not all at the same time. The Hittite princess Matnefrure, mentioned in the Marriage Stele and the Princess of Bekhten story, was his last.

Salat: Islamic ritual prayers done facing the holy city of Mecca. A standing position is alternated with inclinations (*ruku*) and prostrations (*sujud*). According to Muslim tradition, the five daily prayer requirement was set during Muhammad's night ascension to heaven: dawn (*salat as-subh/fadjr*), mid-day (*salat az-zuhr*), afternoon (*salat al-asr*), sunset (*salat al-mughrib*) and evening (*salat al-isha*). The obligation is suspended for the sick, but for all others omitted prayers must be made up. The worshipper must face the direction of Mecca.

Saqqara: The pyramid field near the ancient site of Memphis, about forty-five minutes south along the Nile from Cairo, where the Third Dynasty Step pyramid and Fifth-Sixth Dynasty tombs were built.

Sayed / asyad (pl): An Egyptian term for possession spirits, often used to indirectly refer to the jinn. Derived from *as-siyaada,* "power or authority," "master," something that takes control.

Shaabi: An Arabic adjective meaning "popular, of the people" or "traditional, folk." Used to describe activities or attributes of ordinary people.

Sufi/Sufism, or *tasawwuf* in Arabic: "Sufism is nothing other than Islamic mysticism, which means that it is the central and most powerful current

of that tidal wave which constitutes the Revelation of Islam."[412] Islam's esoteric dimension is founded on the principle that God created the universe
from Divine Love so that his creations would return this energy to him: "I
created the jinn and humans that they may worship me" (Quran 51:56).
Essentially, Sufism is the path to infinity and immortality through the Divine gift of love. In the words of Celâleddin M. Bâqir Çelebi, the twenty-
first descendent of the Mevlevi founder, "The human being has been created with love in order to love."[413] While all Muslims believe they will find
God after death, adherents of Sufism, or Sufis, believe they can approach
Him while still alive—through love, constant remembrance of his name
(*zikr*), prayer, and trance (*hal*)—hence the raison-d'etre for their rituals.

The word *sufi* originated either from the Arabic word *suf*, "wool"
(from the plain wool capes worn by early Muslim holy men) or the
Greek *sophia*, "wisdom." There are Sufi orders or *turuq* in all branches
of Islam; Sunni, Shia, etc. Historically, a Sufi was someone with religious learning who sought unity with Allah through simplicity, humility, and constant worship. This aesthetic philosophy sprouted soon
after Muhammad's death (632 CE) as a pious reaction against the ma-
terialism of the early Umayyad Caliphate (661–750 CE).

Sumerians: An ancient Chalcolithic and Early Bronze Age civilization
(from Dilmun) who lived in Southern Mesopotamia from roughly
5300–1940 BCE. They are credited with the early development of writing, irrigation, the use of fertilizer, and granaries to store food.

Tafqeer: This is from the root *f-q-r*, to sway rhythmically, as during a zikr
or zar, to nod or rock, as from drowsiness or pain, or to flicker like a
candle flame. The word is used to describe the strenuous movements an
arousa does during a zar ritual, after the *takhmeer* and the *takeer*, a form
of shaabi dancing, where the patient strenuously moves her upper body,

---

412   Lings, *What is Sufism?*, 15.

413   From liner notes of *Wherever You Turn Is the Face of God* by the Mevlevi Ensemble of Turkey.

head, spine and hips from side to side and up and down, until she falls unconscious (*al-ughrma* from the root *ghr-m-y*, to faint).

Takeer: From the root *a-k-r*, to roil, become turbid, or to lose coloring, shape, or original state. In zar speak it refers to the trembling or shaking patients exhibit during a ceremony as they enter deep trance. The sheikha will then push them into the dance ring to "recover their psychological balance"; i.e., trance dance until they collapse.

Takhmeer: From the root *kh-m-r*, to ferment. This zar idiom refers to the section of a ritual where two duffs are played on either side of a patient, one per ear, to push her into trance, or *takeer*. While her body shakes, the sheikha will hold the incense tray under her chin for her to inhale, then lead her to the dance ring (*hilba al-tafqeer*) to begin trance dancing, a stage called *takeera*.

Tanakh: A Hebrew acronym for the *Torah* (the Pentateuch or first five books of the Old Testament), *Nevi'im* (Prophets), and *Ketuvim* (Writings). Together, it contains the books Christians refer to as the "Old Testament."

Zar / zayran (pl): This word has several meanings, all associated with a variety of East African possession spirits. It can refer to a ceremony to placate the spirits; the spirits themselves (zayran are a subspecies of jinn); the cult that believes in the spirits; or the dance done to communicate with the spirits.

Zikr or *dhikr*: This Sufi ritual uses rhythmic breathing, chanting, and verbal repetition (either silent or spoken, performed alone or in a group) to invoke God's presence. Frequently repeated words include "Allah," the pronoun "*hu(wa)*" ("He"), the Tawheed (the confirmation that there is no god but God), and "*hai* [He] lives," but other Quranic words and/or phrases may also be used. Chanting or the use of breath control to enter trance is not unique to Islam. Other religions also use monotonous repetition to reach a sacred mindset—implying that what is said is less important than how it is pronounced—method over content—although Sufis would disagree vehemently with this conclusion.

A basic Sufi tenant is that devotees should constantly acknowledge God's presence, his Divine Love, in the fabric of everyday life. Hence, Sufi rituals—prayer, fasting, simplistic lifestyle, and particularly zikr—are meant to facilitate this, even though practices vary by sect, or tariqa.[414] On a more mundane level (yet just as important), performing zikr also brings physical wellbeing, a phenomenon apparently known during Muhammad's time ... "Hearts become tranquil through the remembrance of Allah" (Quran 13:28).

---

414 Individual tariqa rituals are set by an order's founder, since there is no central Sufi organization. The Mevlevi, for example, are only one branch of a very large tree.

Bibliography

Akstein, David. *Un Voyage a Travers la Transe: Terpsichore-Transe-Therapie.* Paris: Editions Sand, 1992.

Al-Aleemi, Adel. *Az-Zar: Masrah al-Taqous* [The Zar: Ritual Theater]. Cairo: Egyptian Book Organization, 1993.

Al-Ashqar, Umar S. *The World of the Jinn and Devils.* Boulder, CO: Al-Basheer Publications and Translations, 1998.

Aldridge, David, and Jörg Fachner. *Music and Altered States: Consciousness, Transcendence, Therapy and Addictions.* Philadelphia: Jessica Kingsly Publishers, 2006.

Ali, Abdullah Yusuf. *The Meaning of the Holy Quran*, 10th Edition. Beltsville, MD: Amana, 1999.

Al-Masri, Fatima. *Az-Zar: Darasa Nefsiya wa Anthropologia* [The Zar: A Neurological and Anthropological Study]. Cairo, 1975.

American Psychiatric Association. *The Diagnostic and Statistical Manual of Mental Disorders*, 4th edition, text revision. Washington, DC: 2000.

Antelme, Ruth. *Les Secrets d'Hathor.* Paris: Editions du Rocher, 1999.

"Are You Easily Pleased?" *The Economist*, May 2, 2015.

Arthuis, M., et. al. "Impaired Consciousness During Temporal Lobe Seizures Is Related to Increased Long-Distance Cortical-Subcortical Synchronization." *Brain* 132(8), August 2009.

Ashour, Mustafa. *The Jinn in the Quran and the Sunna.* London: Dar al-Taqwa, 1989.

As-Shibli, Badr ad-Din. *Akaam al-Murjaan fi Ahkaam al-Jaan.* Beirut: Dar al-Qalim, 1988.

———. *Ghaa'b wa 3agaa'b al-Jan/Akaam al-Murjaan fi Ahkaam al-Jaan.* Cairo: Maktabah al-Quran, 1939.

Austin, James. *Zen and the Brain.* Cambridge, MA: MIT Press, 1998.

———. *Zen-Brain Reflections:* Cambridge, MA: MIT Press, 2006.

Bahn, Paul, and Paul Pettitt. *Britain's Oldest Art: The Ice Age Cave Art of Creswell Crags.* London: Historic England Publishing, 2009.

Becker, Judith. *Deep Listeners: Music, Emotion, and Trancing.* Bloomington, IN: Indiana University Press, 2004.

Bedawi, Al-Said, and Martin Hinds. *A Dictionary of Egyptian Arabic.* Beirut: Librairie du Liban, 1986.

Belloni, Alessandra. *Rhythm is the Cure: Southern Italian Tambourine.* Fenton, MO: Mel Bay Publications, 2007.

"The Benefits of Slumber: Why You Need a Good Night's Sleep." *NIH: News in Health*, April 2013. https://newsinhealth.nih.gov/issue/apr2013/feature1.

Berna, Francesco, et al. "Microstratigraphic Evidence of In Situ Fire in the Acheulean Strata of Wonderwerk Cave, Northern Cape Province, South Africa." *Proceedings of the National Academy of Sciences of the United States of America*, May 15, 2012.

Birch, S., trans. "The Possessed Princess. Tablet of Rameses XII." *Records of the Past: Being English Translations of the Ancient Monuments of Egypt and Western Asia*, Vol. 4. Edited by A. H. Sayce. London: Samuel Bagster and Sons, 1890.

Blackman, Winifred. *The Fellahin of Upper Egypt.* London: George Harrop & Co, 1927.

Blades, James. *Percussion Instruments and Their History.* New York: Praeger, 1970.

Boddy, Janice. *Wombs and Alien Spirits: Women, Men, and the Zar Cult in Northern Sudan.* Madison, WI: University of Wisconsin Press, 1989.

"Bolts from the Blue." *The Economist*, October 18, 2014.

Bowden, Hugh. *Mystery Cults of the Ancient World*. London: Thames & Hudson, 2010.

Bradshaw, Joseph. *The Night Sky in Egyptian Mythology*. Leicester, UK: Troubador, 1997.

Braun, Joachim. *Music in Ancient Israel/Palestine: Archaeological, Written, and Comparative Sources*. Cambridge, UK: Eerdmans Publishing, 2002.

Breasted, Henry. *Ancient Records of Egypt: Historical Documents from the Earliest Times to the Persian Conquest*, Vol. 3. Chicago: University of Chicago, 1906.

Breuil, Henri. *La Caverne de Font-de-Gaume*. Monaco: Imprimerie A. Chene, 1910.

Brierre de Boismont, Alexandre. *Hallucinations: A Rational History*. Philadelphia: Lindsay & Blakiston, 1853.

Bromage, Bernard. *The Occult Arts of Ancient Egypt*. London: Aquarian Press, 1953.

Budge, E. A. Wallis. *Egyptian Magic*. London: Kegan Paul, 1901.

———. *The Gods of the Egyptians, or Studies in Egyptian Mythology*. London: Methuen, 1904.

———. *Legends of the Gods: The Egyptian Texts, Edited with Translations*. London: Kegan Paul, 1912.

Bulfinch, Thomas. *Myths & Legends: The Golden Era*. Boston: David Nickerson & Co., 1907.

Burton, Richard F. *The Book of the Thousand Nights and a Night: A Plain and Literal Translation of the Arabian Nights Entertainments*. London: The Burton Club, 1885-1905.

Calaprice, Alice, ed. *The Expanded Quotable Einstein*, 2nd edition. Princeton, NJ: Princeton University Press, 2000.

Calder, Nigel. *Magic Universe: The Oxford Guide to Modern Science*. Oxford, UK: Oxford University Press, 2003.

Carus, Paul. *The History of the Devil and the Idea of Evil*. Chicago: Open Court Publishing, 1900.

Clark, Ronald. *Einstein: The Life and Times.* New York: Avon Books, 1971.

Cohen, Jennie. "Human Ancestors Tamed Fire Earlier Than Thought." History .com, April 2, 2012. http://www.history.com/news/human-ancestors-tamed -fire-earlier-than-thought.

"Computer Says 'Try This.'" *The Economist,* October 4, 2014.

Conway, Daniel. *Demonology and Devil Lore.* London: Chatto & Windus, 1879.

Cowan, J. M., ed. *Arabic English Dictionary: The Hans Wehr Dictionary of Modern Written Arabic,* 4th edition. Urbana, IL: Spoken Language Services, 1994.

Crapanzano, Vincent. *The Hamdasha.* Berkley, CA: University of California Press, 1973.

"Dark Matter: Material Answers." *The Economist,* July 7, 2012.

Davidson, Richard. *The Emotional Life of Your Brain.* New York: Penguin, 2012.

Deren, Maya. *Divine Horsemen: The Living Gods of Haiti.* New York: McPherson & Co., 1953.

Dobbins, Frank. *Error's Chains: How Forged and Broken.* New York: Standard Publishing House, 1883.

Dow, Carol. *Sarava!: Afro-Brazilian Magick.* St. Paul, MN: Llewellyn, 1997.

Dinç, Nefin. *I Named Her Angel* (Documentary Film). New York: Filmakers Library, 2007.

"Dr. Albert Einstein Dies in Sleep at 76; World Mourns Loss of Great Scientist," April 19, 1955. On This Day, Obituary: *New York Times* on the Web, Learning Network. http://www.nytimes.com/learning/general/onthisday/bday/0314.html

Drieskens, Barbara. *Living with Djinn: Understanding and Dealing with the Invisible in Cairo.* London: Saqi Books, 2008.

Ebers, Georg. *Egypt: Descriptive, Historical and Picturesque.* London: Cassell, Petter Galpin & Co., 1884.

Ehrenreich, Barbara. *Dancing in the Streets: A History of Collective Joy.* New York: Henry Holt, 2006.

Einstein, Albert. Letter to Beatrice Frohlich, Dec. 17, 1952, Archives, Jerusalem. (AEA) Archival Call # 59–797. http://alberteinstein.info/vufind1/Record/EAR000028552.

Eliade, Mircea. *Shamanism: Archaic Techniques of Ecstasy.* Princeton, NJ: Princeton University Press, 1951.

El-Sabban, Sherif. *Temple Festival Calendars of Ancient Egypt.* Liverpool, UK: Liverpool University Press, 2000.

Erman, Adolf. *Life in Ancient Egypt.* Trans. H. M. Hirard. London: Macmillan and Co., 1894.

Euripides, Vol I. Trans. R. Potter. New York: Harper & Brothers, 1852.

Faulkner, R. O. *The Ancient Egyptian Pyramid Texts.* Oxford, UK: Oxford University Press, 1969.

"Fractional Distillation: The Hunt for the Missing 85% of Matter in the Universe is Closing In on Its Quarry." *The Economist*, April 6, 2013.

Frazer, James. *The Golden Bough: A Study in Magic and Religion.* New York: Macmillan Co., 1935.

Freeman, Scott. *Biological Science*, 4th edition. San Francisco: Pearson, 2011.

Friedlander, M., trans. *The Guide for the Perplexed by Moses Maimonides.* New York: E. P. Dutton & Co., 1904.

Frobenius, L. *Voice of Africa*, Vol. 2. London: Hutchins & Co., 1913.

Gabriel, Richard. *Muhammad: Islam's First Great General.* Norman, OK: University of Oklahoma Press, 2007.

Galison, Peter L., Gerald Holton, and Silvan S. Schweber, eds. *Einstein for the 21st Century: His Legacy in Science, Art, and Modern Culture.* Princeton, NJ: Princeton University Press, 2008.

Gibb, H.A.R. *A Shorter Encyclopedia of Islam.* Leiden, Netherlands: E.J. Brill, 1953.

———. *The Travels of Ibn Battuta.* New York: Robert M. McBride & Co., 1929.

Gilders, William. *Blood Ritual in the Hebrew Bible.* Baltimore, MD: Johns Hopkins Press, 2004.

Giordano, James. "Spirituality, Suffering, and the Self." *Mind and Matter* 6(2), 2008.

———. and Joan Engebretson. "Neural and Cognitive Basis of Spiritual Experience: Biopsychosocial and Ethical Implications for Clinical Medicine." *EXPLORE: The Journal of Science and Healing* 2(3), May 2006.

Goldish, Matt, ed. *Spirit Possession in Judaism: Cases and Contexts from the Middle Ages to the Present.* Detroit: Wayne State University Press, 2003.

Goldman, Jason. "What Do Animals Dream About?" BBC.com, April 2014. http://www.bbc.com/future/story/20140425-what-do-animals-dream-about/.

Goodman, Felicitas. *Ecstasy, Ritual, and Alternate Reality: Religion in a Pluralistic World.* Bloomington, IN: Indiana University Press, 1988.

———. *How About Demons? Possession and Exorcism in the Modern World.* Bloomington, IN: Indiana University Press, 1988.

Gore, Belinda. *The Ecstatic Experience: Healing Postures for Spirit Journeys.* Rochester, VT: Inner Traditions, 2009.

Gorer, Geoffrey. *Africa Dances: A Book about West African Negroes.* London: Faber & Faber, 1935.

Graves-Brown, Carolyn. *Dancing for Hathor: Women in Ancient Egypt.* New York: Continuum, 2010.

Gray, Henry. *Gray's Anatomy, Descriptive and Surgical.* Philadelphia, PA: Lea Brothers, 1905.

Gulizar Turkish Music Ensemble. *Music of the Whirling Dervishes: 800 Years of Mevlana Rumi.* CD with liner notes. East Grinstead, UK: ARC Music, 2007.

"Hacking Your Brain—Neurostimulation of the Brain." *The Economist Technology Quarterly*, March 7, 2015.

Halioua, Bruno, and Bernard Ziskind. *Medicine in the Days of the Pharaohs.* Cambridge, MA: Belknap Press of Harvard University Press, 2002.

Hall, Frederic. *The Pedigree of the Devil.* London: Trubner & Co., 1883.

Harner, Michael. *Cave and Cosmos: Shamanic Encounters with Another Reality.* Berkley, CA: North Atlantic Book, 2013.

———. *The Way of the Shaman.* New York: Harper and Row, 1980.

Hart, George. *Egyptian Gods and Goddesses.* New York: Routledge, 1986.

Hawking, Stephan. *A Briefer History of Time.* New York: Bantam, 2005.

Hazleton, Lesley. *The First Muslim: The Story of Muhammad.* New York: Penguin, 2013.

Henkesh, Yasmin. Liner notes, *Cry to the Moon.* Bethesda, MD: Sands of Time Music, 2005.

———. Liner notes, *Dancing with Genies.* Bethesda, MD: Sands of Time, 2006.

———. Liner notes, *Hymn to Hathor.* Bethesda, MD: Sands of Time Music, 2013.

———. Liner notes, *Pulse of the Sphinx.* Bethesda, MD: Sands of Time Music, 2007.

———. Liner notes, *Turkey / Egypt.* Bethesda, MD: Sands of Time Music, 2011.

———. Liner notes, *The Zar: Trance Music for Women.* Bethesda, MD: Sands of Time Music, 2005.

Herodotus. *History of Herodotus*, Vol. II. Translated by George Rawlinson. New York: Scribner, 1875.

Hickman, Hans. *Catalogue Generale des Antiquites Egyptiennes du Musee du Caire: Instruments de Musique.* Cairo: Institut Francais d'Archeologie Orientale, 1949.

———. *Musicologie Pharaonique.* Kehl, Germany: Librarie Heitz, 1956.

Hooper, Meredith. *An Egyptian Tomb: The Tomb of Nebamun.* London: British Museum Press, 2008.

Hopkin, Michael. "Ethiopia Is Top Choice for Cradle of *Homo sapiens*." *Nature*. Feb. 17, 2005.

Hornung, Erik. *Conceptions of God in Ancient Egypt: The One and the Many.* Trans. John Baines. Ithaca, NY: Cornell University Press, 1982.

Hughes, Thomas. *Dictionary of Islam.* London: WH Allen Co., 1885.

Isbenberg, C. W., and J. L. Krapf. *Journals of the Rev. Messrs. Isenberg and Krapf, Missionaries of the Church Missionary Society, Detailing their Proceedings in the Kingdom of Shoa, and Journeys in Other Parts of Abyssinia, in the Years 1839, 1840, 1841, and 1842.* London: Seeley, Burside & Seeley, 1843.

James, William. *The Varieties of Religious Experience: A Study in Human Nature.* New York: New American Library, 1958.

Jankowsky, Richard. *Stambeli: Music, Trance, and Alterity in Tunisia.* Chicago: University of Chicago Press, 2010.

Jia, Xiaoxuan, and Adam Kohn. "Gamma Rhythms in the Brain." *PLoS Biol* 9(4), April 12, 2011. http://dx.doi.org/10.1371/journal.pbio.1001045

Jia, Xiaoxuan, and Adam Kohn. "Gamma Rhythms in the Brain." *PLoS Biol* 9(4), April 12, 2011. http://dx.doi.org/10.1371/journal.pbio.1001045.

Joseph, R. *Limbic System: Amygdala, Hypothalamus, Septal Nuclei, Cingulate, Hippocampus.* Cambridge, MA: Cosmology Science Publishers, 2012.

Kalat, James W. *Biological Psychology*, 11th edition. Belmont, CA: Wadsworth, 2013.

Kanawati, N., and M. Abder-Raziq. *Mereruka and His Family: Part II, The Tomb of Waatethathor.* Australian Centre for Egyptology. Oxford, UK: Aris and Phillips, 2008.

Kapchan, Deborah. *Traveling Spirit Masters: Moroccan Gnawa Trance and Music in the Global Marketplace.* Middletown, CT: Wesleyan University Press, 2007.

Kennedy, John, ed. *Nubian Ceremonial Life: Studies in Islamic Syncretism and Cultural Change.* Berkeley, CA: University of California Press, 1978.

Khan, Muhammad M, trans. *The Translation of the Meanings of Sahih Al-Bukhari.* Riyadh, Saudi Arabia: Darussalam Publishers, 1997.

Kinnaird, James Bruce. *Travels to Discover the Source of the Nile in 1768: Vol 1&3, Egypt and Abyssinia.* London: J. Ruthven, 1790.

Klunzinger, C. B. *Upper Egypt: Its People and Products.* New York: Scribner, 1878.

Kohls, Nikola, Sebastian Sauer, Martin Offenbächer, and James Giordano. "Spirituality: an Overlooked Predictor of Placebo Effects?" *Philosophical Transactions of the Royal Society B,* June 2011.

Konishi, T. "The Standardization of Hyperventilation on EEG Recording in Childhood. I. The Quantity of Hyperventilation Activation." *Brain Development* 9(1), 1987. http://www.ncbi.nlm.nih.gov/pubmed/3605536.

Lampel, Zvi. *Maimonides' Introduction to the Talmud.* Brooklyn, New York: The Judaica Press, 1975.

Landels, John. *Music in Ancient Greece and Rome.* London: Routledge, 1999.

Lane, Edward. *An Account of the Manners and Customs of Modern Egyptians.* London: Charles Knight & Co., 1836.

———. *Arabian Society in the Middle Ages.* London: Chatto & Windus, 1883. (Dover 2004 unabridged republication.)

———. *The Thousand and One Nights, Commonly Called in England, the Arabian Nights Entertainment.* London: Routledge, 1865.

Lane-Poole, Sophia. *The Englishwoman in Egypt.* London: C. Cox, 1851.

Le Brun, Eugenie. *Harems et Musulmanes d'Égypt.* Paris: Felix Juven, 1902.

Lebling, Robert. *Legends of the Fire Spirits: Jinn and Genies from Arabia to Zanzibar.* London: I. B. Tauris, 2010.

LeDoux, Joseph. *The Emotional Brain: The Mysterious Underpinnings of Emotional Life.* New York: Simon & Schuster, 1996.

———. *Synaptic Self: How Our Brains Become Who We Are.* New York: Penguin, 2002.

Leiris, Michel. *La Possession et ses aspects théâtraux chez les Éthiopiens de Gondar.* Paris: Le Sycomore, 1980.

Levitin, Daniel. *This Is Your Brain on Music: The Science of a Human Obsession.* New York: Knopf, 2006.

Lewis, Franklin. *Rumi Past and Present, East and West: The Life, Teachings and Poetry of Jalâl al-Din Rumi.* Oxford, UK: Oneworld Publications, 2000.

Lewis, I. M., Ahmed al-Safi, and Sayyid Hurreiz, eds. *Women's Medicine: The Zar-Bori Cult in Africa and Beyond.* Edinburgh: Edinburgh University Press, 1991.

Lewis-Williams, David. *The Mind in the Cave: Consciousness and the Origins of Art.* London: Thames & Hudson, 2002.

———— and David Pearce. *Inside the Neolithic Mind: Consciousness, Cosmos and the Realm of the Gods.* London: Thames & Hudson, 2005.

Lexova, Irena. *Ancient Egyptian Dances* (1935). Minneola, NY: Dover Publications, 2000.

Limb, Charles. "Your Brain on Improv." TED.com, January 2011. http://www.ted .com/talks/charles_limb_your_brain_on_improv//transcript?language=en.

Lings, Martin. *Muhammad: His Life Based on the Earliest Sources.* Rochester, VT: Inner Traditions, 1983.

————. *What is Sufism?* Berkeley: University of California Press, 1975.

Manniche, Lise. *Music and Musicians in Ancient Egypt.* London: British Museum Press, 1991.

Masquelier, Adeline. *Prayer Has Spoiled Everything: Possession, Power, and Identity in an Islamic Town of Niger.* Durham, NC: Duke University Press, 2001.

McCaughrean, Geraldine. *Gilgamesh the Hero.* Oxford, UK: Oxford University Press, 2002.

McNamara, Patricia. *Spirit Possession and Exorcism: History, Psychology and Neurobiology.* Santa Barbara, CA: ABC Clio, 2011.

The Mevlevi Ensemble of Turkey. *Wherever You Turn Is the Face of God.* CD with liner notes. Santa Barbara, CA: Water Lily Acoustics, 1995.

Morgan, Doug. *TTT: An Introduction to Trance Dancing.* Canada: Ship Cottage Press, 1988.

NASA. "Dark Energy, Dark Matter." *NASA Science: Astrophysics,* updated June 5, 2015. http://science.nasa.gov/astrophysics/focus-areas/what-is-dark-energy/.

———. "Plasma, Plasma, Everywhere: A New Model of the Plasmaspere Surrounding Our World." *NASA Science: Science News,* Sept. 7, 1999, updated April 6, 2011. http://science.nasa.gov/science-news/science-at-nasa/1999/ast07sep99_1/.

Natale, Frank. *Trance Dance: The Dance of Life.* Salisbury, UK: Element Books, 1995.

Naydler, Jeremy. *Shamanic Wisdom in the Pyramid Texts.* Rochester, VT: Inner Traditions, 2005.

Oesterley, W.O.E. *Sacred Dance in the Ancient World.* UK: Cambridge University, 1923.

Omar, Abdul Mannân. *Dictionary of the Holy Quran,* 3rd edition. Hockessin, DE: Noor Foundation International, Inc., 2005.

Oppenheimer, Stephen. *Out of Eden: The Peopling of the World.* London: Constable & Robinson, 2003.

Papini, Giovanni. *The Devil.* NYC: E.P. Dutton & Co., 1954.

Parkinson, Richard. *The Painted Tomb-Chapel of Nebamun.* London: British Museum Press, 2008.

Peel, J. D. Y. *Religious Encounter and the Making of the Yoruba.* Bloomington, IN: Indiana University Press, 2000.

Philips, Abu Ameenah Bilal. *Ibn Taymiyah's Essay on the Jinn (Demons).* Riyadh, Saudi Arabia: International Islamic Publishing House, 2007.

Pinch, Geraldine. *Egyptian Mythology.* Santa Barbara, CA: ABC-Clio Publishers, 2002.

———. *Magic in Ancient Egypt.* London: British Museum Press, 1994.

Plunket, Emmeline. *Ancient Calendars and Constellations*. London: John Murray, 1903.

Randall-MacIver, D., and A. C. Mace. *El-Amrah and Abydos*. London: Egypt Exploration Society, 1902.

Ray, Benjamin. *African Religions: Symbol, Ritual, and Community*. Upper Saddle River, NJ: Prentice-Hall, 1976.

Robbins, Jim. *A Symphony in the Brain: The Evolution of the New Brainwave Biofeedback*. New York: Atlantic Monthly Press, 2000.

Robinson, Neal. *Discovering the Quran: A Contemporary Approach to a Veiled Text*. Washington, DC: Georgetown University Press, 1996.

Rouget, Gilbert. *Music and Trance: A Theory of the Relations Between Music and Possession*. Chicago: University of Chicago, 1985.

Sachs, Curt. *The Rise of Music in the Ancient World: East and West*. New York: Norton & Co., 1943.

———. *World History of the Dance*. New York: Norton & Co., 1937.

Sacks, Oliver. *Hallucinations*. New York: Alfred Knopf, 2012.

———. *Musicophilia: Tales of Music and the Brain*. New York: Alfred Knopf, 2007.

Sanders, Robert. "160,000-Year-Old Fossilized Skulls Uncovered in Ethiopia Are Oldest Anatomically Modern Humans." *UC Berkeley News*, June 11, 2003. http://www.berkeley.edu/news/media/releases/2003/06/11_idaltu.shtml.

Sandys, John Edwin. *The Bacchae of Euripides*. Cambridge: Cambridge University Press, 1885.

Sayce, A. H., ed. "Babylonian Exorcisms." *Records of the Past: Being English Translations of the Ancient Monuments of Egypt and Western Asia*, Vol. 1. London: Samuel Bagster and Sons, 1888.

Scicurious, "Practice Spinning, Tiny Dancer." The Scicurious Brain, *Scientific American* blog, September 2013. http://blogs.scientificamerican.com/scicurious-brain/practice-spinning-tiny-dancer.

Sengers, Gerda. *Women and Demons: Cult Healing in Islamic Egypt.* Boston: Brill, 2003.

Shaarawi, Hoda. *Harem Years: Memoirs of an Egyptian Feminist.* New York: Feminist Press, 1986.

Shiloah, Amnon. *Music in the World of Islam: A Socio-Cultural Study.* Detroit: Wayne State University Press, 1995.

Shiota, Michelle N., and James W. Kalat. *Emotion,* 2nd edition. Belmont, CA: Wadsworth, 2012.

Spence, Lewis. *Myth and Legends: Ancient Egypt.* Boston: David Nickerson & Co., 1907.

Sylvan, Robin. *Trance Formation: The Spiritual and Religious Dimensions of Global Rave Culture.* New York: Routledge, 2005.

"This Is Your Brain on Jazz: Researchers Use MRI to Study Spontaneity, Creativity." Johns Hopkins Medicine News and Publications. February 26, 2008. http://www.hopkinsmedicine.org/news/media/releases/this_is_your_brain_on_jazz_researchers_use_mri_to_study_spontaneity_creativity.

Thompson, Charles. *The Travels of Charles Thompson, Esq.* Dublin: 1744.

Thorndike, Lynn. *History of Magic and Experimental Science.* New York: Columbia University Press, 1923.

Tishkoff, Sarah A., et al. "The Genetic Structure and History of Africans and African Americans." *Science* 324(5930), May 2009. http://www.ncbi.nlm.nih.gov/pmc/articles/PMC2947357.

Touma, Habib Hassan. *Music of the Arabs.* Portland, OR: Amadeus Press, 1996.

Tremearne, A. J. N. *The Ban of the Bori: Demons and Demon-Dancing in West and North Africa.* London: Heath, Cranton and Ouseley Ltd., 1914.

———. *Hausa Superstitions and Customs.* London: Heath, Cranton and Ouseley Ltd., 1913.

———. *The Tailed Head-Hunters of Nigeria.* London: Heath, Cranton and Ouseley Ltd., 1912.

Trumbull, H. Clay. *Oriental Social Life.* Philadelphia: Sunday School Times, 1907.

Van Nieuwkerk, Karin. "*A Trade Like Any Other*": *Female Singers and Dancers in Egypt.* Austin: University of Texas Press, 1995.

Villoteau, Guillaume-Andre. Book 13 of *Description de l'Egypte.* Panckoucke Edition. Paris, 1823.

Von Bomhard, Anne-Sophie. *The Egyptian Calendar: A Work for Eternity.* London: Periplus, 1999.

Walker, John. *Folk Medicine in Modern Egypt.* London: Luzac & Co., 1934.

Weil, Gustav. *The Bible, The Koran and the Talmud.* London: 1863.

White, Tim D., et al. "Pleistocene *Homo sapiens* from Middle Awash, Ethiopia." *Nature,* June 12, 2003.

Wise, Anna. *The High Performance Mind: Mastering Brainwaves for Insight, Healing and Creativity.* New York: Putnam, 1995.

Wolf, Naomi. *Vagina: A New Biography.* New York: Ecco, 2012.

Wrangham, Richard. *Catching Fire: How Cooking Made Us Human.* New York: Basic Books, 2010.

Zay, Julia. *Ecstasia: An Introduction to Transcendental Music and Dance.* Stafford, UK: Immanion Press, 2008.

Art Credit List

Index